Studies in Diversity Linguistics

Editor: Martin Haspelmath

In this series:

ISSN: 2363-5568

Bridging constructions

Edited by

Valérie Guérin

language
science
press

Guérin, Valérie (ed.). 2019. *Bridging constructions* (Studies in Diversity Linguistics 24). Berlin: Language Science Press.

This title can be downloaded at:
http://langsci-press.org/catalog/book/216
© 2019, the authors
Published under the Creative Commons Attribution 4.0 Licence (CC BY 4.0):
http://creativecommons.org/licenses/by/4.0/
Indexed in EBSCO
ISBN: 978-3-96110-141-2 (Digital)
        978-3-96110-142-9 (Hardcover)

ISSN: 2363-5568
DOI:10.5281/zenodo.2563698
Source code available from www.github.com/langsci/216
Collaborative reading: paperhive.org/documents/remote?type=langsci&id=216

Cover and concept of design: Ulrike Harbort
Typesetting: Felix Anker, Sukanta Basu, Felix Kopecky, Sebastian Nordhoff
Proofreading: Amir Ghorbanpour, Andreas Hölzl, Bev Erasmus, Eitan
Grossman, Felix Anker, Grant Aiton, Ivica Jeđud, Jeroen van de Weijer, Lachlan
Mackenzie, Nerida Jarkey, Stephen Jones, Valerie Guerin, Yvonne Treis
Fonts: Libertinus Serif, Libertinus Math, Arimo, DejaVu Sans Mono
Typesetting software: XƎLATEX

Language Science Press
Unter den Linden 6
10099 Berlin, Germany
langsci-press.org

Storage and cataloguing done by FU Berlin

Freie Universität Berlin

Contents

Preface

This volume is partly the result of a two-day workshop entitled *Bridging Linkage in Cross-linguistic Perspective* organized at the Cairns Institute (James Cook University, Australia), on 25–26 February 2015 by Valérie Guérin and Simon Overall. Our intent at the time was two-fold: (i) to gather data from a variety of languages that would enable us to draw cross-linguistic generalisations about the formal and functional characteristics of bridging constructions, and (ii) to try and delimit the range of constructions that can be subsumed under the term bridging construction. In particular, we found it important to try and separate out bridging constructions from repetition. We aimed to cast our net as widely as possible in order to get a broad picture of bridging constructions and their instantiation across languages. For the workshop, we selected nine genetically-unrelated languages: four languages spoken in South America; four languages of Oceania (Australia, Papua New Guinea, and Vanuatu); and Greek. Some of the presentations are reproduced in this volume in their most recent versions. Other chapters were invited by the volume's editor.

In preparation for the workshop (and subsequently, for this volume), we circulated among the authors (i) a list of core features defining bridging constructions extracted from the literature, reproduced below; (ii) a series of questions to address, if relevant, when describing bridging constructions. They are reproduced in the Appendix of Chapter 1; (iii) and an earlier version of Chapter 1, the introductory chapter. We asked that each author use these notions as a starting point to isolate typical and atypical instances of bridging constructions in their language of study.

Characteristic features of bridging constructions

- Bridging constructions are composed of a reference clause and a bridging clause.
    - The bridging clause is a non-main clause. The dependency can be marked morphologically, syntactically, or prosodically.
    - Prototypically, the reference clause is a main clause.

- In the large majority of cases, the reference clause ends a discourse unit while the bridging clause appears at the beginning of a new discourse unit.
- The bridging clause recapitulates at least one clause in the preceding discourse unit.

• There are three types of bridging constructions, differentiated by the content of the bridging clause:

- Recapitulative linkage: the bridging clause repeats the reference clause more-or-less verbatim.
- Summary linkage: the bridging clause does not repeat the reference clause but anaphorically refers to it with a *summarizing* predicate as the bridging element (i.e., a demonstrative verb, a pro-verb, an auxiliary, or a light verb).
- Mixed linkage: both types of linkage may co-occur in a single instance of bridging, where the bridging clause contains the same lexical verb as the reference clause in addition to a summarizing verb of the type typically found in summary linkage.

• In a stretch of discourse, bridging constructions enable:

- Information backgrounding
- Referent tracking
- Event sequentiality
- Paragraph demarcation

The chapters

Chapter 1 takes a typological look at bridging constructions. After introducing the general concepts, Valérie Guérin and Grant Aiton review the three types of bridging constructions that are reported in the literature and in the current volume, and discuss the form and functions of bridging constructions across languages.

In Chapter 2, Nick Emlen analyses recapitulative linkage in Matsigenka, a Kampan (Arawak) language, and shows how these constructions have been borrowed in Spanish, but not in Quechua, in a trilingual community in Peru. This chapter was presented in parts at *Red Europea para el Estudio de las Lenguas Andinas* (REELA), Leiden, September 2015.

Hannah Sarvasy presents bridging constructions in the Bantu language Logoori in Chapter 3. She argues that these constructions are rarely use in Logoori discourse, restricted to procedural texts, and as stylistic features, their presence in a text is highly dependent on the penchant of the speaker.

Diana Forker and Felix Anker examine bridging constructions in the Nakh-Daghestanian language family in Chapter 4. They show that recapitulative and summary linkages both occur in narratives in the Tsezic language group, and suggest that recapitulative linkage can be found throughout the Nakh-Daghestanian language family. Forker and Anker additionally observe a regular shift in deixis between the reference clause and bridging clause, which results in a regular substitution of an andative verb of motion for an equivalent venitive verb.

In Chapter 5, Nerida Jarkey reveals that in White Hmong recapitulative linkage is more common than summary linkage which is only found in first person narratives. The functions of these constructions are illustrated in the light of three text genres.

Chapter 6 by Grant Aiton describes bridging constructions in Eibela, a language of the Western Province of Papua New Guinea. Features of interest in Eibela include three types of summary linkage and discourse preferences relating summary linkage to paragraphs and recapitulative linkage to episodes. Parts of this chapter were published in the journal *Language and Linguistics in Melanesia* in 2015.

In Chapter 7, Lourens de Vries details bridging constructions in Korowai, a Greater Awyu language of West Papua. Summary and recapitulative linkages are described in the wider context of clausal chains, their subtypes and functions clearly spelled out (whether they are marked or unmarked, carrying switch reference marking or not, indicating thematic continuity or discontinuity).

Valérie Guérin analyzes recapitulative linkage in Mavea, an Oceanic language of Vanuatu. In Chapter 8, she shows that bridging clauses are morphologically main clauses but phonologically marked as dependent and that their function in discourse is mostly to add emphasis.

Finally, Angeliki Alvanoudi takes a conversation analytical framework to study clausal repetitions in modern Greek interactions in Chapter 9. She highlights similarities and differences between recapitulative linkage and clause repetition and hypothesizes that the former is a grammaticalized expression of the latter.

The authors

Grant Aiton's primary research interests are language variation and typology with a current emphasis on documentation and field linguistics. He completed a Master's degree in Linguistics at the University of Alberta where he conducted research on Athabaskan and Salish languages. His PhD project at James Cook University was the documentation of Eibela, a previously undescribed language spoken in Western Province and Southern Highlands Province, Papua New Guinea. <aiton.grant@gmail.com>

Angeliki Alvanoudi is Lecturer at the Aristotle University of Thessaloniki and Adjunct Lecturer in Linguistics at James Cook University, Australia. Her main interests are language and gender, language and cognition, and grammar and interaction. Her recent publications include *Language contact, borrowing and code switching: A case study of Australian Greek* (Journal of Greek Linguistics, 2018) and *The interface between language and cultural conceptualizations of gender in interaction: The case of Greek* (in Advances in cultural linguistics, ed. by F. Sharifian, Springer, 2017). She has written the books *Grammatical gender in interaction: Cultural and cognitive aspects* (Brill, 2014) and *Modern Greek in diaspora: An Australian perspective* (Palgrave, 2018). <alvanoudiag@yahoo.gr>

Felix Anker studies General Linguistics at the University of Bamberg and will complete his studies with a Master's thesis on topological relations in Tsova-Tush. His main research interests are languages of the Caucasus, language typology and morphosyntax. His prospective dissertation will be on various topics of Tsova-Tush syntax. <felix.anker@gmx.de>

Lourens de Vries is professor of general linguistics at the Vrije Universiteit, Amsterdam, The Netherlands. His research focus is the description and typology of Papuan languages. He published grammatical descriptions of Wambon, Korowai, Kombai and Inanwatan. <l.j.de.vries@vu.nl>

Diana Forker teaches Caucasian Studies at the University of Jena. She completed her PhD at the Max Planck Institute for Evolutionary Anthropology. Her main interests are languages of the Caucasus, typology, and morphosyntax and sociolinguistics. She currently works on the documentation of Sanzhi Dargwa, a Nakh-Daghestanian language. Among her recent publications are *A Grammar of Hinuq* (2013) and several articles on different aspects of Nakh-Daghestanian languages. <diana.forker@uni-jena.de>

Nicholas Q. Emlen is a linguistic anthropologist (PhD University of Michigan, 2014) who has conducted extensive ethnographic research on multilingualism, language contact, and coffee production on the Andean-Amazonian agricultural frontier of Southern Peru. He also works on the reconstruction of Quechua-Aymara language contact in the ancient Central Andes, and on multilingualism among Quechua, Aymara, Puquina, and Spanish in the colonial Andes. He is currently a National Endowment for the Humanities Fellow at the John Carter Brown Library, and a visiting lecturer in anthropology at Brown University. <nqemlen@gmail.com>

Valérie Guérin obtained a PhD from the University of Hawai'i at Mānoa for her work on Mavea, a moribund language of Vanuatu (grammar published by the University of Hawai'i Press in 2011). She currently works on describing Tay-atuk, a language spoken in the YUS conservation area, Morobe Province, Papua New Guinea. In 2013–2016, she was a postdoctoral research associate at the Language and Culture Research Centre, James Cook University, under the Australian Laureate Fellowship awarded to Professor Aikhenvald. She is currently affiliated with the Language and Culture Research Centre as an adjunct fellow researcher. <valerie.guerin@gmail.com>

Nerida Jarkey teaches Japanese Studies at the University of Sydney. Her research focuses on two Asian languages, Japanese and Hmong, and is concerned with the relationships between language, cognition, culture and the expression of social identity. She pays particular attention to multi-verb constructions, and is author of *Serial Verb Constructions in White Hmong*, published by Brill in 2015. Address: School of Languages and Cultures (A18), University of Sydney, NSW 2006, Australia. <nerida.jarkey@sydney.edu.au>

Hannah Sarvasy received her PhD in 2015 from James Cook University. She has conducted immersion fieldwork on Nungon (Papuan), Kim and Bom (Atlantic; Sierra Leone), and Tashelhit Berber and ran a pioneering longitudinal study of children's acquisition of Nungon. Her publications include *A Grammar of Nungon: A Papuan Language of Northeast New Guinea* (Brill, 2017), *Word Hunters: Field Linguists on Fieldwork* (John Benjamins, 2018), and articles and book chapters on topics in Nungon grammar, fieldwork methodology, Bantu linguistics, and ethnobiology, as well as Kim and Bom language primers. She taught at UCLA, served as a Research Fellow at the Australian National University, and currently holds an Australian Research Council Discovery Early Career Researcher Award for the study of clause chains from typological, acquisition, and psycholinguistic angles. Address: MARCS Institute, Western Sydney University. <h.sarvasy@westernsydney.edu.au>

Acknowledgments

I would like to thank Alexandra Aikhenvald for her generous support to help organize the workshop entitled "Bridging Linkage in Cross-linguistic Perspective" at the Language and Culture Research Center (the Cairns Institute, James Cook University, Australia) from which this volume originates. Special thanks to Simon Overall who helped me co-organize the workshop and got me started on this book, and to Grant Aiton for helping me putting this book together. Many thanks to Sukanta Basu and Felix Anker, and especially to Felix Kopecky and Sebastian Nordhoff who helped me formatting this book with X∄LATEX. Thanks to the copy-editors who volunteer at the Language Science Press. And, finally, a heartfelt "Merci!" to all authors involved with this volume for their long-lasting commitment and support during this intercontinental adventure.

Chapter 1

Bridging constructions in typological perspective

Valérie Guérin
James Cook University

Grant Aiton
James Cook University

In this chapter, we undertake a cross-linguistic examination of bridging constructions, which we define as the sequence of two clauses: the first clause (called the reference clause) ends a discourse unit, the second clause (called the bridging clause) typically repeats the first clause at the beginning of a new discourse unit. Based on published language data and data from the volume, we identify three different types of constructions subsumed under the label bridging construction (§2 and §3): recapitulative linkage, summary linkage, and mixed linkage. They differ in the form that the bridging clause takes on: broadly speaking, verbatim lexical recapitulation of the reference clause; a light verb summarizing the reference clause; or a mix of these two strategies. Because bridging constructions lie at the interface of discourse and syntax, we dedicate §4 to explaining their discourse functions. Amid the cross-linguistic variation, we found two recurrent discourse functions: emphasizing sequentiality and cohesively structuring discourse. Finally, we establish a list of questions to guide the documentation of these linguistic patterns.

1 Preliminaries

While reference grammars and the typological literature have a long tradition describing syntactic phenomena within a clause, cross-linguistic research beyond the level of the clause, especially the role that clause-level phenomena play in discourse structure, is comparatively scarce. This volume presents a case study

Valérie Guérin & Grant Aiton. 2019. Bridging constructions in typological perspective. In Valérie Guérin (ed.), *Bridging constructions*, 1–44. Berlin: Language Science Press. DOI:10.5281/zenodo.2563678 of one such phenomenon, variously labelled in the literature as *tail-head linkage* (de Vries 2005), *head-tail linkage* (Fabian et al. 1998: 163), *tail-head recapitulation* (Farr 1999: 197) *recapitulation clauses* (Genetti 2007: 438; Stirling 1993: 17), *echo clauses* (Heath & Hantgan 2018), or *backgrounding repetition* (McKay 2008: 10), and the less-described variant *generic verb recapitulation* (Farr 1999: 204, 337) or *summary-head linkage* (Thompson et al. 2007: 274) to refer to constructions which contribute to discourse cohesion and structuring in that they "link sentences or paragraphs together, usually by repetition of at least part of the previous clause" (Thurman 1975: 342).[1]

Tail-head linkage is found in a wide number of genetically and geographically diverse languages. It exists in Wolaitta, an Omotic language of Ethiopia (Azeb Ahma, p.c.) and is attested in Bangime (isolate, eastern Mali; Heath & Hantgan 2018); Biak (Austronesian, Indonesia; Plattèl 2013); Cavineña (Tacanan, Bolivia; Guillaume 2011); Creek (Muskogean, USA; Martin 1998); Evenki (Tungusic, Russia; Grenoble 2012); Ngandi (southeastern Arnhem Land, Australia; Heath 1985); Rembarrnga (central Arnhem Land, Australia; McKay 2008); Tariana (Arawak, Brazil; Aikhenvald forthcoming); Tirax (Oceanic, Vanuatu; Brotchie 2009); and Yurakaré (unclassified, Bolivia; van Gijn 2014), to name a few (see also the list in Guillaume 2011: 111). But to the best of our knowledge, this type of linkage has never been the subject of any substantial cross-linguistic study. It is the intent of this volume to partly fill this gap, proposing in this introductory chapter general characteristics of this type of linkage and presenting in subsequent chapters descriptive studies of the phenomenon in unrelated languages.

To compare tail-head linkage across languages, we survey the relevant published literature and extract the features which define this linguistic pattern. We then formulate a comparative concept (in the sense of Haspelmath 2010; 2016; and Croft 2016) presented in (1). As the data revealed the existence of three distinct types of linkage, we adopt the term BRIDGING CONSTRUCTION as a hypernym to avoid terminological confusion between *heads* and *tails*, and to capture the full range of patterns, of which only a subset may be subsumed under the labels *tail-* or *summary-head linkage*.[2]

(1) Bridging constructions: A comparative concept

A bridging construction is a linkage of three clauses. The first clause of the construction (i.e., the reference clause) is the final clause in a unit of

---

[1]The origin of the term *tail-head linkage* is unclear. Although this term has a long tradition in chemistry, its first usage in linguistics could be Longacre (1968).
[2]Not to be confused with the bridging implicature of Clark (1975). We thank Martin Haspelmath for this reference.

discourse. The second clause (i.e., the bridging clause) recapitulates the reference clause. It usually immediately follows the reference clause but it acts as the initial (albeit non-main) clause of a new discourse unit. The primary discourse function of a bridging construction is to add structure and cohesion: recapitulation backgrounds the proposition of the reference clause and foregrounds the clause following the bridging clause. This third clause is discourse-new and typically sequentially ordered.

In the rest of this section, we refine the concepts in (1), while in the following sections we review the formal properties (§2 and §3) and discourse functions (§4) of bridging constructions across individual languages. The distinction between repetition and bridging construction is discussed in §5. We include suggestions for future research in §6. Lastly, the Appendix lists a series of questions that should be addressed when describing bridging constructions in individual languages.

1.1 The constructions

The structure of a bridging construction is represented schematically in (2). There are two discourse units linked by the construction. We call the final clause of the first unit the REFERENCE CLAUSE (a clause which is generally known as the *tail*). The second discourse unit begins with what we label the BRIDGING CLAUSE (that is, traditionally the *head*), a clause which refers back to the reference clause. We adopt the convention of underlining the reference clause and bolding the bridging clause throughout this volume.

(2) [...[Reference Clause]]_{discourse unit} [[**Bridging Clause**]...]_{discourse unit}

The linked discourse units are typically, though not necessarily, multiclausal. The nature of these units (variously referred to in the literature as sentences or clause-chains, paragraphs or discourse episodes) remains an open question, which we address in §4. But importantly, it is the presence of both the reference and bridging clauses, their formal representation, the semantic relationship between these two clauses, and their functions in discourse that create a bridging construction and that set it apart from other clause linking techniques.

The three types of bridging constructions that we distinguish consist of a reference clause and a bridging clause. Their differences lie in the formulation of the bridging clause. The first type, called RECAPITULATIVE LINKAGE (formerly *tail-head linkage*), involves the repetition of the predicate of the reference clause in the bridging clause, as shown in (3).

(3)   Nahavaq (Oceanic, Vanuatu; Dimock 2009: 259)

    a.   *...en re-tur-gcor   no-pon   no-qond.*
       and 3PL-sew-block N.PREF-opening N.PREF-basket

       '...and they sewed up the opening of the basket.'

    b.   ***Re-tur-gcor   no-pon   no-qond,***   *re-gcur   i-gcisgces.*
       3PL-sew-block N.PREF-opening N.PREF-basket 3PL-cause 3SG-tight

       'After they sewed up the opening of the basket, they tightened it.'

The second type is here called SUMMARY LINKAGE (formerly *summary-head linkage*). It does not repeat the predicate of the reference clause but contains in the bridging clause an anaphoric predicate, a light verb, a generic verb, or a demonstrative verb, such as *tangamba* 'do thus' in (4b), which anaphorically refers to the reference clause.

(4)   Siroi (Papua New Guinea; van Kleef 1988: 150)

    a.   *Piro   mbolnge ngukina.*
       garden LOC   planted

       'She planted it in the garden.'

    b.   ***Tangamba*** *nu kinyna*
       doing.thus she slept

       'After having done thus, she slept.'

We call the third type of bridging construction MIXED LINKAGE. This type of construction, exemplified in (5), is a combination of recapitulative and summary linkages in that the bridging clause contains both the lexical predicate of the reference clause and a generic or demonstrative predicate. The bridging clause in (5b) includes the verb *reke* 'cross' of the reference clause in addition to a manner demonstrative *jadya* 'thus' and the auxiliary *ju* 'be' (which are used in a type of summary linkage in that language).

(5)   Cavineña (Tacanan, Bolivia; Guillaume 2011: 129)

    a.   *Ji-da=dya=di   ka-reke-ti-kware*
       good-ADJ.SUF=FOC=EMPH REFL-cross-REFL-REM.PST

       'I crossed well.'

    b.   ***Ka-reke-ti   jadya ju-atsu*** *tapeke=piji   ara-kware*
       REFL-cross-REFL thus   be-ss   trip.food=DIM eat-REM.PST

       'After crossing, I ate the food.'

1.2 The clause

We take the CLAUSE to be a comparative concept (following Haspelmath 2010: 672), involving a predicate (verbal or non-verbal) and its argument(s). A FINAL CLAUSE is taken to be the last clause in a series of formally linked clauses. A final clause can be a MAIN CLAUSE or a NON-MAIN CLAUSE. By main clause we mean a clause that can stand by itself as an independent complete utterance. The verbal predicate of a main clause is inflected for all required grammatical categories (i.e., it is finite), and (generally) has a falling intonation (Fitzpatrick 2000). A main clause can be seen as the equivalent of an independent sentence; however, we avoid the term "sentence" itself, as it is not readily applicable to many languages (Dixon 2010: 132–133; Longacre 1970; Miller 1981; Mithun 2005a). A non-main clause cannot stand by itself as an independent complete utterance; it is dependent on another clause.[3] The dependency can be marked in any level of the grammar, typically either (i) in the morpho-syntax: e.g., a linker marks a clause as dependent; the verbal predicate of the clause is only partially inflected or not inflected at all (i.e., it is non-finite); or both a linker and reduced inflection occur, etc.; or (ii) in the prosody: morpho-syntactically, the clause is inflected like a main clause but the continuation intonation reveals the dependency (Bolinger 1984; Chafe 2003: 9–10; Genetti & Slater 2004: 23–24, 31; Mithun 2005b). The syntactic status of non-main clauses is notoriously difficult to define especially for some of the languages in this volume which make use of CLAUSE CHAINS (i.e., non-main clauses in series). Non-main clauses have been described as adverbial clauses, pseudo-subordinate, co-subordinate, pseudo-coordinate clauses, medial clauses, or converbs. To avoid language-specific analysis of dependency types, we use the term NON-MAIN CLAUSE as a typologically generic cover term in this introductory chapter.[4]

1.3 Bridging constructions in discourse

Some languages possess only one type of bridging construction while others have developed more. Nahavaq seems to only use recapitulative linkage, but in Siroi, recapitulative and summary linkages co-exist, while Cavineña shows all three types of linkage. Needless to say, the functions that bridging constructions can fulfil in discourse are varied. However, there are also some common

---

[3]We do not consider here insubordinate clauses (Evans 2012), which are formally non-main clauses that have gained independent status.

[4]On clausal dependencies, see Cristofaro 2005; Culicover & Jackendoff 1997; Haiman & Thompson 1984; Haspelmath 1995, Haspelmath 2004; Longacre 2007a: 398–417; Van Valin Jr 1984; or Yuasa & Sadock 2002; among others.

trends across languages. The discursive function that is most often associated with bridging constructions is THEMATIC CONTINUITY (in de Vries' 2005 terminology). That is, the linkage is used to highlight the succession of events, as in Nahavaq (Dimock 2009: 259); it supports the continuous flow of the story's main events, such as in Siroi (van Kleef 1988: 151–153); and it foregrounds the "important milestones in the story" and "advances the action of the narrative" in Cavineña (Guillaume 2011: 118–120). This trend is possible owing to the fact that recapitulation "transforms the repeated item from new into given information" (Brown 2000: 224–225) which adds discourse cohesion. The concept of givenness in this context is closest to the sense of SALIENCY outlined by Prince (1981: 228) where "the speaker assumes that the hearer has or could appropriately have some particular thing/entity in his/her CONSCIOUSNESS at the time of hearing the utterance." In this sense, a bridging construction ensures that the event described in the reference clause is salient in the mind of the hearer.

2 Bridging constructions: formal characteristics

In §2.1, we discuss the position of the reference and bridging clauses in a bridging construction, before addressing the syntactic status of these clauses in §2.2 and §2.3 respectively.

2.1 Layout

A common assumption regarding the position of the clauses is that the reference clause is "repeated in the first clause of the next chain" (de Vries 2005: 363); that is, the reference clause and the bridging clause are parts of two distinct discourse units, with the bridging clause a constituent of the second unit. This assumption holds in all languages we have seen so far. While it is typically the case that the reference clause *immediately* precedes the bridging clause, it is also possible for a clause to intervene between reference and bridging clause. A case in point is the bridging clause in (6c) which is separated from the reference clause in (6a) by another clause in (6b). A similar phenomenon is reported in Korowai (de Vries 2019 [this volume]).

(6) Jingulu (non-Pama-Nyungan, Australia; Pensalfini 2015)
  a. *Buba-ngka dakard karuma-nya-yi*
     fire-ALL   warm warm-2SG-FUT
     'You warm it in the fire.'

b. *Nyirrma-nya-yi,*
make-2SG-FUT

'You'll make it (then)'

c. ***dakard karuma-nya-yi,***
warm   warm-2SG-FUT

'having warmed it,'

d. *ila-nya-yi   langa kijurlurlu.*
put-2SG-FUT PREP stone

'you'll put it on the stone.'

In the corpus assembled for this volume, composed mostly of monologue nar-ratives, a maximum of four clauses can separate the reference and the bridging clause, as in White Hmong (Jarkey 2019 [this volume]).

2.2 Morphosyntactic properties of reference clauses

The reference clause is typically cast in the declarative mood. This can arise from the discourse function of bridging constructions, linking discourse units in narrative texts, but it may be simply a result of a data bias, as the data for this study have been drawn mainly from narratives. Occasional examples of non-declarative reference clauses include exclamative clauses in Mavea (Guérin 2019 [this volume]), interrogatives in Tsezic languages (Forker & Anker 2019 [this volume]) and imperatives in Korowai, shown in (7).

(7)   Korowai (Papua New Guinea; de Vries 2019 [this volume])

a.   *...if-e=xa   bando-xe-nè le-mén=é*
here-TR=CONN bring-go-ss eat-IMP:2PL=EX

'...you should take this and eat it!'

b.   ***le-mén=daxu*** *noxu lép-telo-xai=xa...*
eat-IMP:2PL=SS 1PL   ill-be[NON1SG]-IRR=CONN

'You must eat it and if we fall ill...'

When reference clauses are main clauses, they show no restrictions in terms of the tense, aspect, modality, negation, predicate type, etc. They can contain a verbal predicate (as in the examples cited to this point) or a nominal predicate, as shown in (8). The bridging clause then repeats the nominal with a copula verb which bears a dependency marker.

(8) Eibela (Papua New Guinea; Aiton 2019 [this volume])

    a. *[ɛjaːgɛ   do-si=ki]*_{*medial*}   *[uʃu]*_{*final*}

       butterfly STAT-MED:PFV=CONT egg

       'There being a butterfly then there is an egg.'

    b. **[uʃu do-si=ki]**_{*medial*}   *[kɛkɛbɛaːnɛ]*_{*final*}

       egg STAT-MED:PFV=CONT caterpillar

       'There being an egg then there is a caterpillar.'

2.3 Morphosyntactic properties of bridging clauses

As mentioned in (1), bridging clauses are, at some level or other in the grammar, dependent clauses. We found three different dependency relations. First, the dependency is marked in the morphology. In some of the languages we investigated, dependent clauses show morphological modifications or morphological restrictions relative to main clauses in the tense, aspect, modality markers, etc., that they can be specified for. For example, in (7) above, there is no change in mood between the reference and bridging clauses; however, the bridging clause bears a switch-reference marker, which identifies it as a dependent (and non-main clause). In Tsezic languages (Forker & Anker 2019 [this volume]), bridging clauses all use converbs, which is the default strategy in these languages to express dependency (or in these languages, subordination). In White Hmong, bridging clauses are reduced main clauses: they cannot contain pragmatic markers usually occurring at the edge of a main clause nor coordinators or markers of temporal sequence (Jarkey 2019 [this volume]).

Second, the dependency is marked in the prosody. Some languages do not use morphological means to mark dependent clauses but utilize instead continuation prosody to indicate the dependency. Consider Rembarrnga (McKay 2008: 5, 10). As in many Australian languages, a clause boundary is best defined by prosody. All elements in a single intonation contour are considered part of one clause. In Rembarrnga, bridging clauses are part of the same intonation contour as the clause that follows, indicating that they are not independent clauses. In our corpus, three languages use prosody to indicate dependency: Mavea (Guérin 2019 [this volume]), Logoori (Sarvasy 2019 [this volume]) and Jingulu (Pensalfini 2015). In Mavea, both reference and bridging clauses are morphologically equivalent to main clauses. Bridging clauses are overtly marked as dependent clauses by their intonation. The reference clause ends in a falling or level intonation, while the bridging clause ends in a rising intonation to indicate continuation. This is visible in Figure 1 representing the sequence in (9).

(9)   Mavea (Oceanic, Vanuatu; Guérin 2019 [this volume])

a.   *Ko-viris*   *i-si*   *na kuku. [1s]*
     2SG-squeeze 3SG:IRR-go.down LOC pot
     'You squeeze (out the juice) down in a pot.'

b.   **Ko-viris**   *i-si*   *na **kuku*** ro   *[1.15s]*
     2SG-squeeze 3SG:IRR-go.down LOC pot   then
     'You squeeze (out the juice) down in a pot then,'

c.   *ko-ku-a.*
     2SG-boil-3SG
     'you boil it.'

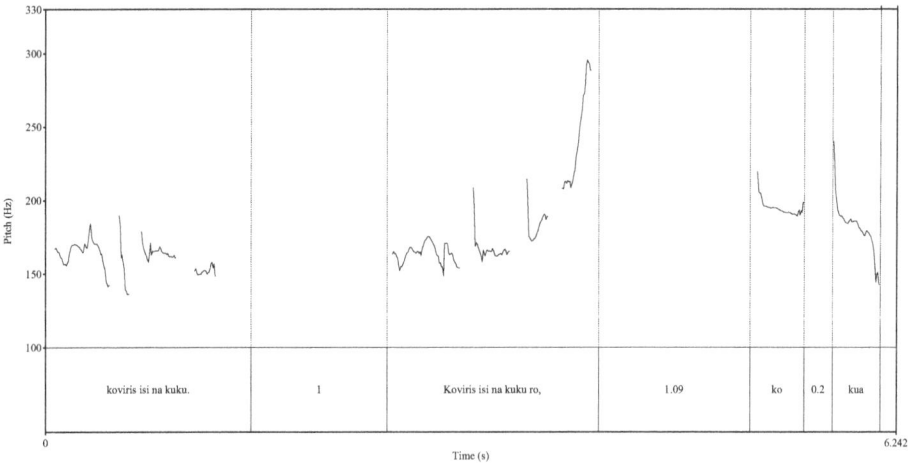

Figure 1: Intonation contour of example (9) extracted with PRAAT.

In Mavea, dependent clauses need not be marked morphologically. Adverbials also seldom make use of overt non-main clause markers (e.g., complementizer or subordinator). They resort instead to prosody (e.g., rising intonation) to mark continuation and indicate grammatical or discourse dependency. The Jingulu data concur: the bridging clause is marked with the same intonation that encodes given information. However, in the absence of fluent speakers today, the Jingulu data is less conclusive (Rob Pensalfini, p.c.).

Logoori is interesting in that respect. In this language (as in other Bantu languages), the predicate of the first clause in the chain is finite, the medial and final clauses of the chain are non-finite. Thus, in Bantu bridging constructions, the reference clause is non-finite (being the last in the chain) and the bridging clause is finite (being the first in the chain). However, bridging clauses in Logoori are also prosodically dependent, while reference clauses are prosodically main clauses (see Sarvasy 2019 [this volume]).

Third, the dependency is marked both in the morphology and the prosody. Some languages may use both morphology and non-final intonation to mark clause dependency. In the Australian language Ngandi, the bridging clause contains a morpheme indicating subordination. In addition, the clause ends on a rising continuation pitch while the clause following it has falling terminal pitch (Heath 1985: 99).

As these different dependency strategies reveal, the general profile of a language influences the formal characteristics of the bridging constructions in that language (see de Vries 2005; Seifart 2010: 898). It is worth mentioning too that in some cases, a subordinator is present to overtly mark the bridging clause as dependent. Thus in White Hmong, the temporal relationship between the reference and the bridging clause can be explicit, as in (10) with *thaum* 'when' or implied, as in (11).

(10) White Hmong (Hmong-Mien, Laos; Jarkey 2019 [this volume])

    a. *...ces   nws poj.niam thiaj   xauv.xeeb tau ob leeg tub ntxaib.*
        and.then 3SG woman so.then give.birth get two CLF son twin

        '...and so then his wife gave birth to twin boys.'

    b. ***Thaum xauv.xeeb tau nkawd...***
        when   give.birth get 3DU

        'When she had given birth to them...'

(11) a. *CES   txawm mus ntsib nraug zaj.*
        and.then then go meet young dragon

        'and then (she) went (and) met a young dragon.'

    b. ***Ntsib nraug zaj,***
        meet young dragon

        '(She) met the young dragon...'

In this volume, we do not separate out bridging clauses with an overt lexical subordinator such as (10) from bridging clauses whose sole indicators of dependency are prosodic like (11) or morphological. Although there could be discourse differences between the different dependency markings, we do not have enough data at this stage to argue that (10) is a less prototypical bridging construction than (11) for example.

3 Types of bridging constructions

The two types of bridging constructions most commonly described across languages are RECAPITULATIVE LINKAGE and SUMMARY LINKAGE. They can be distinguished on the basis of the predicate that their bridging clause contains: in recapitulative linkage, the bridging clause repeats at least the predicate of the reference clause either verbatim or with a close paraphrase; whereas the bridging clause of a summary linkage contains an anaphoric predicate recapping the event/state of the reference clause. A third type of bridging construction emerged from our data collection and comparative studies. We call it here MIXED LINKAGE. This type of bridging construction combines both recapitulative and summary linkages. We discuss these three types of linkage in turn below.

3.1 Recapitulative linkage

Every definition of bridging construction that we encountered in the literature refers to a portion of discourse being *repeated* elsewhere. What is generally assumed is that the repetition is more or less exact, i.e., exact enough so that the reference and bridging clauses can be identified as expressing the same proposition with the same lexical items. There exist, however, many different types of repetition (Brown 2000: 224). We take as our starting point a bridging clause with apparent verbatim repetition. In Tirax (as in many other Oceanic languages of Vanuatu), the bridging clause in (12b) is morphologically identical to the reference clause in (12a). The only difference is the rising intonation which marks the bridging clause as non-final, as described for (9).

(12)   Tirax (Oceanic, Vanuatu; Brotchie 2009: 309)

    a.   *tnah haxal i=mɛ*
         devil INDF 3SG:REAL=come
         'and a devil came along.' (falling intonation)

    b.   *tnah haxal i=mɛ*
         devil INDF   3SG:REAL=come
         'A devil came,' (rising intonation)

c. *i=ŋo...*

3SG:REAL=hear

'and he heard...'

The term VERBATIM repetition, then, does not precisely represent the content of a bridging clause (despite this common assumption regarding recapitulative linkage): at the very least, changes required to accord a bridging clause dependent status are generally applied, be they purely intonational as in (9), or morphological as in (13), where the predicate 'become strong' is marked as non-final in (13b).

(13)   Nabak (Papua New Guinea; Fabian et al. 1998: 164)

a.   *...met-me   ku-mann   ma-katik-ngang   be-in*

go-MED:3SG:DS nail-MED:1PL:DS CONT-strong-NMLZ become-3SG:PRS

'...and it goes [in its proper place] and we nail it and [the floor] becomes strong.'

b.   ***Ku-mann   katik-ngang be-me...***

nail-MED:1PL:DS strong-NMLZ become-MED:3SG:DS

'We nail it and it becomes strong...'

The Nabak example also demonstrates that although typically a single reference clause is repeated in the bridging clause, it is possible to find two clauses repeated in their entirety. The clauses with predicates 'nail' and 'become strong' are both repeated in the bridging clause in (13b). We have not yet found more than two clauses repeated.

Departure from verbatim repetition affects different constituents of the reference clause. Adverbials or arguments may be omitted or the verbal inflection may differ. At least implicitly, the predicate of the reference and bridging clauses is expected to remain identical, but as we show below, the predicate is not immune to replacement. In the following sections we review four types of variation found in the languages surveyed: (1) modifications, the bridging and reference clause contain the same information but in different order or form; (2) omission, the bridging clause omits some material present in the reference clause; (3) addition, the bridging clause contains information, whether lexical or grammatical, which was not present in the reference clause; (4) substitution, where some of the information in the reference clause is replaced in the bridging clause; and (5) a mixture of these features. What is common to all cases of variation (and crucial for bridging constructions) is that the propositional content of the bridging clause is equivalent to the content in the reference clause, with no additional information added to the bridging clause.

3.1.1 Modifications

Modification refers to cases where bridging clauses do not contain omissions from the reference clause nor additions per se, but are not strictly verbatim either. Modification may affect the lexical content of the bridging clause. For example, full NPs in a reference clause may be pronominalized in the bridging clause, as in the Oceanic language Lolovoli. The object in the reference clause (*diringigi* 'the stone oven') in (14a), is repeated in pronominal form (=*e* '3SG.O') in the bridging clause (14b). Similar facts apply to Cavineña: the object *tapeke* 'food' in (15a) is pronominalized with the demonstrative *tumeke* 'that' in (15b). Nothing in the grammar of these languages would prevent a full NP from occurring in a dependent clause.

(14) Lolovoli (Oceanic, Vanuatu; Hyslop 2001: 427)

    a. *Da=mo   sio   na diringi-gi*
       1PL:INCL=REAL lay.stones ACC stone.oven-ASSOC

       'We lay stones for the stone oven.'

    b. *Da=mo   sio=e   mo   rovo,*
       1PL:INCL=REAL lay.stones=3SG:O REAL finish

       'We lay all the stones,'

    c. *ale da=mo   goa   na qeta-gi...*
       CONJ 1PL:INCL=REAL scrape.dirt ACC taro-ASSOC

       'then we scrape the dirt off the taro...'

(15) Cavineña (Tacanan, Bolivia; Guillaume 2011: 129)

    a. *Ka-reke-ti   jadya ju-atsu tapeke=piji   ara-kware*
       REFL-cross-REFL thus be-ss   trip.food=DIM eat-REM.PST

       'After crossing, I ate the food.'

    b. *Tumeke ara-tsu era   ijeti peta-ya.*
       that   eat-ss   1SG:ERG sun look.at-IPFV

       'After eating that (food), I looked at the sun (to know what time it was).'

Other modifications include word order: the order of the phrases in the reference and bridging clauses does not match. For example in Sunwar, *aga* is emphasized and placed at the end of the refence clause in (16a), whereas in the bridging clause in (16b), it is restored to its non-emphasized position.

(16) Sunwar (Himalayan, Nepal; Schulze & Bieri 1973: 391)

    a. *Minu meko <u>khuy</u>   <u>oo-ma</u>   ʻ<u>baakt</u> <u>aga</u>*
       and these thieves enter-3PL ?   inside

       'And the thieves entered into the house.'

    b. ***khuy aga   oo-ma   ʻbaakta***
       thieves inside enter-3PL ?

       'The thieves having entered...'

Placement at the end of a clause for emphasis is not a feature associated with a particular clause type in Sunwar. Although more common in reference clauses, it is also found in bridging clauses (Schulze & Bieri 1973: 391).

3.1.2 Omissions

Omissions in the bridging clause target lexical items, in particular arguments and adverbials. This is the case in Ono (Phinnemore 1998: 121) and Wambon (de Vries 2005). In Wambon in (17b), it is the adverbial *alipke* 'afternoon' that is not included in the bridging clause.

(17) Wambon (Papua New Guinea; de Vries 2005: 373)

    a. *Sanopkuniv-eve ilo   nggapmo-kndevan-o ko   <u>alipke-lo</u>*
       Tuesday-that go.down:SS cut-1PL:PRS-CONN   go:SS afternoon-SS
       ndave-levambo
       return-1PL:PST

       'On Tuesday afternoon we went down and cut (trees) until we returned in the late afternoon.'

    b. ***ndano   la-levambon-o...***
       return:SS sleep-1PL:PST-CONN

       'Having returned, we slept and...'

Ellipsis in the bridging clause can also affect grammatical morphemes. In Sunwar, the evidential marker can be omitted from a bridging clause (Schulze & Bieri 1973: 392). Whether it must be omitted in any non-main clause is unclear at this stage. In Paluai in (18b), the bridging clause does not repeat the aspect marker of the reference clause (namely *pe* 'perfective'), although there are no restrictions on aspectual marking in non-main clauses in Paluai (Schokkin 2013: 419).

(18) Paluai (Oceanic, Admiralties; Schokkin 2014: 116)

   a. <u>*Wurê-pe*</u>   <u>*suwen*</u>   <u>*suk*</u>
      1PL:EXCL-PFV move.down shore

      'We went down to the shore.'

   b. **_Wurê-suwen_**   **_suk_**   *a*
      1PL:EXCL-move.down shore and

      'we went down to the shore and'

   c. *wurê-pe*   *pit*   *nêm*   *la*   *kel*
      1PL:EXCL-PFV jump be.finished go.to canoe

      'we boarded a canoe.'

Determining what portion of the reference clause can be repeated or omitted and whether there are functional differences between exact and non-exact repetitions remain open questions. It could be that the choice of verbatim versus partial repetition is constrained by language specific features. In Yurakaré, for example, the verb's arguments are rarely repeated in the bridging clause. This is a general tendency in the language, and not a specific feature of bridging constructions: topical arguments are not repeated (van Gijn 2014: 295–296).

3.1.3 Additions

Additions are instances where information present in the bridging clause is not present in the reference clause. So far, additions we have found are aspectual or lexical (added NPs). An example of lexical addition is given in Ma Manda in (19). The subject argument in the reference clause is expressed in the form of agreement (1PL) on the verb, but in the bridging clause, a full NP is introduced, referring to a different person–number value, namely 3PL.

(19) Ma Manda (Papua New Guinea; Pennington 2015)

   a. *blaakam ta-waam-ang*
      weed   do-PRS:1PL-HAB

      'we do the weeding.'

   b. **_taam-taam=pû blaakam ta-maa-kong-ka_**
      female-PL=NOM weed   do-COMPL-throw-ss

      'The women doing all the weeding, and...'

An example of aspectual addition in the verb phrase is given in (20). The predicate in (20b) is modified in (20c) by the predicate -*v* 'say' which acts, in this construction, as a phasal predicate (Guérin 2011: 342).

(20) Mavea (Oceanic, Vanautu; Guérin 2019 [this volume])

    a. *i-oele,   ko-arvulesi i-lo-v̆a*
       3SG:IRR-oil 2SG-stir   3SG:IRR-IPFV-go

       'it [is becoming] oil, you keep stirring'

    b. *ko-rong <u>sama-na</u>   <u>mo-rororo</u>.*
       2SG-hear froth-3SG:POSS 3SG-IDEO.noise

       '[until] you hear its froth sizzling.'

    c. ***sama-na   mo-v i-rororo***   *mal mo-noa   ne*
       froth-3SG:POSS 3SG-say 3SG-IDEO.noise DEM 3SG-cooked FOC

       '[when] its froth starts to sizzle, IT is cooked.'

Additions may clarify or refine information that is implicit in the reference clause, for instance by expressing an argument as a lexical noun phrase rather than as an agreement marker, or may offer a different aspectual perspective, but additions still express the same fundamental proposition found in the reference clause.

3.1.4 Substitution

Substitutions are replacements targeting elements in the verb phrase of the reference clause. First, we found instances of the substitution of only grammatical information. Consider the Ma Manda example in (19) above. The verbs are lexically identical in both clauses, but the reference clause is cast in the habitual aspect, whereas the bridging clause marks completion. Although habitual aspect is restricted to main clauses in Ma Manda, completive can be found in both clause types. Another case may be seen in Tsezic languages (Forker & Anker 2019 [this volume]): the finite or tensed verb form in the reference clause is replaced with a converb form. Finally, in White Hmong (Jarkey 2019 [this volume]) aspect systematically shifts between the reference clause and the bridging clause for rhetorical effect.

Second, substitution may target the lexical verb. Lexical substitution involves cases where the bridging verb is a synonym of the reference verb. This is shown in (21), where two different verbs 'tie with a knot' and 'bind' are used in the reference and bridging clauses respectively.

(21) Nabak (Papua New Guinea; Fabian et al. 1998: 164)

    a. *mam-be-mti   <u>za-nup</u>*
       CONT-put-MED:SS tie.with.a.knot-1PL:PRS

       '[we] put it [in place on the house] and tie it [down].'

b. ***Eli-mann...***
bind-MED:1PL:DS
'After we bind it...'

Similar facts are reported in Matsigenka-Spanish (Emlen 2019 [this volume]), Ma Manda (Pennington 2015) and Eibela in (22), where both verbs 'shave thin' and 'make flat' refer to the same event and describe two facets of the same procedure.

(22) Eibela (Papua New Guinea; Aiton 2019 [this volume])

  a. [sɛːli   gaːlɛ-mɛi]*final*
      properly shave.thin-HYPOTH

      '(You) should shave it properly'

  b. [sɛli   ɛmɛlɛ-si]*medial*
      properly make.flat-MED:PFV

      'Flatten it properly (by shaving).'

Although hyponymy and (partial) synonymy are not always easily distinguishable from one another, in a few languages, we find cases of hyponymy. The bridging clause contains a verb whose semantics is more general than that of the verb of the reference clause. This is reported in Siroi (van Kleef 1988: 151) and in Ono, shown in (23). The verb 'take' in the bridging clause in (23b) is a hypernym which refers to the more specific hyponym 'grab' in the reference clause in (23a).

(23) Ono (Papua New Guinea; Phinnemore 1998: 122)

  a. *eŋe kiŋzaŋ.kaŋzaŋ wie   ŋerep mararak-ko-i*
      they suddenly   get.up:ss girl grab-3PL-?

      'They suddenly grabbed the girl.'

  b. ***ma-u   paki***
      take-3PL:DS after:DS

      'After they took (her)...'

On the other hand, in White Hmong (Jarkey 2019 [this volume]) and in Timbe, reported in (24), the verb of the bridging clause is more specific in meaning than the verb of the reference clause (here, *climb > get to*). In Foster's (1981) words, (24) acts "as if it is a correction or a refinement of the final verb" of the previous clause.

(24) Timbe (Papua New Guinea; Foster 1981: 42)

    a. *hikakmâ emelâk <u>Bondâ</u> <u>meyeat</u>.*
       carrying already Bondâ they.got.to

       'and carrying (her child) they made it to Bondâ.'

    b. **Bondâ gayeat**   *âmâ ga...*
       Bondâ they.climbing.to when climbing

       'When they had climbed to Bondâ they climbed to...'

Constructions with non-matching verbs in the reference and bridging clauses raise challenging questions about the limits of bridging constructions: if the predicates in the reference and bridging clause are not identical but are synonyms, should we still consider the constructions involving substitution as bridging constructions, albeit "atypical"? What if the predicates are not synonyms but show different facets or perspectives of the same event? Consider example (25) from Tsez:

(25) Tsez (Nakh-Daghestanian; Forker & Anker 2019 [this volume])

    a. *...<u>kid</u> <u>xan-däyor</u>   <u>y-ik'i-n</u>*
       girl(II) khan-APUD.VERS II-go-PST.UW

       '...the girl went to the king.'

    b. ***elo-r***   *y-ay-nosi...*
       there-LAT II-come-ANT.CVB

       'After she arrived there,...'

In this example, a verb of movement in the reference clause is replaced by another in the bridging clause (go > come) resulting in a different deictic orientation. Should these instances be considered less like bridging constructions and more like PARAPHRASES defined by Longacre (2007a: 382–383) as inexact repetition with a gain or loss of information? The boundary here is fuzzy, and it is not immediately obvious whether there is a clear and categorical distinction between bridging constructions with separate predicates and paraphrases. The answer, we believe, lies in the function of these types of constructions: by looking at both formal and functional features, we assume it is possible to distinguish bridging constructions from paraphrases and other forms of repetition. This rationale, however, requires further research (see also §5).

3.2 Summary linkage

At the extreme end of the substitution spectrum, we reach cases where the lexical verb of the reference clause, its argument, and accompanying adjuncts are replaced with a generic light verb that has no lexical relation to the verb of the reference clause. The relation between the reference and the bridging clause is nevertheless maintained because the verb of the bridging clause is understood to summarize or anaphorically refer to the preceding discourse unit.

Across languages, two major types of verbs are used to form the bridging clause of a summary linkage. First, a verb with generic meaning is used, such as *nu* in (26b).

(26) Jingulu (non-Pama-Nyungan, Australia; Pensalfini 2015)

    a. *Marlarluka-rni ganya-marri jad.bili.*
        old.man-ERG   sing-REM.PST block

        'Old people sang them to block them.'

    b. **Marlarluka wurru-nu,...**
        old.man   3PL-AUX:PST

        'The old people did that,...'

This generic or light verb is often accompanied by a deictic element, as in Yurakaré (van Gijn 2014: 295) and Tariana with the manner deictic *kay* 'thus' in (27c) (see also the paragraph markers of Loos 1963: 701).

(27) Tariana (Arawak, northwest Amazonia; Aikhenvald 2003: 578)

    a. 'I went early, there I fished for aracú fish and went round,'

    b. *lape-pe-se   nu-emhani-na*
        muddy.lake-PL-LOC 1SG-walk-REM.PST:VIS

        'I went round in a muddy lake.'

    c. **kay nu-ni**
        thus 1SG-do

        'Having done this,'

    d. *dekina   nu-dia   nu-mara nu-nu-na-pita*
        afternoon 1SG-return 1SG-drift 1SG-come-REM.PST:VIS-AGAIN

        'I drifted downstream again in the afternoon'

The second strategy to form a summary linkage is to use a pro-verb, as in Aguaruna in (28b), or a demonstrative verb expressing manner (see Guérin 2015), such as *kwamun* 'do like that' in (29b). In these cases, the verb itself has deictic or anaphoric reference as part of its meaning.

(28) Aguaruna (Jivaroan, Peru; Overall 2017: 500)

    a. *mi=na*   *apa-hu*   *maŋkahatu-a-u*   *a-yi*
       1SG=ACC father-POSS:1SG kill:1PL:OBJ-PFV-NMLZ COP-REM.PST:3:DECL

       'my father killed a person'

    b. ***nu-ni-ka-mataĩ***
       ANA-VBLZ:INTR-PFV:SEQ-1/3:DS

       '(he) having done that' or 'and because of that'

    c. *auhu-tsu-u=ka*   *papi=na=ka*   *puhu-ya-ha-i*
       study-NEG-NMLZ=TOP book=ACC=TOP live-REM.PST-1SG-DECL

       'I was unable to study'

(29) Yongkom (Papua New Guinea; Christensen 2013: 66)

    a. *Anon ok*   *an-imam-ɛɛn.*
       dog   water eat-HAB-3:M

       'The dog was drinking water.'

    b. ***Kwamun-ɛ*** *yikabom bikn-ɛ...*
       do.like-SM lizard   hid-SM

       'He did that [and then] the lizard hid...'

Eibela uses a third possibility: the durative auxiliary *hɛna:* which forms a bridging clause, as shown in (30c).

(30) a. [*ɛimɛ*   *oga*   *ɛ*   *gɛ-mɛna=ta*]*medial* [*holo*   *anɛ-obo*]*final*
         already pandanus seedling plant-FUT=ATEL DEM:UP go:PST-INFER

         'He had already gone up there to plant pandanus seeds.'

    b. [[*ogu-bi=ja:*]*topic* *nɛ* *nɛ-ɸɛni*   *ɛna ja*   *di*]*final*
         do.thus-DS=TOP 1:SG 1:SG-alone still here PFV

         'He did that, I was still alone here.'

    c. [[*hɛna:-si=ja:*]*topic* *si-ja:*]*final*
         DUR-MED:PFV=TOP move.around-PST

         'That being the case, I was wandering around here.'

So far, we found three languages with more than one summary linkage. The language Aguaruna stands out with eight different demonstrative verbs, two of them commonly used in bridging constructions. The choice of one over the other is determined by the discourse prominence of the participants and the (in)transitivity of the event (Overall 2017: 257, 499, 589). Cavineña forms two types of summary linkage with two different demonstrative predicates, namely *ju-* 'be' and *a-* 'affect' in conjunction with the anaphoric manner demonstrative *jadya* 'thus'. The choice of predicate depends on the transitivity of the event recapitulated: intransitive with *ju-* or transitive with *a-* (Guillaume 2011: 128). Eibela is noteworthy with three different types of summary linkage formed with three different predicates: a demonstrative verb *wogu* 'do thus', a light verb *ɛ* 'do', and a durative auxiliary *hɛna*. These three anaphoric options have clear semantic and functional differences. The durative auxiliary *hɛna* summarizes a reference clause and adds the aspectual meaning of duration to the proposition: the event or state described in the reference clause continues for an extended time period. The light verb *ɛ* 'do' differs in that the reference of the anaphor is not always limited to the event described in the reference clause, and may extend to summarizing an entire preceding series of events. In contrast, the demonstrative verb *wogu* 'do thus' summarizes and expresses only the same proposition as the reference clause and may add morphological indicators of sequentiality or causation (see Aiton 2019 [this volume]).

3.3 Mixed linkage

A mixed linkage is a type of bridging construction which combines the lexical verb of a reference clause (as in recapitulative linkage) with an anaphoric element (as in summary linkage). Mixed linkage is found in Cavineña, in (31), described as containing the verb of the reference clause in a non-finite form, the particle *jadya* 'thus' and an auxiliary (light verb) carrying the dependency marker, in that order (Guillaume 2011: 129).

(31) Cavineña (Tacanan, Bolivia; Guillaume 2011: 129)

    a. *Ji-da=dya=di*   *ka-reke-ti-kware*
       good-ADJ:SUF=FOC=EMPH REFL-cross-REFL-REM.PST

       'I crossed well.'

    b. ***Ka-reke-ti***   *jadya ju-atsu* *tapeke=piji*   *ara-kware.*
       REFL-cross-REFL thus   be-SS   trip.food=DIM eat-REM.PST

       'After crossing, I ate the food.'

The other languages where the lexical verb from the reference clause and a
light verb are combined are Ma Manda in (32c) and Kokota in (33b).

(32)   Ma Manda (Papua New Guinea; Pennington 2015)

    a.   'The day before yesterday I wanted to go to Lae with Gaamiyong,'

    b.   *ku-gûmot*
       go-REM.PST:1DU

       '(so) we went.'

    c.   **ku-gûmot   ta-ng-alû**
       go-REM.PST:1DU do-DS-2/3

       'We went but'

    d.   *na-taam=pû   kadep=mang kam   nûnû-gûng...*
       male-female=NOM road=LOC   down 1PL:OBJ:tell-REM.PST:2/3PL

       'the people down on the road told us...'

(33)   Kokota (Oceanic, Solomon Islands; Palmer 2009: 398)

    a.   *n-e   toga ağe=u   maneri,*
       REAL-3SG arrive go=CONT they

       'They arrived.'

    b.   **toga ğ-e=u**   *tana nogoi lao hure=i   hinage=na...*
       arrive NT-3SBJ=be.thus then VOC go carry=3SG.OBJ boat=that

       'They arrived and then went [and] carried that boat...'

In White Hmong, on the other hand, mixed linkage combines the verb of the
reference clause and the anaphoric adverb *li* 'thus, like'. Other anaphoric elements can be added. In (34), the speech verb *hais* is repeated in the bridging
clause, and the anaphoric adverb *li*, the anaphoric demonstrative *ntawd* 'that,
there' and the particle *tag* 'finish' are added (see Jarkey 2019 [this volume]).

(34)   White Hmong (Hmong-Mien, Laos; Jarkey 2019 [this volume])

    a.   Ces   *Luj Tub thiaj.li hais tias   "Yog tsaug~tsaug.zog thiab*
       and.then Lu Tu so.then say COMP COP REDUP~be.sleepy and
       nqhis~nqhis   nqaij mas yuav.tau rov   mus..."
       REDUP~crave meat TOP must   return go

       'And so then Lu Tu said, "If you are very sleepy and are really craving
       meat, (I) must go back"...'

b. ***Hais li   ntawd tag   ces...***
say   like that   finish and.then

'After saying that, then...'

The status of these mixed bridging constructions remains to be studied in more detail. Evidence that the bridging clause in a mixed linkage is a single clause (and not a sequence of two clauses) comes from clause boundary markers: switch-reference in Cavineña and Ma Manda, agreement marking in Kokota, or the coordination *ces* in White Hmong. Other cases are not so clear. Consider Aguaruna's summary linkage with the anaphoric verb *nu-ni-* 'ANA-VBLZ.INTR-' as the bridging element in (28b) above. In Aguaruna there is also the option of using this anaphoric verb followed by the lexical verb of the reference clause. Whether this construction, shown in (35b), is a mixed linkage is unclear, given that both the anaphoric verb and the lexical verbs are marked with switch-reference.

(35)   Aguaruna (Jivaroan, Peru; Overall 2017: 617)

a.   *...mau-tayami*
kill-NORM

'...we kill it.'

b.   ***nu-ni-ka***   ***ma-a***
ANA-VBLZ.INTR-PFV:SEQ:1PL:SS kill-PFV:SEQ:1PL:SS

'having done that, having killed it'

c.   'if we take it away, we easily take it away.'

Note also that in Ma Manda, the switch-reference agreement on the light verb *ta-* 'do' does not match the subject of the previous verb, thereby suggesting that the light verb could have grammaticalized into a conjunction (see further discussion in §6). This light verb is also typically used in summary linkage, giving us indirect access to the possible historical development of bridging elements into clause linking devices.

4 Discourse functions

Bridging constructions are considered a "discourse strategy rather than a phenomenon of the sentence grammar" (de Vries 2005: 364). They operate beyond the level of the independent clause to serve specific discourse functions, where discourse can be understood both in its structural sense, meaning "grammar above the clause" (i.e., the structural organization of units larger than a main clause), and in its functionalist sense, referring to "language in use", i.e., the general cultural knowledge that is required to (de)code a text (Cameron 2001: 10–13). In the following subsections, we discuss three major discourse features associated with bridging constructions, which are relevant to both definitions of discourse. First, we consider some discourse characteristics that are prone to trigger the use of bridging constructions: the text genre, the medium of communication, and the speaker are discussed in §4.1. The cohesive functions of these constructions are then presented in §4.2. Last, the structuring role that bridging constructions play in discourse is detailed in §4.3.

4.1 Conducive factors

Several factors are conducive to the presence or absence of bridging constructions in discourse. In this section, we concentrate on the text genre, the medium of communication, and the speaker. In Longacre's (1983) discourse typology, four genres of monologue discourse are differentiated: procedural (e.g., how-to-do-it), behavioural (e.g., eulogy, hortatory), narrative (e.g., prophecies, myth), and expository discourse (e.g., scientific paper). These types of monologue discourse correlate with distinctive grammatical markers across languages. In English, for example, narrative discourse uses historical present or past tense, and participants are encoded with 1st or 3rd singular pronouns; while procedural discourse uses imperative, non-focused agent, and 1st plural pronouns (Longacre 1983: 3–17). Of these four genres, both Longacre (1983: 9) and de Vries (2005: 365) acknowledge that bridging constructions are one of the distinctive features of narrative and procedural texts. This may be a reflection of a bias towards this type of data in corpora, since most descriptive grammars often concentrate on these two types of monologue discourse, and not so much a real effect of genre on the distribution of the phenomenon. In this volume, we found bridging constructions to be used in a rather restricted range of texts. In Matsigenka (Emlen 2019 [this volume]) bridging constructions are a prominent feature of myth narration but they are found in no other types of performative oration. Similarly, in Nakh-Daghestanian languages (Forker & Anker 2019 [this volume]), bridging constructions are restricted to traditional fictional narratives (and are not found in historical or autobiographical narratives). In Logoori, bridging constructions are used in some procedural text, but not in other text genres (Sarvasy 2019 [this volume]), while in Greek (Alvanoudi 2019 [this volume]), clause repetition is found to play a major cohesive role in conversations.

In addition, de Vries (2005: 378;2006: 817) indicates that a key function of bridging linkage is to give the speaker an opportunity to plan the subsequent narrative episode, and to give the listener an opportunity to process the events of previous discourse unit. These processing pressures are largely absent from written language, and we would therefore expect bridging constructions to be absent or far less frequent in a written medium, as hinted in Matsigenka and Tsezic languages (see Emlen 2019 and Forker & Anker 2019 [this volume]), a hypothesis that remains to be tested.

We do not have frequency counts of bridging clauses for each genre in each language we investigated, and a quantitative analysis is beyond the scope of this volume. Impressionistically, it seems that in Ma Manda, bridging clauses appear preceding almost every single main clause in a narrative or a procedural text (Pennington 2015), while in Manambu (Aikhenvald 2008: 544–545), the most common way to connect main clauses is with the connectives *ata* 'then' and *atawata:y* 'in summary', and bridging constructions are frequent but not pervasive. More importantly, because bridging constructions can be used as a stylistic device, the rate of their use varies with individual preferences, as noted in Logoori, White Hmong and Mavea (see the chapters by Sarvasy, Jarkey, and by Guérin, in this volume. See also de Vries 2005: 375). The identity of the narrator (Longacre 1983: 17–20), in terms of age, sex, social position, etc., does also affect his/her usage of bridging constructions and these variables should thus be taken into consideration before claims about the frequency of occurrence of bridging constructions in a particular text genre or medium can be made meaningful.

4.2 Adding cohesion

Cohesion refers to "the relation of meaning that exists within a text. [...] Cohesion occurs where the interpretation of some element in the discourse is dependent on that of another" (Halliday & Hasan 1976: 4). Features such as cross-reference, substitution, ellipsis, and semantic relations between propositions are all different instances of cohesion. One of the cohesive relations that bridging constructions instantiate in discourse is cross-reference, as in (36). Bridging constructions help track participants in languages with switch reference marking (de Vries 2005: 373–378). As shown in (36a), reference-tracking information is not encoded on the finite predicate of the reference clause, but on the bridging clause in (36b). This marking indicates whether the subject of the previous and following sentences is the same or different, and at the same time, it types the clause as dependent.

(36) Aguaruna (Jivaroan, Peru; Overall 2017: 499–500)

    a. *yunuma-tu-ka-u-i*

       approach-APPL-PFV-NMLZ-COP:3:DECL

       '(The person) approached (the boa).'

    b. **nu-ni-ka-mataĩ**

       ANA-VBLZ:INTR-PFV:SEQ-1/3:DS

       'When he (the person) had done so'

    c. *nu-na   achi-ka-u-i   aintsu-na paŋkĩ*

       ANA-ACC grab-PFV-NMLZ-COP:3:DECL person-ACC boa

       'the boa grabbed that person.'

Thematic continuity is another cohesive technique that bridging constructions enable. As the story progresses, bridging construction highlight important turning points, or new events on the main event line, and the (sequential) relationship between these events. This function is described in this volume in Eibela, Mavea and White Hmong. In addition, bridging constructions in Mavea and White Hmong can be used to bring the narrative back to the main event line after a digression. In Greek conversations, clause repetition could be said to have a similar role when a speaker repeats a question to pursue a response after being ignored.

Bridging constructions also mark a semantic relation between discourse segments, typically, expressing sequentiality, as shown in (17). The event in (17b) (*la* 'sleep') is temporally subsequent to the event in the reference clause in (17a) (*ndave* 'return'). Bridging constructions expressing a temporal or sequential relation between parts of discourse are found in Dani (Bromley 2003: 314), Murui (Wojtylak 2017: 516), and several languages in this volume (see Table 1). Other semantic relations are concession and consequence in Eibela (Aiton 2019 [this volume]) and in Aguaruna (Overall 2017: 499–502).

4.3 Structuring discourse

What does the linkage link? In our current schema given in (2), we argue that bridging constructions link DISCOURSE UNITS, a notion left intentionally vague as one of the purposes of this volume was to refine what such a discourse segment could be. In chaining languages of Papua New Guinea, de Vries (2005: 363) argues that the discourse segments linked by bridging constructions are clause chains. But more generally, from a discourse perspective, we agree with Thompson et al. (2007: 272–274) that bridging constructions link PARAGRAPHS.

Following Longacre (1983: 14–17), we analyse in this volume monologue discourse which distinguishes two organizational positions: the EVENT LINE which carries the main events forward, and the SUPPORTIVE LINE which adds emotive or depictive information. The event line generally follows the macro-structure or schema: exposition (introduction, orientation), development (inciting moment, complication action), developing conflict, climax, denouement (result, resolution), conclusion (closure, coda).[5] Each of these macro-structural components carries the main story forward through a series of episodes, which are expounded in paragraphs.

We follow Longacre (2007b: 116) who claims that paragraphs are part of any language's discourse patterns as they are the building blocks of discourse. Longacre (1983: 295) goes on to argue that a paragraph is "the developmental unit of discourse". It is the typical unit within which a discourse topic is elaborated (an argument in hortatory discourse, an explanation in expository discourse, or an episode in narrative discourse). As a discourse unit, the paragraph "maintains a uniform orientation" (Hinds 2012: 136) in terms of its spatial, temporal, thematic and participant continuity (Givón 1983: 7–10; Longacre 2007b: 115–120). The paragraph is also a structural unit, showing closure: the onset and coda are overtly marked by particles, connectives, or intonational patterns (van Dijk 1977: Chap. 5; Seifart 2010: 895–896). We argue, in line with Longacre (1983: 9), that bridging constructions are one of the possible patterns that formally outlines a paragraph boundary. This is shown in Korowai, Eibela, White Hmong and Nakh-Daghestanian languages in this volume. However, in some cases, it is the lack of bridging constructions that is the boundary marker (Farr 1999: 337).

For example, in procedural texts, the narrative line is pared down to the main activities (i.e., the procedure) essential to achieving the objective of the text. Each new event is a new step in the procedure, and these steps are seldom explained or expounded into episodes. In these text genres then, a paragraph is reduced to a single clause. Consider (37). From a discourse perspective, the bridging clause in (37b) signals the end of an event, a step in the procedure and the beginning of a new one. From a structural perspective, the bridging clause signals a new paragraph.

(37)   Jingulu (non-Pama-Nyungan, Australia; Pensalfini 2015)

    a.   *kijurlurlu-warndi nangka-marri marlarluka-rni.*
        stone-INS   chop-REM.PST old.men-ERG
        'Olden folk would crush it with a stone.'

---

[5]See Chafe 2001: 277; Johnstone 2001: 637–639; Longacre 1983: 21–24, 38–41; see also Gleason Jr 1968; Labov & Waletzky 1967/2007; and van Dijk 1977.

b. ***kijurlurlu-warndi nangka-marrimi*** *dika ajuwa-marriyimi.*
   stone-INS   chop-REM.PST   fat   throw-REM.PST
   'Once crushed with a stone they'd mix fat in with it.'

In narratives, bridging constructions are often associated with the main event line. They maintain thematic continuity by helping the story unfold. For example, in Iatmul, Jendraschek (2009: 1324) argues that bridging constructions "help to carry the plot forward by providing transitions between linked events", while in Siroi, "by just glancing over the [bridging clauses] of a story you can usually get an accurate impression of the story line" (van Kleef 1988: 153). However, de Vries (2005; 2006) has shown that bridging constructions can also break the event line to add supporting material (e.g., give background information) or to create special effects, such as setting the stage for a climactic or unexpected peak event in the story (de Vries 2005: 373). In Siroi, van Kleef (1988: 151–152) notes that bridging constructions have different discursive functions depending on their placement in discourse: at the beginning of a paragraph, they highlight discontinuity (a change in time, location, or the addition of a new participant), while within a paragraph, which is the most common position in Siroi (as in Cavineña, Guillaume 2011: 123), bridging constructions highlight continuity. The correlation position/meaning also holds in Kasu, another Papuan language, with a notable addition: the type of bridging construction used (summary or recapitulative) also plays a role. In this language, recapitulative linkage occurs inside a paragraph to indicate continuity whereas summary linkage is found across paragraphs to mark the beginning of a new thematic paragraph (Logan 2008: 23–30).

Interestingly, the position of bridging constructions within a text as a whole is no less significant. Van Kleef indicates (1988: 152) that in Siroi bridging constructions never occur around the climax of the story, although they do so in Angave, another Papuan language as well as in Mavea (Guérin 2019 [this volume]).

The discourse functions of the bridging constructions studied in this volume are summarized in Table 1. Empty cells indicate lack of data. Although bridging constructions are in many languages a conspicuous feature of discourse, much light still needs to be shed on the nature and length of the discourse units that these constructions link, their placement in discourse, and their types and functions for each genre in different languages.

We briefly mention here two other constructions with similar discourse functions: nominal repetition in Logoori (Sarvasy 2019 [this volume]) and the connector pronoun in Bora (Seifart 2010). In Logoori, an AVO language, the O of a final clause can be repeated as the S the following clause. If a bridging construction marks event cohesion and continuity, then nominal repetition can be

Table 1: Reported discourse functions of bridging constructions in this volume

	Stylistic	Sequential	Cohesion	Structuring	Emphasis
Eibela		✓		✓	
Greek		✓			✓
Korowai			✓	✓	
Logoori	✓	✓	✓		
Matsigenka	✓	✓		✓	
Mavea	✓	✓		✓	✓
Nakh-Daghestanian	✓			✓	
White Hmong		✓	✓	✓	✓

said to mark referential cohesion and topic continuity. This feature is, however, just as uncommon as bridging clauses in Logoori. In Bora, a language of Peru, paragraphs are almost always introduced by a connector pronoun, which Seifart argues (2010: 900) is the functional equivalent to bridging constructions in Papuan languages. Similarities include the fixed paragraph-initial position of the bridging clause and the connector pronoun; the connector pronoun can assume different forms reminiscent of summary and recapitulative linkages (although no difference in meaning or functions is noted for the connector); and, like bridging constructions, the connector pronoun can indicate causal, adversative, or temporal semantic relations (Seifart 2010: 904–909).

5 Other types of repetition

REPETITION is pervasive in language (Brown 2000) and may serve various functions, depending on the language. Clause repetition can add aspectual meaning, denoting habitual or iterative events in Tuvalu (Besnier 2014: 487) or representing the continuation of a state or activity in Nahavaq (Dimock 2009: 259–260), or it can mark emphasis in Sunwar (Schulze & Bieri 1973: 390). In each language, these functions are distinct from those of bridging constructions, which operate on the level of discourse, and express event sequencing or reference tracking, as discussed in §4. However, the boundary between bridging constructions and clausal repetition may be obscured when repetition is verbatim and pared down to the predicate. This is especially true of some Oceanic languages of Vanuatu, where bridging clauses are morphologically identical to main clauses. Consider data from Nahavaq: clausal repetition, in (38c), and the bridging clause, bolded in (39b), are morphologically main clauses, and in both cases, there is verbatim repetition of a previous clause. Thus, there is no grammatical marker to distinguish a bridging clause from clausal repetition.

(38)   Nahavaq (Oceanic, Vanuatu; Dimock 2009: 261)

   a. *Ru-raq   ne-hew   gcen   wut ru-q-vwul   ni-momoq*
      3DU-work N.PREF-garden because COMP 3DU-IRR-buy N.PREF-woman

      'And they made a garden so they could buy him a wife,'

   b. *sut   migce-n qin, ro-koh, en i-yar   en.*
      NON.SPE to-3SG   3SG 3PL-be and 3SG:REAL-finish and

      'and they stayed.'

   c. *Ro-koh mbey, ro-koh mbey, ro-koh mbey,*
      3PL-be to   3PL-be to   3PL-be to

      'They stayed on and on,'

   d. *en   ru-pir   ni-mbwuwes...*
      and 3DU-look.after N.PREF-pig

      'and they raised pigs...'

(39)   a. *...en i-suq   qin*
         and 3SG:REAL-stab 3SG

         '...and [he] punctured it.'

      b. *i-suq   qin, i-min.*
         3SG:REAL-stab 3SG 3SG:REAL-drink

         'He punctured it, he drank.' Interpreted as: '[...] and punctured it. **And after** he had punctured it, he drank.' (Dimock 2009: 260)

We do, however, expect to find a prosodic distinction, as has been described for Sunwar (Schulze & Bieri 1973: 389–391). In Sunwar, the reference clause has a falling, sentence-final intonation. It is followed by a pause and the bridging clause has level intonation (see also discussion in §2.3). Repetitions in Sunwar have, on the other hand, level or rising intonation on each clause repeated (see also the chapter on Mavea in this volume). Further formal differences may be present. Bridging constructions are typically composed of a single bridging clause, as we saw in (9), whereas repetitions are more numerous. In Tuvaluan, the verb phrase can be repeated up to eight times, "the number of times the verb is repeated is iconic of the degree of habituality" (Besnier 2014: 487).

Teasing apart clause repetition from bridging constructions is not always problematic. In Murui, the distinction is unequivocally marked in the morphology: the repeated clause is a main clause in (40c), whereas a bridging clause, as in (41c), is a nominalized clause (Wojtylak 2017: 518), thus a non-main clause.

(40)   Murui (Witotoan, Columbia; Wojtylak 2017: 514)

    a. *bai-e*   *ɨi-ñɨaɨ*   *kobeda ui-t-e*
       this-CLF:GENL man-COLL shotgun take-LK-3

       'The men took weapons.'

    b. *naɨ-do   do-ri-ta-kana*   *jai-d-e*
       path-INS shoot-DUR-CAUS-OVLP go-LK-3

       'Shooting along the way, they walked the path.'

    c. *naɨ-do   do-ri-ta-kana*   *jai-d-e*
       path-INS shoot-DUR-CAUS-OVLP go-LK-3

       'Shooting along the way, they walked (and walked).'

    d. *naɨ-do   bai-e*   *joma-nɨaɨ*   *do-ri-ta-kana*
       way-INS that-CLF:GENL monkey-COLL shoot-DUR-CAUS-OVLP

       ui-t-e
       bring-LK-3

       'Along the path shooting at monkeys, they brought (them)'

(41)   a. 'And, after pounding (it), after mixing (it),'

    b. *kome jai   nai-e*   <u>*du-t-e*</u>   *jmm...*
       person already ANA.SP-CLF:GENL chew.coca-LK-3 INTERJ

       'a person already chews it.'

    c. ***du-a-no-na***   *kome kome-kɨ*   *faka-d-e*
       chew.coca-E.NMLZ-SEQ-N.S/A.TOP person heart-CLF:RND think-LK-3

       jmm
       INTERJ

       'After chewing (it), a person meditates (lit. thinks).'

Arguments in Murui are also generally omitted from bridging clauses but not from repetition. The two constructions' functions in discourse do not overlap: repetitions have aspectual overtones, while bridging clauses mark sequentiality (Wojtylak 2017: 513–522). Thus, although there may be a formal overlap between repetition and bridging constructions, by looking at both formal and functional features we can distinguish the two.

6 Summary and directions for future research

Bridging constructions represent an interface between sentence and discourse. As sentence-level structures, they display the morphosyntactic categories of a language's clauses, whether final or non-final. As part of a language's discourse patterns, bridging constructions add coherence and cohesion by demarcating discourse units such as paragraphs and/or by highlighting semantic relationships between or within these units. For example, aspectual differences in a reference clause and bridging clause serve to communicate the relative temporal relationships of disparate events in Eibela (Aiton 2019 [this volume]) and White Hmong (Jarkey 2019 [this volume]). Bridging constructions also perform specific pragmatic functions. For example, categories such as topic and focus attached to a bridging clause in Eibela (Aiton 2019 [this volume]) and Korowai (de Vries 2019 [this volume]) convey the pragmatic relevance of the bridging clause, and by extension of the previous discourse unit.

The languages examined in this volume all use at least one type of bridging construction in texts, except Greek, which replaces bridging constructions in conversations with clause repetition, to achieve overall the same effect (i.e., discourse cohesion). The majority of languages in our dataset have more than one type of bridging constructions (e.g., Cavineña and Ma Manda use recapitulative and mixed linkages). Few languages have more than one type of summary linkage (e.g., Aguaruna, Cavineña, Eibela).

What is revealing here (as alluded in de Vries 2005 for Papuan languages) is that languages which exploit several bridging techniques also ascribe specific functions to each form of linkage. In particular, if a language has both recapitulative and summary linkage, it seems to us that recapitulative linkage is the default construction and summary linkage the marked construction, for two main reasons. First, because of its form, recapitulative linkage refers specifically to an identifiable chunk of text. In Korowai (de Vries 2019 [this volume]), recapitulative linkage is a recurrent textual construction feature. It is its absence or the use of a different type of linkage that signals discontinuity in the narrative flow. On the other hand, summary linkage uses a generic verb, thus the chunk of text that this linkage refers to is much more difficult to pinpoint. In Korowai (de Vries 2019 [this volume]), summary linkage may refer back to the final clause of the previous clause chain, to the previous clause chain, or to the preceding chain of clause chains. In a similar vein in Eibela (Aiton 2019 [this volume]), a summary linkage found in the penultimate line of a narrative can summarize the whole narrative and not just the previous clause. It is up to the addressee to infer from the context which information the speaker refers to. The second piece of evidence is that summary linkage seems to be associated with direct speech and verbs of saying. In Cavineña, Guillaume (2011: 128–131) argues that summary linkage is most exclusively "restricted to the recapitulation of quotation events [...] direct speech, thoughts, or expression of feeling", a finding that is echoed in Tsezic languages (Forker & Anker 2019 [this volume]) and in White Hmong (Jarkey 2019 [this volume]). Jarkey notes that summary linkage is more likely associated with unplanned personal narrative and conversation than with literary style and third person narration. However, Guillaume also admits that he cannot pinpoint clear contrasts between mixed linkage and summary linkage (2011: 130). At the time van Kleef wrote her article, she had not yet found what separated the use of recapitulative and summary linkages in van Kleef (1988: 155). Thus, research in this area is still crucially needed. It is likely that exploring the type of events and generic verbs used in summary linkage will yield insightful results.

Further questions that are beyond our reach at this stage but need to be addressed are listed here. First and foremost, as we prepared this volume, we were often asked to pinpoint the typological characteristics that bridging constructions correlate with (e.g., SOV syntax, NP density, switch-reference, demonstrative verbs, etc.). For example, Guillaume (2011: 113) notes that bridging constructions are prevalent in polysynthetic languages or languages favouring null arguments. They have often been associated with chaining languages exhibiting switch reference in general (after Stirling 1993) and Papuan languages in particular, following de Vries 2005. Seifart (2010) links bridging constructions to "verby languages" and pronoun connector to "nouny languages". However, none of these features seem to be sufficient or necessary. Logoori, an SVO Bantu language with clause chains barely uses bridging construction in discourse, as shown by Sarvasy (2019 [this volume]). In our opinion, defining the typological features that correlate with bridging constructions is only relevant if bridging constructions are an integral part of the grammar. We assume that to be part of a language's grammar, a bridging construction must be a conventionalized pattern with a productive formal representation paired with a consistent and predictable semantic contribution. It could be that bridging constructions are part of the grammar of some languages, but this subset of languages still needs to be established. Siroi and Aguaruna are, in our view, good candidates for this subset as virtually every clause chain in these languages starts with a bridging clause promoting discourse cohesion (van Kleef 1988: 152, Overall 2017: 589). But in other languages we have studied, bridging constructions lie at the interface between discourse and syntax. They are restricted to certain genres, are not pervasive and not reliably or consistently employed. They are considered a stylistic feature, used more by certain speakers than others in the same language community, and are in no case mandatory (as for example in Mavea or Logoori). A caveat is that these constructions could be unreported for a particular language because they only occur in a special genre that has not been documented in that language (yet); because the "right" speakers have not been recorded (as described by Grenoble 2012); or because they are not sufficiently distinctive to be recognized as a conventionalized construction.

The historical development of bridging constructions into grammatical markers seems to us a promising line of research. Our thoughts on this topic stem from a few descriptive studies noting that bridging clauses function as clausal coordinators (Bromley 2003: 314; Jendraschek 2009: 1327). In Yongkom, the demonstrative verb *kwan* 'do like that' is extensively used in bridging constructions. In medial form it is lexicalized as the adverbial 'likewise, also' but with additional causative morphology, it has grammaticalized as the connective 'therefore' (Christensen 2013: 29). Based on these remarks, it is conceivable that the bridging component of the construction becomes a conventionalized means of transitioning between discourse episodes, which ultimately fully grammaticalizes into a coordination marker, as discussed for Ma Manda in (32c) and possibly in Bora (Seifart 2010: 909, 913) and Kombai (de Vries 2005: 376–377). Interestingly, Alvanoudi (2019) further alludes to the possibility that bridging constructions may result from the grammaticalization of repeated discourse practices that serve to provide discourse cohesion.

The diffusion of bridging constructions through language contact is a research area for which we do not have enough data. The phenomenon is reported and discussed in the Arawak language studied in the volume, Matsigenka (Emlen 2019 [this volume]), corroborating the fact that bridging constructions as discourse devices are not immune to borrowing (Aikhenvald 2006: 15, 17).

Last, de Vries (2005: 378; 2006: 817) also mentions "ease of processing" as an additional function of bridging constructions: the bridging construction allows the speaker to hold the floor long enough to process their next narrative move and gather his/her thoughts too, and it gives listeners time to process the information of the paragraph it follows. Indirect evidence could possibly be found in Mavea (Guérin 2019 [this volume]), but overall, experimental data to confirm these claims are at present lacking.

Appendix

As more research needs to be devoted to the topic, we have established a preliminary list of questions that researchers interested in describing bridging constructions should consider.

1. Content of bridging clause

    a) What is repeated? The lexical verb of the reference clause? Verbal complex? Any arguments?

    b) What is omitted? Are the omissions dictated by the grammar (e.g., lack of morphology associated with non-main clauses) or optional?

    c) Is there a dedicated verb instead of a repetition? If so, what kind of verb can be used?
    If a generic verb, what are its properties?

    d) Is there no verb at all referring to the reference clause but instead a pronoun? How does this linkage fit in with anaphora in general?

    e) Any special marking on the bridging element?
    E.g., topic marker, case marking, focus, etc. Do bridging clauses occur with preceding discourse particle (e.g., *now, then, so*)?

2. Syntactic status

    a) Is the bridging clause a non-main clause?
    Are the tense and/or aspectual markings the same as the reference clause? Any restrictions in tense/aspect/modality, polarity, or person marking?

    b) What is the status of the bridging clause? E.g., is it subordinated? Juxtaposed? Coordinated? Is the bridging clause a special clause type?

3. Position

    a) Is the bridging clause in initial position? Or in what Longacre (2007a) calls the "sentence margin".

    b) Is the bridging clause placed immediately after the reference clause?

    c) What do bridging clauses link? Clauses? Paragraphs?
    How often do they occur in a text? Where do they occur in a text? Where do they not occur? Are bridging constructions obligatory? Optional? If optional, what other strategy, if any, is used instead?

4. Intonation

    a) Is there a break/pause between the reference and the bridging clauses?

    b) What is the intonation pattern of the bridging clause? Any other particular intonation pattern?

Valérie Guérin & Grant Aiton

5. Semantics

   a) Does the bridging clause mark any semantic relation to its controlling clause? Repetition; simultanity, describing concomitant activities; sequentiality, expressing a state of affair in addition to another, etc.

6. Discourse function

   a) Do bridging constructions:

      - Connect two unrelated sections, thus, carry forward the event line: a new topic is introduced after the bridging clause (topic-shifting)?
      - Provide textual boundary (event sequencing)?
      - Provide lexical cohesion through repetition or summary?
      - Act as participant-tracking devices, especially in languages with switch reference marking?

   b) If the language only has one bridging construction, does the linkage fulfil a single semantic function? A single discourse function? Or more than one functions?

   c) If the language has several types of bridging constructions, which linkage fulfils which semantic function? Which discourse function?

7. Cohesive strategies

   a) How do bridging constructions compare or contrast with other linking strategies? E.g., subordination, coordination

   b) How similar/different are bridging constructions from repetitions? From paraphrase? In terms of frequency, function, position, obligatoriness, etc.

8. Text genres

   a) Do bridging constructions appear in different text genres? Conversation, procedural texts, narratives, etc.

   b) For languages with different types of bridging constructions, does the same type of bridging construction appear across text genres? Or are there different types of bridging constructions associated with different texts?

9. Historical and areal questions

    a) Is the bridging clause reduced (and grammaticalized) to the point where it becomes a discourse particle, subordinator, or coordinator? This could be especially relevant for summary linkage, where the bridging element contains a generic verb.

    b) In contact situations, is there any evidence that bridging constructions could be areally diffused?

Abbreviations

:	portmanteau	COP	copula
-	separates root and suffix	DECL	declarative
=	separates root and clitic	DEM	demonstrative
1	first person	DIM	diminutive
2	second person	DS	different subject
3	third person	DU	dual
1/3:DS	different subject, from third person to first person	DUR	durative
		EMPH	emphatic
2/3	second or third person	ERG	ergative
I-V	gender	EX	exclamative
ACC	accusative	EXCL	exclusive
ADJ.SUF	adjective suffix	FOC	focus
AGAIN	again	FUT	future
ALL	allative	GENL	general
ANA	anaphoric pronoun	HAB	habitual
ANT.CVB	anterior converb	HYPOTH	hypothetical
APPL	applicative	IDEO	ideophone
APUD	apudessive case	IMP	imperative
ASSOC	associative	INCL	inclusive
ATEL	atelic	INDF	indefinite
AUX	auxiliary	INS	instrumental
CLF	classifier	INFER	inferred
COLL	collective	INTERJ	interjection
COMP	complementizer	INTR	intransitive
COMPL	completive	IPFV	imperfective
CONN	connective	IRR	irrealis
CONJ	conjunction	LAT	lative case
CONT	continuous/continuative	LOC	locative

M	masculine	PST.UW	unwitnessed past tense
MED	medial	REAL	realis
NEG	negation	REDUP	reduplicated
NMLZ	nominalizer	RND	round
NOM	nominative	REFL	reflexive
NON1	second or third person (non-speaker)	REM.PST	remote past
		SEQ	sequential
NON.SPE	non-specific	SG	singular
N.S/A	non S/A subject	SM	sentence medial verb ending
NORM	normative	SS	same subject
N.PREF	nominal prefix	STAT	stative
NT	neutral modality	SJB	subject
OBJ	object	TOP	topic/topical
OVLP	overlap	TR	transitional sound
PFV	perfective	UP	higher elevation
PL	plural	VBLZ	verbalizer
POSS	possessive	VIS	visual
PREP	preposition	VOC	vocative
PRS	present tense		
PST	past tense		

Acknowledgements

We wish to thank Simon Overall for his contribution to an earlier version of this chapter. Special thanks to Angeliki Alvanoudi, Diana Forker, Spike Gildea, Martin Haspelmath, Nick Piper, and Lourens de Vries for constructive feedback.

References

Aikhenvald, Alexandra Y. Forthcoming. Bridging linkage in Tariana, an Arawak language from North-West Amazonia. *International Journal of American linguistics*.

Aikhenvald, Alexandra Y. 2003. *A grammar of Tariana, from Northwest Amazonia*. Cambridge: Cambridge University Press.

Aikhenvald, Alexandra Y. 2006. Grammars in contact: A cross-linguistic perspective. In Alexandra Y. Aikhenvald & R. M. W. Dixon (eds.), *Grammars in contact: A cross-linguistic typology*, 1–66. Oxford: Oxford University Press.

Aikhenvald, Alexandra Y. 2008. *The Manambu language of the East Sepik, Papua New Guinea.* Oxford: Oxford University Press.

Aiton, Grant. 2019. The form and function of bridging constructions in Eibela discourse. In Valérie Guérin (ed.), *Bridging constructions,* 157–184. Berlin: Language Science Press. DOI:10.5281/zenodo.2563688

Alvanoudi, Angeliki. 2019. Clause repetition as a tying technique in Greek conversation. In Valérie Guérin (ed.), *Bridging constructions,* 239–267. Berlin: Language Science Press. DOI:10.5281/zenodo.2563694

Besnier, Niko. 2014. *Tuvaluan: A Polynesian language of the Central Pacific.* London: Routledge.

Boersma, Paul & David Weenink. 2019. *Praat: Doing phonetics by computer. Computer program, version 6.0.46.* http://www.praat.org, accessed 2019-1-3.

Bolinger, Dwight. 1984. Intonational signals of subordination. *Proceedings of the tenth annual meeting of the Berkeley Linguistics Society.* 401–413.

Bromley, H. Myron. 2003. *A grammar of Lower Grand Valley Dani* (Pacific Linguistics C63). Canberra: Australian National Universtity.

Brotchie, Amanda. 2009. *Tirax grammar and narrative: An Oceanic language spoken on Malakula, North Central Vanuatu.* The University of Melbourne PhD Dissertation.

Brown, Penelope. 2000. Repetition. *Journal of Linguistic Anthropology* 9(1–2). 223–226.

Cameron, Deborah. 2001. *Working with spoken discourse.* London: Sage.

Chafe, William. 2001. The analysis of discourse flow. In Deborah Schiffrin, Deborah Tannen & Heidi Hamilton (eds.), *The handbook of discourse analysis,* 673–687. Malden, MA: Blackwell.

Chafe, William. 2003. Linking intonation units in spoken English. In John Haiman & Sandra A. Thompson (eds.), *Clause combining in grammar and discourse,* 1–27. Amsterdam: John Benjamins.

Christensen, Steve. 2013. *Yongkom reference grammar.* Ukarumpa: SIL.

Clark, Herbert H. 1975. Bridging. *Proceedings of TINLAP 75, the 1975 workshop on theoretical issues in natural language processing.* 169–174. http://dl.acm.org/citation.cfm?id=980237, accessed 2018-10-19.

Cristofaro, Sonia. 2005. *Subordination.* Oxford: Oxford University Press.

Croft, William. 2016. Comparative concepts and language-specific categories: Theory and practice. *Linguistic Typology* 20(2). 377–393.

Culicover, Peter W. & Ray Jackendoff. 1997. Semantic subordination despite syntactic coordination. *Linguistic Inquiry* 28(2). 195–217.

de Vries, Lourens. 2005. Towards a typology of tail-head linkage in Papuan languages. *Studies in Language* 29(2). 363–384.

de Vries, Lourens. 2006. Areal pragmatics of New Guinea: Thematization, distribution and recapitulative linkage in Papuan narratives. *Journal of Pragmatics* 38(6). 811–828.

de Vries, Lourens. 2019. Online and offline bridging constructions in Korowai. In Valérie Guérin (ed.), *Bridging constructions*, 185–206. Berlin: Language Science Press. DOI:10.5281/zenodo.2563690

Dimock, Laura Gail. 2009. *A grammar of Nahavaq (Malakula, Vanuatu)*. New Zealand: Victoria University of Wellington PhD Dissertation.

Dixon, R. M. W. 2010. *Basic linguistic theory*. Vol. 1. Oxford: Oxford University Press.

Emlen, Nicholas Q. 2019. The poetics of recapitulative linkage in Matsigenka and mixed Matsigenka-Spanish myth narrations. In Valérie Guérin (ed.), *Bridging constructions*, 45–77. Berlin: Language Science Press. DOI:10.5281/zenodo.2563680

Evans, N. J. 2012. Insubordination and its uses. In Irina Nikolaeva (ed.), *Finiteness: Theoretical and empirical foundations*, 366–431. Oxford: Oxford University Press.

Fabian, Grace, Edmund Fabian & Bruce Waters. 1998. *Morphology, syntax and cohesion in Nabak, Papua New Guinea* (Pacific Linguistics C144). Canberra: Australian National Universtity.

Farr, Cynthia J. M. 1999. *The interface between syntax and discourse in Korafe, a Papuan language of Papua New Guinea* (Pacific Linguistics 148). Canberra: Australian National Universtity.

Fitzpatrick, Jennifer. 2000. On intonational typology. *STUF–Language Typology and Universals* 53(1). 88–96.

Forker, Diana & Felix Anker. 2019. Bridging constructions in Tsezic languages. In Valérie Guérin (ed.), *Bridging constructions*, 99–128. Berlin: Language Science Press. DOI:10.5281/zenodo.2563684

Foster, Michael. 1981. *Timbe grammar sketch: Cohesion in Timbe texts*. Ukarumpa: SIL.

Genetti, Carol. 2007. *A grammar of Dolakha Newar*. Berlin: Mouton de Gruyter.

Genetti, Carol & Kenneth Slater. 2004. An analysis of syntax and prosody interactions in a Dolakhā Newar rendition of The Mahābhārata. *Himalayan Linguistics* 1. 1–91.

Givón, Talmy. 1983. Topic continuity in discourse: An introduction. In Talmy Givón (ed.), *Topic continuity in discourse: A quantitative cross-language study*, 1–41. Philadelphia: John Benjamins.

Gleason Jr, Henry A. 1968. Contrastive analysis in discourse structure. In James E. Alatis (ed.), *Report of the nineteenth annual round table meeting on linguistics and language studies. Contrastive linguistics and its pedagogical implications*, 39–63. Washington DC: Georgetown University.

Grenoble, Lenore A. 2012. From clause to discourse: The structure of Evenki narrative. In Andrej L. Malchukov & Whaley Lindsay J. (eds.), *Recent advances in Tungusic linguistics*, 257–277. Wiesbaden: Harrassowitz.

Guérin, Valérie. 2011. *A grammar of Mavea, an Oceanic language of Vanuatu*. Honolulu: University of Hawai'i Press.

Guérin, Valérie. 2015. Demonstrative verbs: A typology of verbal manner deixis. *Linguistic Typology* 19(2). 141–199.

Guérin, Valérie. 2019. Recapitulative linkage in Mavea. In Valérie Guérin (ed.), *Bridging constructions*, 207–238. Berlin: Language Science Press. DOI:10.5281/zenodo.2563692

Guillaume, Antoine. 2011. Subordinate clauses, switch-reference, and tail-head linkage in Cavineña narratives. In Rik van Gijn, Katharina Haude & Pieter Muysken (eds.), *Subordination in native South American languages*, 109–140. Amsterdam: John Benjamins.

Haiman, John & Sandra A. Thompson. 1984. "Subordination" in universal grammar. *Proceedings of the tenth annual meeting of the Berkeley Linguistics Society.* 510–523.

Halliday, M. A. K. & Ruqaiya Hasan. 1976. *Cohesion in English*. London: Longman.

Haspelmath, Martin. 1995. The converb as a cross-linguistically valid category. In Martin Haspelmath & Ekkehard König (eds.), *Converbs in cross-linguistic perspective*, 1–55. Berlin: Mouton de Gruyter.

Haspelmath, Martin. 2004. Coordinating constructions: An overview. In Martin Haspelmath (ed.), *Coordinating constructions*, 3–39. Amsterdam: John Benjamins.

Haspelmath, Martin. 2010. Comparative concepts and descriptive categories in crosslinguistic studies. *Language* 86(3). 663–687.

Haspelmath, Martin. 2016. The serial verb construction: Comparative concept and cross-linguistic generalization. *Language and Linguistics* 17(3). 291–319.

Heath, Jeffrey. 1985. Discourse in the field: Clause structure in Ngandi (Australia). In Johanna Nichols & Anthony Woodbury (eds.), *Grammar inside and outside the clause*, 89–110. Cambridge: Cambridge University Press.

Heath, Jeffrey & Abbie Hantgan. 2018. *A grammar of Bangime*. Berlin: Mouton de Gruyter.

Hinds, John. 2012. Organizational patterns in discourse. In Talmy Givón (ed.), *Semantics and syntax: Discourse and syntax*, 135–157. New York: Academic Press.

Hyslop, Catriona. 2001. *The Lolovoli dialect of the North-East Ambae language, Vanuatu* (Pacific Linguistics 515). Canberra: The Australian National University.

Jarkey, Nerida. 2019. Bridging constructions in narrative texts in White Hmong (Hmong-Mien). In Valérie Guérin (ed.), *Bridging constructions*, 129–156. Berlin: Language Science Press. DOI:10.5281/zenodo.2563686

Jendraschek, Gerd. 2009. Switch-reference constructions in Iatmul: Forms, functions, and development. *Lingua* 119(9). 1316–1339.

Johnstone, Barbara. 2001. Discourse analysis and narrative. In Deborah Schiffrin, Deborah Tannen & Heidi Hamilton (eds.), *The handbook of discourse analysis*, 635–649. Malden, MA: Blackwell.

Labov, William & Joshua Waletzky. 1967/2007. Narrative analysis: Oral versions of personal experience. In Teun A. van Dijk (ed.), *Discourse studies*, 359–390. London: Sage.

Logan, Tommy. 2008. *Kasua sketch grammar*. Ukarumpa, PNG: SIL. http://www-01.sil.org/pacific/png/abstract.asp?id=50999, accessed 2018-8-10.

Longacre, Robert E. 1968. *Philippine languages: Discourse, paragraph and sentence structure*. Vol. 21. Santa Ana: Publications in Linguistics & Related Fields. SIL.

Longacre, Robert E. 1970. Paragraph and sentence structure in New Guinea Highland languages. *Kivung* 3(3). 153–243.

Longacre, Robert E. 1983. *The grammar of discourse*. New York: Plenum Press.

Longacre, Robert E. 2007a. Sentences as combinations of clauses. In Timothy Shopen (ed.), *Language typology and syntactic description: Complex constructions*, vol. 2, 372–420. Cambridge: Cambridge University Press.

Longacre, Robert E. 2007b. The paragraph as a grammatical unit. In Talmy Givón (ed.), *Semantics and syntax: Discourse and syntax*, 115–134. New York: Academic Press.

Loos, Eugene E. 1963. Capanahua narration structure. *Texas Studies in Literature and Language* 7. 697–742.

Martin, Jack. 1998. Notes on switch-reference in Creek. *Santa Barbara papers in linguistics: Proceedings from the first workshop on American indigenous languages* 8. 97–107.

McKay, Graham. 2008. Cohesive features in Rembarrnga narratives. In Timothy J. Curnow (ed.), *Selected papers from the 2007 conference of the Australian Linguistic Society*.

Miller, Jim. 1981. Does spoken language have sentences? In Palmer Frank R. (ed.), *Grammar and meaning: Essays in honour of Sir John Lyons*, 116–135. Cambridge: Cambridge University Press.

Mithun, Marianne. 2005a. On the assumption of the sentence as the basic unit of syntactic structure. In Zygmunt Frajzyngier, A. Hodges & David S. Rood (eds.), *Linguistic diversity and language theories*, 169–183. Amsterdam: John Benjamins.

Mithun, Marianne. 2005b. Re(e)volving complexity: Adding intonation. In Talmy Givón & Masayoshi Shibatani (eds.), *Syntactic complexity: Diachrony, acquisition, neuro-cognition, evolution*, 53–80. Amsterdam: John Benjamins.

Overall, Simon E. 2017. *A grammar of Aguaruna*. Berlin: Mouton de Gruyter.

Palmer, Bill. 2009. *Kokota grammar*. Honolulu: University of Hawai'i Press.

Pennington, Ryan. 2015. *Bridging linkage in Ma Manda*. Paper presented at the special workshop of the Language and Culture Research Centre entitled "Bridging linkage in cross-linguistic perspective", James Cook University, Cairns, Australia, 24–25 February 2015.

Pensalfini, Rob. 2015. *Canonical and non-canonical bridging constructions in Jingulu*. Paper presented at the special workshop of the Language and Culture Research Centre entitled "Bridging linkage in cross-linguistic perspective", James Cook University, Cairns, Australia, 24-25 February 2015.

Phinnemore, Penny. 1998. Coordination in Ono. *Language and Linguistics in Melanesia* 19(1–2). 97–123.

Plattèl, Marieta. 2013. *Tail-head linkage in het Biak vergeleken met herhalingen in het Nederlands*. The Netherlands: Universiteit Utrecht MA thesis.

Prince, Ellen. 1981. Towards a taxonomy of given-new information. In Peter Cole (ed.), *Radical pragmatics*, 223–256. New York: Academic Press.

Sarvasy, Hannah. 2019. Short, finite and one-sided bridges in Logoori. In Valérie Guérin (ed.), *Bridging constructions*, 79–98. Berlin: Language Science Press. DOI:10.5281/zenodo.2563682

Schokkin, Dineke. 2014. Discourse practices as an areal feature in the New Guinea region? Explorations in Paluai, an Austronesian language of the Admiralties. *Journal of Pragmatics* 62. 107–120.

Schokkin, Gerda. 2013. *A grammar of Paluai, the language of Baluan Island, Papua New Guinea*. Cairns, Australia: James Cook University PhD Dissertation.

Schulze, Marlene & Dora Bieri. 1973. Chaining and spotlighting: Two types of paragraph boundaries in Sunwar. In Irvine Davis (ed.), *Clause, sentence, and discourse patterns in selected languages of Nepal*, 389–399. Tribhuvan University, Kathmandu: SIL Oklahoma & Tribhuvan Universtity Press.

Seifart, Frank. 2010. The Bora connector pronoun and tail-head linkage: A study in language-specific grammaticalization. *Linguistics* 48(2). 893–918.

Stirling, Lesley. 1993. *Switch-reference and discourse representation*. Cambridge: Cambridge University Press.

Thompson, Sandra A., Robert E. Longacre & Shin Ja J. Hwang. 2007. Adverbial clauses. In Timothy Shopen (ed.), *Language typology and syntactic description: Complex constructions*, vol. 2, 237–300. Cambridge: Cambridge University Press.

Thurman, Robert C. 1975. Chuave medial verbs. *Anthropological Linguistics* 17(7). 342–352.

Van Valin Jr, Robert D. 1984. A typology of syntactic relations in clause linkage. *Proceedings of the tenth annual meeting of the Berkeley Linguistics Society.* 542–558.

van Dijk, Teun A. 1977. *Text and context: Explorations in the semantics and pragmatics of discourse.* London: Longman.

van Gijn, Rik. 2014. Repeated dependent clauses in Yurakaré. In Rik van Gijn, Jeremy Hammond, Dejan Matić, Saskia van Putten & Ana Vilacy Galucio (eds.), *Information structure and reference tracking in complex sentences*, 291–308. Amsterdam: John Benjamins.

van Kleef, Sjaak. 1988. Tail-head linkage in Siroi. *Language and Linguistics in Melanesia* 20. 147–156.

Wojtylak, Katarzyna I. 2017. *A grammar of Murui (Bue): A Witotoan language of Northwest Amazonia.* Cairns, Australia: James Cook University PhD Dissertation.

Yuasa, Etsuyo & Jerrold M. Sadock. 2002. Pseudo-subordination: A mismatch between syntax and semantics. *Journal of Linguistics* 38(1). 87–111.

Chapter 2

The poetics of recapitulative linkage in Matsigenka and mixed Matsigenka-Spanish myth narrations

Nicholas Q. Emlen

John Carter Brown Library, Brown University

In a small community in the Andean-Amazonian transitional zone of Southern Peru, speakers of Matsigenka use recapitulative linkages in myth narrations. These constructions establish a kind of rhythm, distinctive to the myth narration discourse genre, through which the events of the narrative unfold, information is introduced and elaborated, and suspense and surprise are achieved. This chapter describes the structural and discursive properties of these linking devices and their use in myth narrations. Bridging clauses generally recapitulate reference clauses verbatim or with minor modifications, and are usually linked to discourse-new information as simple juxtaposed clauses (though there is much variation in the structure and pragmatic functions of these constructions). Though the constructions contribute to discourse cohesion, their function is primarily poetic in nature. Furthermore, when Matsigenka speakers narrate the same myths in Spanish and in mixed Matsigenka-Spanish speech, they use the same kinds of linking constructions (which are otherwise uncommon in Spanish). Thus, the transfer of this kind of pattern from Matsigenka to Spanish is regimented by discourse genre, and offers an illustration of the cultural (i.e., metapragmatic) mediation of language contact.

1 Introduction

This chapter describes a type of recapitulative linkage used in Matsigenka myth narrations in a small, multiethnic community on the Andean-Amazonian agricultural frontier of Southern Peru. It also briefly presents the use of this construction in Spanish and mixed Matsigenka-Spanish myth narrations by the same speakers.

Nicholas Q. Emlen. 2019. The poetics of recapitulative linkage in Matsigenka and mixed Matsigenka-Spanish myth narrations. In Valérie Guérin (ed.), *Bridging constructions*, 45–77. Berlin: Language Science Press. DOI:10.5281/zenodo.2563680

The most common form of the construction is as follows: a proposition is uttered (the reference clause, indicated in underlined text throughout this chapter), followed by a pause (indicated in brackets). Then, the proposition in the reference clause is recapitulated in the bridging clause (indicated in boldface text) and followed immediately by discourse-new information, usually in the form of a simple juxtaposed clause without any subordinating morphology. A simple Matsigenka example is given in (1):[1]

(1) a. *Impogini maika <u>oaigake</u>.* [0.6]
        impogini maika o-a-ig-ak-i
        then   now   3F-go-PL-PFV-REAL
        'Then they went.'

     b. ***Oaigake** agaiganake oviarena.*
        o-a-ig-ak-i   *o-ag-a-ig-an-ak-i*   *o-piarena*
        3F-go-PL-PFV-REAL 3F-get-EP-PL-ABL-PFV-REAL 3F-gourd
        'They went (and) they got their gourds.'

These recapitulative linkages often express continuity between a single character's simultaneous or immediately sequential actions (as in *oaigake* 'they went' in (1a) and *agaiganake oviarena* 'they got their gourds' in (1b)); for this reason, the recapitulated clause and the discourse-new clause usually have the same subject. However, there is substantial variation in the structure and pragmatic function of these constructions. For instance, in many cases the discourse-new information clarifies or elaborates the preceding proposition instead of offering a new one, and less frequently, the subject of the discourse-new clause is different from that of the recapitulated clause. More rarely, the recapitulated element does not contain a verb at all, but still follows the discursive patterns described here and thus must be considered part of the same phenomenon.

Among some speakers in the community, these linkages are employed very frequently in myth narrations – sometimes more than a dozen times over the course of a brief five- or ten-minute narrative, and many more times in longer narratives. The frequent use of these pause/repetition sequences to structure the events and introduce new information creates a particular kind of narrative rhythm that is a salient poetic characteristic of the myth narration discourse genre. The association between myth narrations and recapitulative linkages is so close that the one is rarely found without the other – even personal narratives about one's own

---

[1]Matsigenka morphemic analyses are adapted from Michael (2008) and Vargas Pereira & Vargas Pereira (2013).

life or family history, which are similar in other respects to myth narrations, do not include them. Thus, while recapitulative linkages certainly contribute to discourse cohesion – a common function of such constructions (see Guérin & Aiton 2019 [this volume]) – their exclusive association with the myth narration discourse genre suggests that they should be understood primarily as a poetic or stylistic feature of that genre.

Linkage constructions similar to the kind described in this chapter (also known as head-tail linkages or tail-head linkages, among other terms) have been identified in a number of indigenous Amazonian languages, particularly in Western Amazonia. These include Cavineña (Guillaume 2011), Tariana (Aikhenvald 2002: 169–171), Yurakaré (van Gijn 2014), Aguaruna (Overall 2014), Murui (Wojtylak 2017: 515–522), and Ese Ejja (Vuillermet 2017: 598–599). Note, however, that my analysis differs from these cases in focusing on the poetic function of such constructions in Matsigenka (and in both Spanish and mixed Matsigenka-Spanish speech). The ubiquity of linkage constructions across Western Amazonia suggests that they might be an areal phenomenon attributable to language contact (Seifart 2010: 916), as indeed we see in the transfer of such a construction from Eastern Tucanoan to Tariana in the Vaupés region (Aikhenvald 2002: 169–171). This would certainly be consistent with the proposal of Beier et al. (2002) that Amazonia constitutes a "discourse area," in which particular ways of speaking have diffused broadly across languages and language families in that region (though this notion has usually been applied to contact between indigenous languages instead of between indigenous and European colonial languages). However, linkage constructions are a common enough discourse strategy among the languages of the world (for instance, in Papuan languages; see de Vries 2005) that it may be difficult to distinguish the effects of areal diffusion from chance except in very clear cases.

There is a more specific sense in which the Matsigenka linkage constructions discussed in this chapter are relevant to the topic of language contact – namely, that their regimentation by the myth narration discourse genre is what licenses their portability between languages (I use the linguistic anthropological senses of the terms *regimentation* and *discourse genre*; see Briggs & Bauman 1992; Silverstein 1993; and §2.2). As young Matsigenka-Spanish bilinguals in the community have taken up interest in myths, they have begun to perform such narrations in Spanish and in mixed Matsigenka-Spanish speech (though this is not as common as Matsigenka narrations). When this happens, they use the very same kinds of linkage constructions as in the Matsigenka narrations, even though this creates utterances that are considered unusual in Spanish (see §4). I argue that because these recapitulative linkages are regimented by the local metapragmatic conventions of myth narration, they are also used when that discourse genre is invoked in a different lexico-grammatical code. In other words, since such linkages are understood to be part of a well executed myth performance, they are transferred to another language when speakers perceive themselves to be engaged in the same myth performance discourse genre in that language. While these Spanish and mixed Matsigenka-Spanish performances are not considered exemplary of Matsigenka verbal art, they often draw on other poetic conventions of Matsigenka myth performance as well, including (among others) the frequent use of ideophones, reported speech and special voices, and a common set of prosodic features and facial expressions for the indication of surprise, apprehension, and intensity. This case thus gives one example of how the effects of language contact can be culturally (i.e., metapragmatically) mediated. However, as I mentioned earlier, this case is different from the kind of inter-indigenous language contact commonly associated with an Amazonian discourse area. Furthermore, since myth narration is not practiced much among the younger generations, and since many Matsigenka speakers are shifting to Spanish, this contact feature is not likely to persist.

This chapter begins with an introduction to Matsigenka, Andean Spanish, and the discourse genre of myth narration on the Andean-Amazonian frontier of Southern Peru (§2.2). Then, in §3, I give a formal characterization of recapitulative linkages (§3.1), including relations between the reference clause and the bridging clause (§3.2), and the composition of the second discourse unit (§3.3). In §3.4, I discuss some atypical cases. Next, in §4, I go on to describe how the Matsigenka recapitulative linkages discussed thus far are borrowed in Spanish and mixed Matsigenka-Spanish performances of the same discourse genre. §5 offers some concluding comments.

2 Matsigenka, Spanish, and myth narration on the Andean-Amazonian frontier

2.1 Languages and communities

Matsigenka is an Arawak language, of the Kampan sub-group, spoken by a few thousand people in the Amazonian lowlands adjacent to the Southern Peruvian Andes (for more on the classification of Matsigenka, see Aikhenvald 1999; Michael 2008: 212–219; Michael 2010; and Payne 1981). Most speakers of Matsigenka have at least some exposure to Spanish, and many people in the Andean contact zone (as in the community described in this chapter) also speak Southern Peruvian Quechua (Emlen 2017). Matsigenka is head-marking with a rich polysynthetic structure, and it uses verbal suffixes and enclitics, as well as a few prefixes and proclitics, for most of its grammatical functions. For more on the typological profile of the Kampan languages, see Michael (2008) and Mihas (2015). This chapter also discusses Andean Spanish, a set of contact varieties spoken by millions of people across Western South America. Andean Spanish features notable phonological and structural influence from Quechua (for more, see Adelaar & Muysken 2004: 593–595; Babel 2018; Cerrón-Palomino 2001; Escobar 2003). For more information about the heterogeneous forms of Spanish in this area, see Emlen (2019).

The community where these recordings were made occupies a small, remote hillside in the Alto Urubamba Valley of Southern Peru, part of traditional Matsigenka territory that abuts the Andes. This region has been a conduit for the movement of goods, people, and languages between the Andes and Amazonia since the Inka period and likely long before (Gade 1972; Camino 1977). Today the Alto Urubamba is an agricultural frontier, and as the road network has expanded into Amazonia since the 1950s, tens of thousands of Quechua-speaking migrants from the Andes have come to Matsigenka territory in search of land for the cultivation of coffee and other tropical crops. This migratory wave has displaced many Matsigenka people to remote corners of the valley, while others have intermarried with Andean settlers and joined the multiethnic agrarian society.

The community where this research was conducted came together in the 1980s and 1990s through the intermarriage of Matsigenka people from across the region and Andean settlers from the nearby highlands. These people come from a wide variety of sociolinguistic backgrounds, and many are trilingual in Matsigenka, Quechua, and Spanish. Matsigenka and Quechua are associated with domestic life and kin relations (depending on the family background), while Quechua is used in interactions relating to the coffee economy and rural agrarian society. Spanish is the language of the community's political and institutional life. Most people can speak, or at least understand, all three languages. For more about how the three languages are used in the community, see Emlen (2014; 2015; 2017).

2.2 Myth narration

Myth narration is one of many locally recognized discourse genres in the community. I mean the term *discourse genre* both in the formal sense of "constellations of co-occurrent formal elements and structures that define or characterize particular classes of utterances" (Briggs & Bauman 1992: 141), and in the metapragmatic sense of culturally constructed "orienting frameworks, interpretive procedures, and sets of expectations" (Hanks 1987: 670) that regiment the production and interpretation of speech (see also Bakhtin 1986; Silverstein 1993).

Myth narration is something of a specialized discursive skill in the community, and the oldest members who grew up beyond the coffee frontier and the Dominican missionary sphere are considered to be its most authoritative performers. These performances are usually relatively monologic, unlike in other places where they tend to be more dialogic (e.g., among speakers of the nearby and closely related Nanti language; Michael 2008: 44). This is due in part to the fact that many young Matsigenka speakers are shifting to Spanish and Quechua and are increasingly directing their attention to the rural agrarian social world instead of the cultural practices of their parents and grandparents. The performances usually take place at the home in the evening, and can last for hours, depending on the stamina and skill of the speaker and the engagement of the audience. Others are briefer, and last only a few minutes. The best performances (as judged by local metapragmatic standards) are quite long, feature virtuosic displays of creativity and improvisation, and are "keyed" (see Goffman 1974; Bauman 1977) – that is, signaled as instances of a particular discourse genre – by special formal and narrative features. These features include frequent ideophones and other iconic phenomena, reported speech (often with special voices), a particular set of prosodic features and facial expressions, cameos by characters from other myths that create intertextual links across the dense web of Matsigenka cosmology, and the kind of narrative rhythm that emerges from the frequent use of the bridging constructions discussed here. Matsigenka myth narration in the community has come to be constructed around a language ideology that conceives of such discourse as an exemplary model (Kroskrity 1998) of traditional Matsigenka language, culture, and knowledge, and it is generally subject to a regime of purism in which code-switching is discouraged (a fact that distinguishes it from all other domains of Matsigenka language use in the community).

However, during my field work in 2009–2012, Matsigenka myths were occasionally performed in Spanish and in mixed Matsigenka-Spanish speech, particularly by younger people who were interested in traditional Matsigenka culture and were not deterred by the ideology of linguistic purism. These narrations usually came with disclaimers about their non-authoritativeness, and tended to offer a brief, *just the facts* versions of the stories rather than the kind of lengthy, virtuosic performances described above. Some of these Spanish and mixed Matsigenka-Spanish performances were given upon my request (sometimes to the puzzled amusement of older and more authoritative narrators), but many speakers also performed them among their friends and families, and in spaces of explicit cultural exposition such as community festivals and visits from municipal officials. Note that I never witnessed or successfully elicited a Matsigenka myth in Quechua, a language that is associated with a different tradition of verbal art, and that is understood by the local ideologies of language to be incompatible with explicit expressions of Matsigenka culture. This is part of a larger tension in the conflicted and contested space of the agricultural frontier, where Quechua and Matsigenka are connected to opposite sides of an ethnically-inflected struggle over land and legitimacy, and where Spanish represents a (relatively) unmarked common ground (see Emlen 2015; 2017).

Most Matsigenka myths tell a story of "cosmological transformism" (Viveiros de Castro 1998: 471), an ontological principle common in indigenous South American societies by which many animals, plants, and supernatural beings were once human before taking their current form, in which they now retain their essentially human subjectivity. This phenomenon has been described among Matsigenka people by Rosengren (2006) and Johnson (2003), among others. These are origin stories, but since the moment of transformation often hinges on a moral transgression of one or another character in the myth, they also serve as "morality tales" (Johnson 2003: 118–124, 220) that warn Matsigenka speakers about particular types of dangerous emotions or behavior (Izquierdo & Johnson 2007; Johnson 1999; Rosengren 2000; Shepard 2002). Matsigenka stories have been collected in translation and in Matsigenka by anthropologists (e.g., Baer 1994; Renard-Casevitz & Pacaia 1981; Renard-Casevitz 1981) and by missionaries (e.g., de Cenitagoya 1944; Davis & Snell 1999[1968]), usually as source of information regarding Matsigenka culture and ontology rather than as a representation of the language and verbal art per se. However, a thorough recent compilation of 170 written Matsigenka texts (Vargas Pereira & Vargas Pereira 2013) gives a closer look at Matsigenka linguistic structure and the verbal artistry associated with myths, as well as a rich perspective on Matsigenka culture. However, those myths do not appear to exhibit the recapitulative linkages discussed in this chapter, either because of the particular sociolinguistic circumstances of the narrators, or because those myths were collected in written rather than oral form.

The data used in this chapter come from audio and video recordings of 35 myth narrations in the community, performed by seven people from a range of different ages and sociolinguistic backgrounds. These were collected over the course of 19 months of field work in 2009–2012. Additionally, 11 myth performances from speakers in five other communities in the Alto Urubamba were included in the corpus as a basis of regional comparison; however, only data from the community of focus are presented in this chapter. Some myths were told for me in my house, while others were recorded in the narrators' homes as they performed the myths for their families. Several recordings were also made by Matsigenka speakers themselves, whom I had trained to use the equipment in my absence. The use of the bridging constructions appears to be consistent across these contexts, and does not vary by the age or gender of the narrator. The 35 performances each ranged from several minutes to nearly an hour in length, and I identified a total of around 300 bridging constructions in the myth corpus. Note that these constructions also appear, using the same structures and in roughly the same frequency, in my recordings from across the Alto Urubamba, though I do not know how widespread they are beyond that region. For instance, bridging constructions following this pattern do not appear in Nanti (Lev Michael, p.c.) nor in Caquinte (Zachary O'Hagan, p.c.), two of the nearest Arawak languages, and I have not noted similar constructions in the local variety of Quechua.

2.3 Recapitulative linkages in myth narrations

By way of an example of bridging constructions in Matsigenka myth performances, consider a passage from the *pakitsa* 'harpy eagle' myth, told in November 2011 by one of the community's most authoritative practitioners of Matsigenka verbal art. She told the story one evening to me and several of her family members, and it featured all of the elements of virtuosic performance mentioned above. In this sequence the *pakitsa* 'harpy eagle,' who had recently been transformed from a man into an eagle, swoops down upon the house of his human wife, daughter, and son (the man mentioned in 2a). He snatches up his daughter, who had been walking around outside the house, and carries her off to his nest across the river. The sequence contains two bridging constructions, in (2) and (3). The passages in (2) and (3) are directly sequential in the narrative.

 The narrator first sets the tone of this scene in (2a) by describing the mother, who is occupied by routine domestic work inside the house and is unaware of the fate that is about to befall her daughter. In (2b), this context is restated in the bridging clause and linked to a description of the daughter's vulnerable position outside the house (note that this case is unusual in linking clauses with different subjects). In this case, the bridging construction serves to express the simultaneous unwitting actions of the mother and the daughter, a calm scene that will be interrupted by the violent arrival of the *pakitsa* in (3).

(2) a. *Impogini otarogavagetake iroro oga irotyo iriniro yoga matsigenka.* [1.1]
      impogini o-tarog-a-vage-t-ak-i   iroro o-oga   iro-tyo
      then   3F-sweep-EP-DUR-EP-PFV-REAL she   3F-that she-AFFECT

iriniro   i-oga   matsigenka
his.mother 3M-THAT person

'Then she was sweeping, she, the mother of the man.'

b. **Impogini otarogavageti**, *inti oga oshinto anuvagetakeroka oga oga*
  sotsiku. [1.0]
  impogini o-tarog-a-vage-t-i   i-nti   o-oga o-shinto
  then   3F-sweep-EP-DUR-EP-REAL 3M-COP 3F-that 3F-daughter
  o-anu-vage-t-ak-i-roka   o-oga o-oga sotsi-ku
  3F-walk-DUR-EU-PFV-REAL-EPIS.WK 3F-that 3F-that outside-LOC

  'Then she was sweeping, [and] her daughter must have been walking
  around, um, outside.'

Then, in (3), the eagle-man dives in and grabs his daughter, an abrupt turn
of events that the narrator punctuates with a stark and deliberate 1.3 second
pause. Once this development has been introduced, the narrator restates it in the
bridging clause in (3b) and links it to the *pakitsa's* next act of carrying the girl
across the river to his nest. Both events are related as witnessed by the mother,
which invites the listeners to contemplate the horror of such an experience. In (3),
the bridging construction allows the eagle-man's sudden attack to stand alone in
dramatic tension before it is restated to express continuity with the girl's removal
to the nest.

(3) a. *Okemiri maika yarapaake <u>yagapanutiro pe oga oshinto otyomiani</u>.* [1.3]
     o-kem-i-ri   maika ı-ar-apa-ak-ı
     3F-listen-REAL-3M now   3M-fly-ALL-PFV-REAL
     i-ag-apanu-t-i-ro   pe o-oga o-shinto   o-tyomia-ni
     3M-get-DIR:DEP-EP-REAL-3F EMPH 3M-that 3F-daughter 3F-small-ANIM

     'She heard him [as] he flew in and he grabbed her young daughter.'

   b. *Yagapanutiro, opampogiavakeri koa yarakaganake anta*
     yovetsikakera ivanko intati anta.
     i-ag-apanu-t-i-ro   o-pampogi-av-ak-i-ri   koa
     3M-get-DIR:DEP-EP-REAL-3F 3F-watch-TR-PFV-REAL-3M more
     i-ar-akag-an-ak-i   anta i-ovetsik-ak-i-ra   i-panko
     3M-fly-CAUS-ABL-PFV-REAL there 3M-make-PFV-REAL-SBD 3M-house
     intati   anta
     other.side there

     'He grabbed her, [as] [the mother] watched him, [and] he quickly flew her away to where he had made his house on the other side [of the river].'

The effect of these constructions is to establish a narrative rhythm through which the plot unfolds and information is introduced and elaborated (for another extended example, see (13) below). This rhythm creates tension, suspense, and surprise in the narrative, and (in the best performances) holds the listeners in rapt attention. In some myth narrations these bridging constructions appear between every two or three clauses – sometimes twice a minute or more – and this narrative rhythm is only heard within such performances. Note that these constructions are not communicatively necessary, strictly speaking, for the functional purposes of discourse cohesion; indeed, the discourse would be perfectly intelligible and easy to follow without them. Instead, these bridging constructions are oriented toward the poetic function of language, which, by Jakobson's definition (1960), prioritizes the form of the message above its purely referential ends (particularly through the co-occurrence of formal features in a given stretch of discourse). Thus, this analysis follows the long linguistic anthropological tradition of research on verbal art and ethnopoetics (Bauman 1977; Hymes 1981; for a recent review, see Webster & Kroskrity 2013).

3 Formal characterization

3.1 Basic template

This section gives a formal characterization of recapitulative linkages in Matsigenka myth performances in the Andean-Amazonian frontier community. The basic template for these constructions is given in (4):

(4)   [...[Reference clause]]_discourse unit

[0.5–4.0 second pause]

[[**Bridging clause**] [Discourse-new information]]_discourse unit

Here, discourse units are understood as stretches of discourse that present particular events in the narrative, and that are marked off by pauses and special intonational contours. In addition to a 0.5–4.0 second pause between the discourse units, speakers sometimes utter a validating *mmhmm* or *aha*, as in (5), and in (12) below. These pauses are seen as appropriate moments for backchannel. In some of the recordings in the corpus that were made by native speakers of Matsigenka themselves, a listener supplied the validating *mmhmm* or *aha* instead of the narrator (however, there are no cases in my data in which a listener repeats a reference clause). The example in (5) is from a different speaker's performance of the *pakitsa* 'harpy eagle' myth, and refers to the same events in (2) and (3) above. Note that the emphatic particle *pe* in (5a) comes from Andean Spanish (for more, see §4).

(5) a. *Yamanakero pe.* [2.4]
         i-am-an-ak-i-ro   *pe*
         3M-carry-ABL-PFV-REAL-3F EMPH
         'He carried her away.'

     b. *mmhmm.* [0.5]

     c. *Yamanakero imenkotakara imperitaku.*
         i-am-an-ak-i-ro   *i-menko-t-ak-a-ra*
         3M-carry-ABL-PFV-REAL-3F 3M-make.nest-EP-PFV-REAL-SBD
         imperita-ku
         cliff-LOC
         'He carried her away [to] where he had made his nest in the cliff.'

In addition to bridging constructions that take place in the narrator's voice, the phenomenon also appears in the reported speech of characters in the narrative, as in (6):

(6) a. *Okantiro maika, "noshinto, gaigakite nia."* [1.1]
         o-kant-i-ro   *maika no-shinto*   *n-ag-a-ig-aki-t-e*
         3F-say-REAL-3F now   1-daughter IRR-get-EP-PL-TRNLOC.PFV-EP-IRR
         nia
         water
         'She said to her, "my daughter[s], go get water."'

     b. *"Gaigakite nia maika nontinkakera ovuroki."*
         n-ag-a-ig-aki-t-e   *nia*   *maika*
         IRR-get-EP-PL-TRNLOC.PFV-EP-IRR water now
         no-n-tink-ak-e-ra   *ovuroki*
         1-IRR-mash-PFV-IRR-SBD masato
         '"Go get water, I'm going to mash up masato."'

Within the template given in (4), bridging constructions can take a variety of forms. Linkages between the reference clause and the bridging clause are discussed in §3.2; relationships between the bridging clause and the discourse-new information in the second discourse unit are discussed in §3.3; and some atypical cases are described in §3.4.

3.2 Reference clause/bridging clause relations

Before discussing the relationship between the reference clause and the bridging clause, it is necessary to first characterize typical reference clauses. These units are usually simple clauses (e.g., *oaigake* 'they went' in 1a). However, it bears mentioning that in some cases, the reference unit itself is a more complex construction, as in the example in (7). This case comprises a reference unit of two juxtaposed clauses (7a) that are both repeated verbatim in the bridging clause (7b). Such juxtapositions are common in Matsigenka (see §3.3).

(7) a. <u>*Agake omonkigakero.*</u> [1.4]
    o-ag-ak-i   o-monkig-ak-i-ro
    3F-get-PFV-REAL 3F-carry.in.clothing-PFV-REAL-3F
    'She caught [it] [and] carried it in her cushma.'

  b. ***Agake omonkigakero*** *sokaitakero oga shitatsiku...*
    o-ag-ak-i   o-monkig-ak-i-ro
    3F-get-PFV-REAL 3F-carry.in.clothing-PFV-REAL-3F
    sokai-t-ak-i-ro   o-oga   shitatsi-ku
    dump.out-EP-PFV-REAL-3F 3F-that mat-LOC
    'She caught [it] [and] carried it [in her cushma], [and then] she dumped it out onto the mat...'

Bridging clauses are usually verbatim repetitions of the reference clause – that is, *recapitulative linkages* – as in (7) and in most of the other examples given in this chapter. Summary linkages, in which the reference clause is referred to anaphorically with a summarizing verb rather than repeated (Guérin & Aiton 2019 [this volume]), do not appear. This is apparently because the construction's poetic function is built on repetition. However, in some cases the bridging clause presents a modified order or form of the information, or information is omitted, added, or substituted. For instance, in the passage from the first *pakitsa* 'harpy eagle' myth given in (2) and (3) above, the reference clause *yagapanutiro pe oga oshinto otyomiani* 'he grabbed her young daughter' (3a), with its full direct object noun phrase, is shortened to *yagapanutiro* 'he grabbed her' (3b). Similarly, in (8) the adverbial *inkenishiku* 'in the forest' in the reference clause is omitted in the bridging clause:

(8) a. *Iaigake imagavageigi inkenishiku.* [2.0]

        i-a-ig-ak-i   *i-mag-a-vage-ig-i*   *inkenishi-ku*

        3M-go-PL-PFV-REAL 3M-sleep-EP-DUR-PL-REAL forest-LOC

        'They went [and] they slept in the forest.'

  b. ***Imagavageigi*** *ipokaigai okutagitanake ikantiri "tsame"...*

        i-mag-a-vage-ig-i   *i-pok-a-ig-a-i*

        3M-sleep-EP-DUR-PL-REAL 3M-come-EP-PL-DIR:REG-REAL

        o-kutagite-t-an-ak-i   *i-kant-i-ri*   *tsame*

        3F-be.dawn-EP-ABL-PFV-REAL 3M-say-REAL-3M go.HORT

        'They slept [and then] they came back the next day, and he said to him, "let's go."'

Some information is omitted in the bridging clauses in (3b) and (8b), though they both retain enough similarity to the reference clauses to serve the poetic function of repetition. Similarly, in (9), the Spanish reportative evidential particle *dice* in the reference clause is omitted in the bridging clause, because it is unnecessary to mark the evidential status of the same information more than once in the same stretch of discourse (for a similar case in Sunwar, see Schulze & Bieri 1973: 392).[2]

(9) a. *Itentaigari dice.* [1.8]

        i-tent-a-ig-a-ri   *dice*

        3M-accompany-EP-PL-REAL-3M EVID.REP

        'He brought him along, they say.'

  b. ***Itentaigari*** *ya itasonkake...*

        i-tent-a-ig-a-ri   *ya*   *i-tasonk-ak-i*

        3M-accompany-EP-PL-REAL-3M at.that.point 3M-blow.on-PFV-REAL

        'He brought him along, and then he blew [on him]...'

A case of substitution can be seen in the Spanish example in (15) below, whereby the reference clause *sigue caminando* 'she kept walking' is restated in the

---

[2]This reportative evidential particle, which has been borrowed from Spanish into Matsigenka in some parts of the Alto Urubamba, is common in some varieties of Andean Spanish (as well as its variant *dizque*; see Babel 2009).

bridging clause as *sigue avanzando* 'she kept moving forward'. Such lexical substitutions, however, are uncommon.

3.3 Relations within the second discourse unit

Relations within the second discourse unit – that is, between the bridging clause and the discourse-new information that follows it – can take a number of forms. As discussed above, the second discourse unit often expresses simultaneity or immediate temporal continuity between the action in the reference/bridging clause and a discourse-new proposition, as in 'he flew away' and 'he went into the forest in order to hunt' in (10):

(10) a. *Oneiri yaranake.* [2.1]
   o-ne-i-ri   *i-ar-an-ak-i*
   3F-see-REAL-3M 3M-fly-ABL-PFV-REAL
   'She saw him [as] he flew away.'

  b. **Yaranake iatake inkenishiku anta inkovintsatera iriro aikiro irityo**
   pakitsa.
   i-ar-an-ak-i   *i-a-t-ak-i*   *inkenishi-ku anta*
   3M-fly-ABL-PFV-REAL 3M-go-EP-PFV-REAL forest-LOC there
   i-n-kovintsa-t-e-ra   *iriro aikiro iri-tyo* *pakitsa*
   3M-IRR-hunt-EP-IRR-SBD he also he-AFFECT harpy.eagle
   'He flew away [and] went into the forest in order to hunt, the harpy
   eagle too.'

Often, the bridging clause and discourse-new clause are simply linked as juxtaposed (or apposite) clauses, with no subordinating morphology. This is a common means of clause-linking in Matsigenka and other Kampan languages (e.g., Michael 2008: 435). This can be seen in several of the examples given so far, including (10b).

The expression of continuity and immediate temporal succession between two actions most often refers to the actions of a single character; for this reason, the subject of the reference/bridging clause and the subject of the discourse-new clause in the second discourse unit are usually the same. However, speakers sometimes express such a link between the actions of two different characters, as in sentence (3a) above: *impogini otarogavageti, inti oga oshinto anuvagetakeroka oga oga sotsiku* 'Then she was sweeping, [and] her daughter must have been walking around, um, outside'. Matsigenka does not mark switch reference morphologically, and the change in subjects is simply expressed through person marking.

But while the Matsigenka bridging constructions described here usually express continuity and quick temporal succession between two actions, in other cases the discourse following the bridging clause instead offers an additional clarification or elaboration of the first action. For instance, in example (11), the discourse-new information in the second discourse unit is the reported utterance *ipokai piri* 'your father came back' (11c), which clarifies what one man called out to another man in the reference clause (11a):

(11) a. *Ikaemakotapaakeri.* [1.8]
   i-kaem-ako-t-apa-ak-i-ri
   3M-call-APPL-EP-ALL-PFV-REAL-3M

   'He called out to him.'

   b. *mmhmm.* [0.3]

   c. **Ikaemakotapaakeri** *"ipokai piri."*
   i-kaem-ako-t-apa-ak-i-ri   i-pok-a-i   piri
   3M-call-APPL-EP-ALL-PFV-REAL-3M 3M-come-DIR:REG-REAL your.father

   'He called out to him, "your father came back."'

Similarly, in (5) discussed above, the clause *yamanakero* 'he carried her away' (5a) is clarified by the additional discourse-new information *imenkotakara imperitaku* '[to] where he had made his nest in the cliff' (5c), marked with the subordinator *-ra*. In such cases, the discourse-new information is linked to the reference/bridging clauses through a broader range of constructions than just the simple juxtapositions described above; however, this is less common.

3.4 Some atypical cases

It is important to note here two related variations of this poetic phenomenon that do not fall under the category of inter-clausal bridging constructions per se. First, in some cases a reference clause is simply repeated in a second discourse unit, within the same stylistic parameters described above, but is not linked to any discourse-new information at all, as in (12). Such cases are therefore not bridging construction at all, but since they follow the same poetic structure, they thus must be considered in the same analysis. Note that the second discourse unit (12b) differs from the reference clause (12a) only by fronting the object, creating a pre-verbal focus construction (Michael 2008: 385).

(12) a. <u>*Yagaigake aryopaturika chakopi.*</u> [1.3]
     i-ag-a-ig-ak-i   *aryopaturika chakopi*
     3M-grab-EP-PL-PFV-REAL large.(sheaf) arrow
     'They grabbed a big sheaf of arrows.'

    b. ***Aryopaturika chakopi yagaigake.***
     aryopaturika chakopi i-ag-a-ig-ak-i
     large.(sheaf) arrow   3M-grab-EP-PL-PFV-REAL
     'A big sheaf of arrows, they grabbed.'

A second variation is a kind of construction in which the reference unit does not contain a verb at all, but is still an instance of the same poetic pattern discussed in this chapter. For instance, passage (13) includes an ideophone *kong kong* 'whistle sound' that serves as a reference unit linking (13a) and (13c). The linkage in (13c) reestablishes the flow of the narrative after it is interrupted by a clarifying digression in (13b). Note that the bridging discourse unit is followed by another, canonical bridging construction (13c and 13d).

(13) a. *Okemake isonkavatapaake <u>kong kong</u>.* [1.0]
     o-kem-ak-i   *i-sonkava-t-apa-ak-i*   *kong*
     3F-hear-PFV-REAL 3M-whistle-EP-ALL-PFV-REAL whistle.sound
     kong
     whistle.sound
     'She heard him whistle, kong kong.'

    b. *Tera iravise ampa ipokapaake aka pankotsiku.* [3.6]
     tera   *i-r-avis-e*   *ampa*   *i-pok-apa-ak-i*   *aka*
     NEG.REAL 3M-IRR-approach-IRR bit.by.bit 3M-come-ALL-PFV-REAL here
     panko-tsi-ku
     house-ALIEN-LOC
     'He didn't approach [the house], he came slowly to the house.'

    c. ***Kong kong** <u>yogonketapaaka</u>.* [2.4]
     kong   *kong*   *i-ogonke-t-apa-ak-a*
     whistle.sound whistle.sound 3M-arrive-EP-ALL-PFV-REAL
     'Kong kong, [and] he arrived.'

    d. ***Yogonketapaaka** ikaemakotapaakero.*
     i-ogonke-t-apa-ak-a   *i-kaem-ako-t-apa-ak-i-ro*
     3M-arrive-EP-ALL-PFV-REAL 3M-call-APPL-EP-ALL-PFV-REAL-3F
     'He arrived [and] he called out to her.'

4 Spanish and mixed Spanish-Matsigenka speech

As I discussed in §2, Matsigenka myths are usually performed in Matsigenka with very little code-switching in Spanish (though a number of other Spanish discourse features, including the reportative evidential particle *dice* (9a), and the emphatic particle *pues* or *pe* (3a), (5a), often pass below the threshold of a speaker's awareness). However, because of the community's complex sociolinguistic constitution, ongoing language shift, and uneven distribution of discursive skills, the narration of Matsigenka myths in Spanish or in mixed Matsigenka-Spanish speech has become more common. This is particularly true among young people who wish to engage with traditional Matsigenka culture, but who do not feel that they possess the requisite Matsigenka language competence. These performances are strictly distinguished from the monolingual Matsigenka performances discussed so far in this chapter, which are considered authoritative and culturally exemplary.

What is interesting about these Spanish and mixed Spanish-Matsigenka performances is that they usually employ the same poetic and stylistic features that "key" the discourse genre of Matsigenka myth performance (in the sense of Goffman 1974), including ideophones, prosodic and facial expressions, reported speech, and bridging linkages. That is, once a narrator "breaks through" into full performance (Hymes 1975), the metapragmatic conventions of Matsigenka myth narration – that is, the local cultural expectations about what makes a "good story" – can be applied in Spanish as well.

For instance, consider the mixed Matsigenka-Spanish example in (14). This young narrator acquired a great deal of cultural information while listening to his mother perform Matsigenka myths over the course of his childhood, and he enjoys listening to such performances for hours on end; but while he cares deeply about Matsigenka stories, he is not comfortable performing them entirely in Matsigenka. He recorded himself recounting the story of the *oshetoniro* demon to his wife one evening in their home while I rested outside:

(14)   a.   *Al medio se ha ido la canoa y se ha hundido pe ese oshetoniro.* [1.3]

      al   medio se   ha   ido

      PREP+DET.DEF.M.SG center REFL have.3SG.PRS go.PST.PTCP

      la   canoa y   se   ha   hundido   pe

      DET.DEF.F.SG canoe and REFL have.3SG.PRS sink.PST.PTCP EMPH

      ese   oshetoniro

      that.ADJ.DEM.M.SG oshetoniro.demon

      'The canoe went out into the center (of the river) and that oshetoniro demon sank.'

> b. ***Se ha hundido pe*** *mataka ya está maika yokaataka.*
> se   ha   hundido   pe   mataka ya   está
> REFL have.3SG.PRS sink.PST.PTCP EMPH that's.it already be.3SG.PRS
> *maika i-okaa-t-ak-a*
> now   3M-drown-EP-PFV-REAL
> 'He sank, that's it, that's it, he drowned.'

Here, the reference clause in (14a), *se ha hundido pe ese oshetoniro* 'that os-hetoniro demon sank', is in Spanish (except for the name of the demon itself), and it is recapitulated in the bridging clause with the subject omitted: *se ha hundido pe* 'he sank'. The code switch to Matsigenka appears at the beginning of the discourse-new information in the second discourse unit in (14b) (*mataka ya está maika yokaataka* 'that's it, that's it, he drowned'), directly after the bridging clause. It is significant that the reference clause and the bridging clause are the parts of the discourse that coincide in language choice: the poetic function of the constructions discussed in this chapter depends on the latter's similarity with the former, so we would expect them to be in the same language. It is not until immediately after the repetition of the reference clause that the narrator switches to Matsigenka.

Another example comes from a performance by the same man's wife (15):

(15)   a. <u>*Sigue caminando.*</u> [2.1]
             sigue   *caminando*
             continue.3SG.PRS walk.PRS.PTCP
             'She kept walking.'

        b. ***Sigue avanzando*** *oneapaakeri timashitake grande ya pe imaarane.*
             sigue   *avanzando*   *o-ne-apa-ak-i-ri*
             continue.3SG.PRS go.forward.PRS.PTCP 3F-see-ALL-PFV-REAL-3M
             timashi-t-ak-i   *grande ya*   *pe*   *i-maarane*
             sneak.up.on-EP-PFV-REAL big   already EMPH M-big
             'She kept going forward [and] she saw [it] sneaking up on her, a big one, a really big one.'

Again here, the code switch from Spanish to Matsigenka in (15b) takes place after the reference clause is recapitulated in the bridging clause, with the introduction of the discourse-new information. Note also that just as in most of the Matsigenka examples given so far, the two propositions in the second discourse unit are linked as simple juxtaposed clauses (*sigue avanzando oneapaakeri* 'She kept going forward [and] she saw [it]'), which would be considered unusual in

Spanish. However, unlike in (14), the verb *caminar* 'to walk' in the reference clause is substituted with the verb *avanzar* 'to go forward'. This substitution, in a parallel construction following *sigue...* 'she kept...', was similar enough to serve the poetic purposes of the linkage.[3]

In addition to these examples of bridging linkages that feature Matsigenka-Spanish code-switching, we also find examples in myths performed entirely in Spanish. For instance, one woman told a story to a group of family members, children, and visitors who did not speak Matsigenka (16):

(16)   a. *La había cogido y la había tetado.* [0.9]
   la   había   cogido   y   la
   her.PN.OBJ.F.3SG have.3SG.PST pick.up.PST.PTCP and her.PN.OBJ.F.3SG
   había   tetado
   have.3SG.PST nurse.PST.PTCP
   'She picked up [the baby] and she nursed her.'

   b. ***La había tetado*** *entonces la ha empezado a coger...*
   la   había   tetado   entonces la
   her.PN.OBJ.F.3SG have.3SG.PST nurse.PST.PTCP then   it.PN.OBJ.F.3SG
   ha   empezado   a   coger
   have.3SG.PRS begin.PST.PTCP TO take.INF
   'She nursed her, and then [the baby] began to take [the breast]...'

As in many of the examples given so far in this chapter, the reference clause in (16a) is repeated verbatim in the bridging clause; however, in this case the bridging clause is linked to the discourse-new information in the second discourse unit (16b) by a conjunction *entonces* 'then', a more familiar construction in Spanish than the simple juxtaposed clauses above. As in other cases throughout this chapter, the reference clause in (16a) was produced with falling intonation, and the bridging clause was produced with rising intonation to signal that the proposition would be followed by discourse-new information.

Another example from a Spanish performance of a Matsigenka myth comes from the same narrator (17). More information about the variety of Andean Spanish spoken in the community is available in Emlen (2019).

(17)   a. *Así se habrá echado pues así, y de su pie le ha empezado a tragarle pe.*
   [1.0]
   así   se   habrá   echado   pues así
   like.that self.PN.REFL.3 have.3SG.FUT lie.down.PST.PTCP EMPH like.that

---

[3]When Matsigenka/Spanish bilinguals speak Spanish, they often use present tense marking to express past events.

> *y   de   su pie le   ha   empezado   a*
> and from her foot him.PN.OBL.3SG have.3SG.PRS begin.PST.PTCP to
> *tragarle   pe*
> swallow.INF+PN.3SG EMPH
>
> 'She must have laid down like that, and it began swallowing her from her foot.'

b. ***De su pie le ha empezado a tragar,*** *ha llegado hasta acá.*

> *de   su   pie le   ha   empezado   a*
> from her foot him.PN.OBL.3SG have.3SG.PRS begin.PST.PTCP to
> *tragar   ha   llegado   hasta acá*
> swallow.INF have.3SG.PRS arrive.PST.PTCP until here
>
> 'It began swallowing her from her foot, [and] it got this far.' [Points to leg with finger.]

Here, the reference clause in (17a) is repeated nearly verbatim in (17b), with the exception of the emphatic particle *pe*, which is omitted in the bridging clause, and the object enclitic *le* 'her' at the end of the infinitive verb *tragar* 'to swallow'. However, in this case the speaker does not use a conjunction between the bridging clause and the discourse-new information, but rather uses the typically Matsigenka juxtaposed verb construction in (17b).

5 Conclusion

This chapter presented a type of bridging construction that is ubiquitous in the narration of Matsigenka myths in a small community on the Andean-Amazonian agricultural frontier of Southern Peru. The construction appears primarily in Matsigenka language discourse, but it is also heard in Spanish and in mixed Spanish-Matsigenka performances of the same genre. While these constructions surely contribute to discourse cohesion, they must be understood primarily as a poetic feature distinctive to the discourse genre of myth narration.

The fact that these constructions are a property of the myth narration discourse genre – rather than of a particular lexico-grammatical code – means that they can be transferred from one language to another (in this case, Spanish) when that genre is invoked. In fact, they must be transferred, to the extent that they are considered by the local metapragmatic standards to be an essential part of successful myth performance. In other words, because these constructions are limited to the genre of myth narration but cross-cut languages, they should be understood not as a property of the Matsigenka language per se, but rather of the myth narration discourse genre – which may also cross-cut languages. The fact that the metapragmatic regimentation of discourse genres enables the circulation of features across languages shows how discourse areas might emerge from local cultures of language (as in Amazonia; Beier et al. 2002), and it also illustrates how contact-induced language change can be mediated by locally meaningful categories of discursive behavior (i.e., 'culture'; Silverstein 1976). This case thus supports the proposition that *language contact is culturally mediated*. However, this contact effect is only as stable as the community's multilingualism, and it will likely not long outlast the language shift from Matsigenka to Spanish currently under way in the community.

Appendix

Excerpt of Pakitsa (Harpy Eagle) story, Alto Urubamba Matsigenka, November 2011. Analyzed by Nicholas Q. Emlen and Julio Korinti Piñarreal.

This narration of the Matsigenka *pakitsa* 'harpy eagle' story was recorded in November 2011 in the Alto Urubamba region of Southern Peru. The narrator (whose name is withheld per the arrangement with the community) grew up speaking Matsigenka and, to a lesser degree, Spanish. She lived in various places across the Alto Urubamba Valley as Quechua-speaking coffee farmers gradually colonized the region since the 1950s, and she lived for a brief time as an adult in a nearby Dominican mission. More information about this history and sociolinguistic situation can be found in Emlen (2014; 2015; 2017; 2019).

The *pakitsa* story is popular across the region, and deals with themes of incest and cannibalism. The harpy eagle is a renowned hunter, which is a recurrent part of this story. A summary of this version of the story is excerpted from Emlen (2014: 255–256): "a man requests fermented yuca beer from his wife before going out to burn his *chacra* for planting. However, the night before his son had had a dream that his father would become too drunk and be killed in the fire, so he warned his mother not to give him too much beer. But the man drank too much and was burned up in the fire. The son reprimanded his mother and instructed her to wake him up if the man appeared at the door of the house during the night – his body would be composed of ash, and a small amount of water would restore him. When the man appeared, the mother did not wake up her son, but rather threw an excessive quantity of water on her husband, disintegrating him into a puddle of ash on the ground. The ash that remained became the *pakitsa* 'harpy eagle' (with its distinctive puffy, ash-like white feathers around its neck)."

The excerpt below picks up at this point in the story. Here, the *pakitsa*-man abducted his daughter and impregnated her. After this excerpt, Emlen (2014: 256) continues, the man and his daughter "lived together in his nest and became cannibals. The *pakitsa*-man was eventually killed while hunting for humans, and upon hearing of his death, his daughter ate their newborn son and disappeared into a river to join the mythical tribe of cannibalistic female *maimeroite* warriors."

The story, which lasted about sixteen minutes in total, was considered an exemplary instance of myth narration. Recapitulative linkages are indicated with underlined and bolded text, as in the accompanying chapter. The morpheme glossing conventions mostly follow Vargas Pereira & Vargas Pereira (2013), which is the most complete accounting of Alto Urubamba Matsigenka morphology to date. However, a full descriptive grammar of Matsigenka remains to be written, and some of the morphemic analyses are preliminary.

(A1)   *Impo ikimotanake yoga pakitsa aryompa aryompa yantavankitanake.*
       impo i-kimo-t-an-ak-i   i-oga   pakitsa   aryompa
       then 3M-grow-EP-ABL-PFV-REAL 3M-that harpy.eagle gradually
       aryompa i-anta-vanki-t-an-ak-i
       gradually 3M-mature-NI:wing-EP-ABL-PFV-REAL
       'Then the eagle grew bit by bit, [and] his wings matured.'

(A2)   *Impogini maika iatake ikovintsavagetakera otomi anta iaigake*
       yanuvageigakitira.
       impogini maika i-a-t-ak-i   i-kovintsa-vage-t-ak-i-ra
       then   now   3M-go-EP-PFV-REAL 3M-hunt-DUR-EP-PFV-REAL-SBD
       o-tomi anta i-a-ig-ak-i
       3F-son there 3M-go-PL-PFV-REAL
       i-anu-vage-ig-aki-t-i-ra
       3M-walk-DUR-PL-ASSOC.MOT:DIST-EP-REAL-SBD
       'Then her sons went to hunt, they went on hunting trips.'

(A3)   *Iatake yagaigi komaginaro inti iriro kishiatanatsi anta pankotsiku.*
       i-a-t-ak-i   i-ag-a-ig-i   komaginaro   i-nti   iriro
       3M-go-EP-PFV-REAL 3M-get-EP-PL-REAL monkey.species 3M-COP 3M.PRO
       kishia-t-an-ats-i   anta panko-tsi-ku
       comb-EP-ABL-SUBJ.FOC-REAL there house-ALIEN-LOC
       'He went and caught monkeys, and [the eagle] kept combing [his feathers] at the house.'

(A4) *Okantiri maika "kishiatanatsivi maika pinkovintsatakitera*
pinkovintsatakitera komaginaro anta onkimotanakera pinampina
irokona irokona pashi" okantakerira.
o-kant-i-ri   maika kishia-t-an-ats-i-vi   maika
3F-say-REAL-3M now   comb-EP-ABL-SUBJ.FOC-REAL-2 now
pi-n-kovintsa-t-aki-t-e-ra
2-IRR-hunt-EP-ASSOC.MOT:DIST-EP-IRR-SBD
pi-n-kovintsa-t-aki-t-e-ra   komaginaro   anta
2-IRR-hunt-EP-ASSOC.MOT:DIST-EP-IRR-SBD monkey.species there
o-n-kimo-t-an-ak-i-ra   pi-nanpina iro-kona   iro-kona
3F-IRR-grow-EP-ABL-PFV-IRR-SBD 2-side   3F.PRO-INCR 3F.PRO-INCR
pi-ashi o-kant-ak-i-ri-ra
2-POSS 3F-say-PFV-REAL-3M-SBD
'Then she said to him, "you keep on combing yourself, today you have
to go hunting, you have to go hunt a monkey, so that your partner will
grow a little bit" she said to him.'

(A5) *Ipotevankitanake*
i-pote-vanki-t-an-ak-i
3M-flap-NI:wing-EP-ABL-PFV-REAL
'He flapped his wings.'

(A6) *Oneiri yaranake.*
o-ne-i-ri   i-ar-an-ak-i
3F-see-REAL-3M 3M-fly-ABL-PFV-REAL
'She saw him [as] he flew away.'

(A7) **Yaranake** *iatake inkenishiku anta inkovintsatera iriro aikiro irityo*
pakitsa.
i-ar-an-ak-i   i-a-t-ak-i   inkenishi-ku anta
3M-fly-ABL-PFV-REAL 3M-go-EP-PFV-REAL forest-LOC   there
i-n-kovintsa-t-e-ra   iriro aikiro iri-tyo   pakitsa
3M-IRR-hunt-EP-IRR-SBD he   also   he-AFFECT harpy.eagle
'He flew away [and] went into the forest in order to hunt, the harpy
eagle too.'

(A8) *Iaigi itomiegi aikiro ikovintsaigi yagaigi yamaigi komaginaro ikanti "neri*
ina komaginaro kote sekataigakempara."
i-a-ig-i   i-tomi-egi aikiro i-kovintsa-ig-i   i-ag-a-ig-i
3M-go-PL-REAL 3M-son-PL also   3M-hunt-PL-REAL 3M-get-EP-PL-REAL
i-am-a-ig-i   komaginaro   i-kant-i   neri ina
3M-bring-EP-PL-REAL monkey.species 3M-say-REAL take.it my.mother
komaginaro   n-onko-t-e   Ø-n-sekat-a-ig-ak-empa-ra
monkey.species IRR-cook-EP-IRR 1.INCL-IRR-eat-EP-PL-PFV-IRR-SBD
'His sons also went to hunt, they caught and brought a monkey, they
said "take the monkey, mother, cook it so that we can eat."'

(A9) *Inti iriro yami yovuokiri en kapashipankoku yoginoriiri yoga*
yashiriapaaka.
i-nti   iriro i-am-i   i-ovuok-i-ri   en kapashi
3M-COP 3M.PRO 3M-carry-REAL 3M-drop-REAL-3M in palm.species
panko-ku i-ogi-nori-i-ri   i-oga   i-ashiri-apa-ak-a
house-LOC 3M-CAUS-lie.down-REAL-3M 3M-that 3M-fall-ADL-PFV-REAL
'He brought it, he dropped it on top of the thatched-roof house and laid
it down, he made it fall down on top.'

(A10) *Agiri onkotakeri aikiro iriro iriro aikiro iati ikovintsatira iriro aikiro*
pakitsa.
o-ag-i-ri   o-onko-t-ak-i-ri   aikiro iriro iriro aikiro
3F-get-REAL-3M 3F-cook-EP-PFV-REAL-3M again 3M.PRO 3M.PRO also
i-a-t-i   i-kovintsa-t-i-ra   iriro   aikiro pakitsa
3M-GO-EP-REAL 3M-hunt-EP-REAL-SBD 3M.PRO also   harpy.eagle
'She took it in order to cook it, and the eagle went out to hunt again.'

(A11) *Onkotakeri impo oka onianiatakeri okisavitakerira itomi.*
o-onko-t-ak-i-ri   impo o-oka o-nia-nia-t-ak-i-ri
3F-cook-EP-PFV-REAL-3M then 3F-this 3F-speak-speak-EP-PFV-REAL-3M
o-kis-a-vi-t-ak-e-ri-ra   i-tomi
3F-make.angry-EP-MOT.OBL-EP-PFV-REAL-3M-SBD 3M-son
'She cooked it later, and she made his son mad by talking to [the eagle].'

(A12)   *"Pinianiatanakeri maika pakitsa inkaontake matsigenka*
   nianianiataerini."

   pi-nia-nia-t-an-ak-i-ri   *maika pakitsa*
   2S-speak-speak-EP-ABL-PFV-REAL-3M now harpy.eagle

   i-n-kaont-ak-e   *matsigenka*
   3M-IRR-be.like-PFV-IRR person

   n-nia-nia-nia-t-a-e-ri-ni
   IRR-speak-speak-speak-EP-DIR:REG-IRR-3M-RECP

   '[He said], "you keep on talking to the eagle as if he were a person that
   you could talk to."'

(A13)   *Impogini tataka isuretaka iriro irityo yoga pakitsa?*

   impogini tata-ka   *i-sure-t-ak-a*   *iriro* *iri-tyo*
   then   what-INDEF 3M.think.EP.PFV.REAL 3M.PRO 3M.PRO-AFFECT

   i-oga *pakitsa*
   3M-that harpy.eagle

   'What must the eagle have thought?'

(A14)   <u>*Iatake intati anta itinkaraakero oga yovetsikakera imenko ivanko yoga*</u>
   <u>*pakitsa.*</u>

   i-a-t-ak-i   *intati*   *anta i-tinkara-ak-i-ro*   *o-oga*
   3M-go-EP-PFV-REAL other.side there 3M-snap-PFV-REAL-3F 3F-that

   i-ovetsik-ak-i-ra   *i-menko i-panko i-oga* *pakitsa*
   3M-make-PFV-REAL-SBD 3M-nest 3M-house 3M-that harpy.eagle

   'The eagle went across to break off [sticks] to build his nest, his house.'

(A15)   **Itinkaraake itinkaraake** *terong terong yovetsikake aryomenkorika*
   kara.

   i-tinkara-ak-i   *i-tinkara-ak-i*   *terong*   *terong*
   3M-snap-PFV-REAL 3M-snap-PFV-REAL snapping.sound snapping.sound

   i-ovetsik-ak-i   *aryo-menko-rika*   *kara*
   3M-make-PFV-REAL truly-NI:nest-INDEF there

   'He snapped off more and more [sticks] 'terong terong' and made his
   big nest there.'

(A16) <u>*Impogini otarogavagetake iroro*</u> *oga irotyo iriniro yoga matsigenka.*
impogini o-tarog-a-vage-t-ak-i   iroro o-oga   iro-tyo
then   3F-sweep-EP-DUR-EP-PFV-REAL she   3F-that she-AFFECT
iriniro   i-oga   matsigenka
his.mother 3M-that person
'Then she was sweeping, she, the mother of the man.'

(A17) **Impogini otarogavageti,** *inti oga oshinto anuvagetakeroka oga oga sotsiku.*
impogini o-tarog-a-vage-t-i   i-nti   o-oga   o-shinto
then   3F-sweep-EP-DUR-EP-REAL 3M-COP 3F-that 3F-daughter
o-anu-vage-t-ak-i-roka   o-oga   o-oga sotsi-ku
3F-walk-DUR-EU-PFV-REAL-EPIS.WK 3F-that 3F-that outside-LOC
'Then she was sweeping, [and] her daughter must have been walking around, um, outside.'

(A18) *Okemiri maika yarapaake <u>yagapanutiro pe oga oshinto otyomiani.</u>*
o-kem-i-ri   maika i-ar-apa-ak-i
3F-listen-REAL-3M now   3M-fly-ALL-PFV-REAL
i-ag-apanu-t-i-ro   pe   o-oga   o-shinto   o-tyomia-ni
3M-get-DIR:DEP-EP-REAL-3F EMPH 3M-that 3F-daughter 3F-small-ANIM
'She heard him [as] he flew in and he grabbed her young daughter.'

(A19) **Yagapanutiro** *opampogiavakeri koa yarakaganake anta yovetsikakera ivanko intati anta.*
i-ag-apanu-t-i-ro   o-pampogi-av-ak-i-ri   koa
3M-get-DIR:DEP-EP-REAL-3F 3F-watch-TR-PFV-REAL-3M more
i-ar-akag-an-ak-i   anta i-ovetsik-ak-i-ra   i-panko
3M-fly-CAUS-ABL-PFV-REAL there 3M-make-PFV-REAL-SBD 3M-house
intati   anta
other.side there
'He grabbed her, [as] [the mother] watched him, [and] he quickly flew her away to where he had made his house on the other side [of the river].'

(A20)   *Okanti "yamanakeroni noshinto."*
        o-kant-i   i-am-an-ak-i-ro-ni   no-shinto
        3F-say-REAL 3M-bring-ABL-PFV-REAL-3F-RECP 1-daughter
        'She said, "he took away my daughter."'

(A21)   *Ipokapaake itomi ikantiro "virotakani maika kantage-*
        kantagetakovagetanatsivi."
        i-pok-apa-ak-i   i-tomi i-kant-i-ro   viro-takani maika
        3M-come-ADL-PFV-REAL 3M-son 3M-say-REAL-3F you-CULP   now
        kant-a-ge   kant-a-ge-t-ako-vage-t-an-ats-i-vi
        do-EP-DSTR do-EP-DSTR-EP-APPL:INDR-DUR-EP-ABL-SUBJ.FOC-REAL-2
        'His son came [and] said to her, "it's your fault, you keep on doing it
        [i.e., talking]."'

(A22)   *"Pine gara yagapanutiro incho"*
        pi-ne gara   i-ag-apanu-t-i-ro   incho
        2-see NEG.IRR 3M-get-DIR:DEP-EP-REAL-3F my.sister
        '"Otherwise he wouldn't have taken my sister away."'

(A23)   *Impo aryompa aryompa anta yogimonkanakero iriro anta intati anta*
        ipegakagakero ikovintsavageti komaginaro
        impo aryompa aryompa anta i-ogimonk-an-ak-i-ro   iriro   anta
        then gradually gradually there 3M-raise-ABL-PFV-REAL-3F 3M.PRO there
        intati   anta i-peg-akag-ak-i-ro
        other.side there 3M-turn.into-CAUS-SOC-PFV-REAL-3F
        i-kovintsa-vage-t-i   komaginaro
        3M-hunt-DUR-EP-REAL monkey.species
        'But little by little he raised her there on the other side of the river, he
        hunted monkey.'

71

(A24) *Aryompa aryompa oneiro iriniro antarotanake ya iroro irishinto antarotanake ya.*
      aryompa aryompa o-ne-i-ro   iriniro
      gradually gradually 3F-see-REAL-3F their.mother
      o-antaro-t-an-ak-i   ya   iroro iri-shinto
      3F-be.adult-EP-ABL-PFV-REAL already 3F.PRO 3M-daughter
      o-antaro-t-an-ak-i   ya
      3F-be.adult-EP-ABL-PFV-REAL already
      'And bit by bit her mother saw her, she was already grown up.'

(A25) *Okantiro maika "noshinto aryo oga antarotanake" okantiro "hehe".*
      o-kant-i-ro   maika no-shinto aryo o-oga
      3F-say-REAL-3F now   1-daughter truly 3F-that
      o-antaro-t-an-ak-i   o-kant-i-ro   hehe
      3F-be.adult-EP-ABL-PFV-REAL 3F-say-REAL-3F yes
      'She said "my daughter, you've grown up", and she said, "yes."'

(A26) *Aryompa aryompa onamonkitanake.*
      aryompa aryompa o-onamonki-t-an-ak-i
      gradually gradually 3F-be.pregnant-EP-ABL-PFV-REAL
      'Little by little, her belly began to grow.'

(A27) *Yonamonkitagakero irityo pakitsa oga tsinane.*
      i-onamonki-t-ag-ak-i-ro   iri-tyo   pakitsa
      3M-be.pregnant-EP-CAUS.SOC-PFV-REAL-3F 3M.PRO-AFFECT harpy.eagle
      o-oga tsinane
      3F-that woman
      'The eagle had impregnated the woman [lit. made her belly grow].'

(A28) *Yonamonkitagakero.*
      i-onamonki-t-ag-ak-i-ro
      3M-be.pregnant-EP-CAUS.SOC-PFV-REAL-3F
      'He had impregnated her.'

Abbreviations

1.INCL	first person inclusive	F	feminine
1	first person	HORT	hortative
2	second person	INCR	incremental
3	third person	INDEF	temporally indefinite
ABL	ablative	INF	infinitive
ADJ	adjective	IRR	irrealis
ADL	adlative	LOC	locative
AFFECT	affect	M	masculine
ALIEN	alienable possession	NEG	negation
ALL	allative	NEG.IRR	irrealis negation
ANIM	animate	NI:NEST	incorporated noun: nest
APPL	applicative	NI:WING	incorporated noun: wing
APPL:INDR	indirective applicative	OBJ	object
ASSOC.MOT:DIST	distal associated motion	OBL	oblique
		PFV	perfective
CAUS	causative	PL	plural
CAUS.SOC	sociative causative	PN	pronoun
COP	copula	PREP	preposition
CULP	culpable	PRO	pronoun
DEF	definite	PRS	present
DEM	demonstrative	PST	past
DEP	departative	PTCP	participle
DET	determiner	REAL	realis
DIR:DEP	directional: departative	RECP	recipient
DIR:REG	directional: regressive	REFL	reflexive
DSTR	distributive	SBD	subordinate
DUR	durative	SG	singular
EMPH	emphasis	SUBJ.FOC	subject focus
EP	epenthesis	TR	transitive
EPIS.WK	weak epistemic modality	TRNLOC	translocative

Acknowledgments

Thanks to my Matsigenka friends and colleagues in the Alto Urubamba, Julio Korinti Piñarreal, Valérie Guérin, Simon Overall, and two anonymous reviewers. This research was supported by a Fulbright-Hays Doctoral Dissertation Research Abroad (DDRA) Fellowship and an NSF Doctoral Dissertation Improvement Grant (1021842). Any opinions, findings, conclusions, or recommendations expressed in this material are those of the author and do not necessarily reflect the views of the National Science Foundation. The research leading to these results also received funding from the European Research Council under the European Union's Seventh Framework Programme (FP7/2007–2013)/ERC grant agreement number 295918. Thanks also to the John Carter Brown Library at Brown University.

References

Adelaar, Willem F. H. & Pieter Muysken. 2004. *The languages of the Andes.* Cambridge: Cambridge University Press.

Aikhenvald, Alexandra Y. 1999. The Arawak language family. In R. M. W. Dixon & Alexandra Y. Aikhenvald (eds.), *The Amazonian languages,* 65–106. Cambridge: Cambridge University Press.

Aikhenvald, Alexandra Y. 2002. *Language contact in Amazonia.* Oxford: Oxford University Press.

Babel, Anna M. 2009. Dizque, evidentiality, and stance in Valley Spanish. *Language in Society* 38(4). 487–511.

Babel, Anna M. 2018. *Between the Andes and the Amazon: Language and social meaning in Bolivia.* Tuscon: The University of Arizona Press.

Baer, Gerhard. 1994. *Cosmología y shamanismo de los Matsiguenga.* Quito, Ecuador: Ediciones Abya-Yala.

Bakhtin, Mikhail M. 1986. The problem of speech genres. In Mikhail M. Bakhtin, Michael Holquist, Vern McGee & Caryl Emerson (eds.), *Speech genres and other late essays,* 60–102. Austin: University of Texas Press.

Bauman, Richard. 1977. *Verbal art as performance.* Rowley, MA: Newbury House.

Beier, Christine, Lev Michael & Joel Sherzer. 2002. Discourse forms and processes in indigenous lowland South America: An areal-typological perspective. *Annual Review of Anthropology* 31. 121–145.

Briggs, Charles L. & Richard Bauman. 1992. Genre, intertextuality, and social power. *Journal of Linguistic Anthropology* 2(2). 131–172.

Camino, Alejandro. 1977. Trueque, correrías e intercambios entre los Quechuas Andinos y los Piro y Machiguenga de la montaña Peruana. *Amazonía Peruana* 1(2). 123–140.

Cerrón-Palomino, Rodolfo. 2001. *Castellano andino: Aspectos sociolingüísticos, pedagógicos y gramaticales.* Lima: Fondo Editorial PUCP.

Davis, Harold & Betty E. Snell. 1999[1968]. *Kenkitsatagantsi Matsigenka: Cuentos folklóricos de los Machiguenga.* Pucallpa: Ministerio de Educación & Instituto Lingüístico de Verano.

de Cenitagoya, Vicente. 1944. *Los Machiguengas.* Lima: Sanmarti y Cia.

de Vries, Lourens. 2005. Towards a typology of tail-head linkage in Papuan languages. *Studies in Language* 29(2). 363–384.

Emlen, Nicholas Q. 2014. *Language and coffee in a trilingual Matsigenka-Quechua-Spanish frontier community on the Andean-Amazonian borderland of Southern Peru.* Ann Arbor, USA: University of Michigan PhD Dissertation.

Emlen, Nicholas Q. 2015. Public discourse and community formation in a trilingual Matsigenka–Quechua–Spanish frontier community of Southern Peru. *Language in Society* 44(5). 679–703.

Emlen, Nicholas Q. 2017. Multilingualism in the Andes and Amazonia: A view from in-between. *Journal of Latin American and Caribbean Anthropology* 22(3). 556–577.

Emlen, Nicholas Q. 2019. The many Spanishes of an Andean-Amazonian crossroads. In Stephen Fafulas (ed.), *Amazonian Spanish: Language contact and evolution.* Amsterdam: John Benjamins.

Escobar, Anna María. 2003. *Contacto social y lingüístico.* Lima: Pontificia Universidad Católica del Perú.

Gade, Daniel W. 1972. Comercio y colonización en la zona de contacto entre la sierra y las tierras bajas del Valle del Urubamba en el Perú. *Actas y memorias del XXXIX congreso internacional de Americanistas* 4. 207–221.

Goffman, Erving. 1974. *Frame analysis: An essay on the organization of experience.* New York: Harper Colophon.

Guérin, Valérie & Grant Aiton. 2019. Bridging constructions in typological perspective. In Valérie Guérin (ed.), *Bridging constructions*, 1–44. Berlin: Language Science Press. DOI:10.5281/zenodo.2563678

Guillaume, Antoine. 2011. Subordinate clauses, switch-reference, and tail-head linkage in Cavineña narratives. In Rik van Gijn, Katharina Haude & Pieter Muysken (eds.), *Subordination in native South American languages*, 109–140. Amsterdam: John Benjamins.

Hanks, William F. 1987. Discourse genres in a theory of practice. *American Ethnologist* 14(4). 668–692.

Hymes, Dell H. 1975. Breakthrough into performance. In Dan Ben-Amos & Kenneth Goldstein (eds.), *Folklore: Performance and communication*, 11–74. New York: Routledge.

Hymes, Dell H. 1981. *"In vain I tried to tell you": Essays in Native American ethnopoetics.* Philadelphia: University of Pennsylvania Press.

Izquierdo, Carolina & Allen W. Johnson. 2007. Desire, envy and punishment: A Matsigenka emotion schema in illness narratives and folk stories. *Culture, Medicine and Psychiatry* 31. 419–444.

Jakobson, Roman. 1960. Linguistics and poetics. In Thomas Sebeok (ed.), *Style in language*, 350–359. Cambridge: MIT Press.

Johnson, Allen W. 1999. The political unconscious: Stories and politics in two South American cultures. In Stanley Renshon & John Duckitt (eds.), *Political psychology: Cultural and crosscultural foundations*, 159–181. New York: New York University Press.

Johnson, Allen W. 2003. *Families of the forest: The Matsigenka Indians of the Peruvian Amazon*. Berkeley: University of California Press.

Kroskrity, Paul V. 1998. Arizona Tewa kiva speech as a manifestation of a dominant language ideology. In Bambi B. Schieffelin, Kathryn A. Woolard & Paul V. Kroskrity (eds.), *Language ideologies: Practice and theory*, 103–122. Oxford: Oxford University Press.

Michael, Lev. 2008. *Nanti evidential practice: Language, knowledge, and social action in an Amazonian society*. Austin, USA: University of Texas PhD Dissertation.

Michael, Lev. 2010. *Phonological reconstruction of the Kampan branch of Arawak*. Paper presented at the Workshop on American Indian Languages, 29 April 2010.

Mihas, Elena. 2015. *A grammar of Alto Perené (Arawak)*. Berlin: Mouton De Gruyter.

Overall, Simon E. 2014. Clause chaining, switch reference, and nominalizations in Aguaruna (Jivaroan). In Rik van Gijn, Jeremy Hammond, Dejan Matić, Saskia van Putten & Ana Vilacy Galucio (eds.), *Information structure and reference tracking in complex sentences*, 309–340. Amsterdam: John Benjamins.

Payne, David L. 1981. *The phonology and morphology of Axininca Campa*. Arlington, TX: Summer Institute of Linguistics.

Renard-Casevitz, France-Marie. 1981. *Le banquet masqué: Une mythologie de l'étranger chez les indiens Matsiguenga*. Paris: Lierre & Coudrier.

Renard-Casevitz, France-Marie & Cristóbal Pacaia. 1981. *El dios Yabirebi y su cargado Yayenshi/Yaviteri inti yayenshi igíane*. Edición bilingüe Matsiguenka-Español. Biblioteca Andina de Bolsillo, 21. Lima: IFEA/Lluvia Editores.

Rosengren, Dan. 2000. The delicacy of community: On kisagantsi in Matsigenka narrative discourse. In Joanna Overing & Allan Passes (eds.), *The anthropology of love and anger: The aesthetics of conviviality in Native Amazonia*, 309–340. London: Routledge.

Rosengren, Dan. 2006. Transdimensional relations: On human-spirit interaction in the Amazon. *Journal of the Royal Anthropological Institute* 12(4). 803–816.

Schulze, Marlene & Dora Bieri. 1973. Chaining and spotlighting: Two types of paragraph boundaries in Sunwar. In Irvine Davis (ed.), *Clause, sentence, and discourse patterns in selected languages of Nepal*, 389–399. Tribhuvan University, Kathmandu: SIL Oklahoma & Tribhuvan Universtity Press.

Seifart, Frank. 2010. The Bora connector pronoun and tail-head linkage: A study in language-specific grammaticalization. *Linguistics* 48(2). 893–918.

Shepard, Glenn H. 2002. Three days for weeping: Dreams, emotions, and death in the Peruvian Amazon. *Medical Anthropology Quarterly* 16(2). 200–229.

Silverstein, Michael. 1976. Shifters, linguistic categories, and cultural description. In Keith Basso & Henry A. Selby (eds.), *Meaning in anthropology*, 1–53. Albuquerque: University of New Mexico Press.

Silverstein, Michael. 1993. Metapragmatic discourse and metapragmatic function. In John A. Lucy (ed.), *Reflexive language: Reported speech and metapragmatics*, 33–58. Cambridge: Cambridge University Press.

van Gijn, Rik. 2014. Repeated dependent clauses in Yurakaré. In Rik van Gijn, Jeremy Hammond, Dejan Matić, Saskia van Putten & Ana Vilacy Galucio (eds.), *Information structure and reference tracking in complex sentences*, 291–308. Amsterdam: John Benjamins.

Vargas Pereira, Haroldo & José Vargas Pereira. 2013. *Matsigenka texts.* http://www.cabeceras.org/ldm_publications/mcb_text_collection_30jun2013_v1.pdf, accessed 2018-9-7.

Viveiros de Castro, Eduardo. 1998. Cosmological deixis and Amerindian perspectivism. *Journal of the Royal Anthropological Institute* 4(3). 469–488.

Vuillermet, Marine. 2017. *A grammar of Ese Ejja, a Takanan language of the Bolivian Amazon.* Lyon, France: Université Lumière Lyon 2 PhD Dissertation.

Webster, Anthony K. & Paul V. Kroskrity. 2013. Introducing ethnopoetics: Hymes's legacy. *Journal of Folklore Research* 50(1). 1–11.

Wojtylak, Katarzyna I. 2017. *A grammar of Murui (Bue): A Witotoan language of Northwest Amazonia.* Cairns, Australia: James Cook University PhD Dissertation.

Chapter 3

Short, finite and one-sided bridges in Logoori

Hannah Sarvasy

MARCS Institute, Western Sydney University

The Luyia Bantu language Logoori shows a genre-based split in bridging construction distribution. Examination of a small corpus of Logoori texts of various genres told by diverse speakers shows that recapitulative linkage is limited to the genre in which actions are most central: procedural texts. In descriptive texts, where concepts rather than actions are topical, recapitulation occurs in the vessel of NPs, not verbs. Both types of recapitulation are largely absent from narratives. In Logoori recapitulative linkage, the predicate in the bridging clause uniformly takes the Immediate Perfect inflection, meaning "X having just Ved". The semantics of this inflection entail that bridging constructions cement a tight sequential relationship between the action described in the reference clause and the clause after the bridging clause. But even within the procedural text genre, recapitulative linkage is unevenly distributed and is apparently replaceable: one speaker uses the Immediate Perfect within a procedural text to effect the same sequential relationship as recapitulative linkage, but without lexical repetition. The intra-genre uneven distribution of bridging constructions, and their absence from narratives, point to their non-essentiality to Logoori discourse coherence.

1 Introduction

Logoori is a northeastern Bantu language spoken in Kenya, part of the Luyia language group (Mould 1981). The Luyia languages are highly of-a-piece lexically and grammatically, but no grammar of any one language exists. Logoori is an under-described variety. Published work on the language includes a short pedagogical grammar published by the Church Missionary Society (Appleby 1961) and a Master's thesis on Logoori tone (Leung 1991). Michael Diercks commissioned a

Hannah Sarvasy. 2019. Short, finite and one-sided bridges in Logoori. In Valérie Guérin (ed.), *Bridging constructions*, 79–98. Berlin: Language Science Press. DOI:10.5281/zenodo.2563682 corpus of Logoori oral narratives and songs; these recordings were transcribed by Logoori speakers in Kenya. In 2014–2015, the target language of the UCLA graduate Field Methods course, taught by the author, was Logoori; speaker Mwabeni Indire served as consultant for the course.

Logoori is far from monolithic, with a high degree of dialect mixing. Logoori phonology is distinguished by a seven-vowel inventory, multiple place distinctions for nasals, including a dental nasal, and for some speakers, an unusual interdental glide [j̪], (equivalent to [j] for other speakers). Although Logoori is tonal, like other Luyia languages, tone does not have a high functional load. It plays no role to my knowledge in lexical distinction for nouns, or for basic grammatical distinctions in verbs such as TAM, which are mostly marked through morphology, as in other Luyia languages (e.g., Marlo 2008). Tone will be unmarked in this chapter because a full tonal analysis of Logoori is still pending. The orthography used here is a practical orthography related to the analyses of Leung (1991) and the UCLA Field Methods cohort. It differs from the orthography used by speakers in adding two vowel symbols: ⟨ɛ⟩ and ⟨ɔ⟩. Logoori speakers use a practical orthography in which both front-high and front-mid vowels are represented with ⟨i⟩, but a third, lower front vowel with ⟨e⟩. They use ⟨u⟩ to represent both back-high and back-mid vowels, but ⟨o⟩ for a third, lower back vowel. These are distinguished in the orthography used here, so that the three front vowels are represented as: ⟨i⟩, ⟨e⟩, and ⟨ɛ⟩, and the three back vowels as: ⟨u⟩, ⟨o⟩, and ⟨ɔ⟩. Further, long vowels are represented with doubled vowel symbols: ⟨aa⟩.

Transcriptions here were completed by the author in consultation with Mr. Mwabeni Indire in the 2014–2015 period. The author's experience with Logoori is limited to an intensive twenty-week stretch in which I, along with the PhD students in the UCLA Field Methods cohort, analyzed Logoori grammar based on available reference materials, elicitation with Mr. Indire, and the corpus consulted here. In some respects, then, especially mid- and high-vowel qualities and vowel quantities, these transcriptions are not authoritative. That said, the identification and analysis of bridging constructions here should not be affected by any idiosyncrasies or misspellings, which would primarily be possible confusion of /i/ and /e/, or of /u/ and /o/, or erroneous marking of vowel length.

This chapter draws on a small, diverse corpus of 15 Logoori texts from ten speakers. These come from: a collection of Logoori narratives and songs commissioned by Michael Diercks (nine texts from four men and two women); short narratives recorded during the 2014–2015 UCLA Field Methods course, focused on Logoori, all by native speaker Mwabeni Indire (male, early thirties); and two extended conversational segments in Logoori from the 1976 documentary film *Maragoli* (including three main Logoori speakers; Nichols & Ssenyonga 1976).

All texts were transcribed and glossed during the 2014–2015 UCLA Field Methods course with the assistance of Mwabeni Indire. Genres of the texts range from interviews and conversations (e.g., *Discussion of theft in the region*) to procedural descriptions (e.g., *How I cook vuchima for lunch*), instructions (e.g., *How to care for a cow*), and narratives, including folktales, historical stories, and personal experience narratives. Mwabeni Indire is highly fluent in English and Swahili. The rural Logoori speakers from the documentary *Maragoli* likely had varying levels of literacy and competence in Swahili or English.

Every clause of each text in this small corpus was examined for evidence of bridging constructions. These are rare across the corpus, largely limited to some sections of some procedural and descriptive texts, and uniformly "recapitulative" in the sense of Guérin & Aiton (2019 [this volume]). Folktales and other narrative texts in the small sample lack bridging constructions almost entirely. The descriptive texts with "thematically-organized" discourse (Farr 1999), however, feature occasional lexical repetition of NPs from the end of one clause to the beginning of another. This could be understood as another type of bridging using NPs.

The absence of either type of lexical repetition – in predicates or NPs – from the narrative genre in the corpus is striking. At least one other Bantu-speaking society has been described as placing a very high premium on oratory (Albert 1964), and it is conceivable that a preferred Logoori narrative style discourages recapitulative bridging – which would stand in contrast to Matsigenka (Emlen 2019 [this volume]).

Many Bantu languages have a verb inflection used for sequences of events or actions that lacks tense marking (Dalgish 1979). This inflection is variously called "narrative" or "sequentive", and verbs so inflected can be chained for structures that approach classical "clause chains" in Papuan, Turkic, and Tibeto-Burman languages (Sarvasy, in prep.). An example of a Papuan chain is shown in (1) from Nungon. This example includes five clauses; only the verb in the last clause has tense marking. The other verbs are "medial" or "converb" forms; these lack both tense and subject person/number marking.

(1) Nungon (Papua New Guinea)
     Deerim e-ng-a,   maa-no   maa-no   yiip bög-in
     Deerim come-DEP-MV name-3SG.POSS name-3SG.POSS salt house-LOC
     yoo-ng-a,   iyak   tana-ng-a,   yoo-ng-a,   Deerim
     NSG.O.take-DEP-MV greens pluck-DEP-MV NSG.O.take-DEP-MV Deerim

ongo-go-mong.
go-RP-1PL

'Coming to Deerim, taking up various things at the store, picking greens, taking them, we went to Deerim.' (Sarvasy 2017: 252)

The Bantu chains generally differ from those in Nungon and clause chaining languages of most other families in two ways. First, subject person and number are obligatorily marked on all clausal predicates within the Bantu chains. Second, as noted by Haspelmath (1995) and others for Swahili, in clause chains in Bantu languages it is the predicate of the first clause that is finite (marked for tense), rather than the last, as in the Nungon example above. If Bantu languages have bridging constructions, then, they could pose a challenge for Guérin & Aiton's (2019 [this volume]) assumption that bridging clauses are "non-main" and reference clauses are "main". If the bridging clause begins a new clause chain and the reference clause ends the preceding clause chain, Bantu patterns predict that the bridging clause should be finite and the reference clause, if it ends a clause chain, should be non-finite. But in accordance with Guérin & Aiton's summary, Logoori bridging clauses – albeit finite – are prosodically and semantically dependent, while non-finite reference clauses are prosodically and semantically main clauses (see §2.1).

§2 presents Logoori recapitulative linkage involving verbal predicates. §3 covers linkage through NP repetition and another strategy observed in the corpus for promoting discourse coherence: use of anaphora. §4 gives full counts of all three of these in the corpus and concludes the chapter.

2 Logoori recapitulative bridging

The Logoori bridging construction that complies with the structural definition in Guérin & Aiton (2019 [this volume]) involves lexical recapitulation of verbs. In the 15-text small corpus consulted here, this construction is found solely in the two procedural texts. In every instance in these texts, the verb of the reference clause is repeated in the bridging clause with the lexical verb root, same subject person and number, same object person and number (if present), but different verb inflection, namely the Immediate Perfect.

Bantu verbs are famously agglutinative; Logoori is no exception. Nurse (2003: 90) gives the schema in (2) for Bantu verbs.

(2)   Bantu verb inflection slots (after Nurse 2003: 90)

Initial–Subject–Negative–T(A)–Object–Root–Extension(s)–Final–Suffix

Bantu languages are further renowned for their myriad verbal inflections, often including multiple tense distinctions in both future and past (Botne & Kershner 2008; Nurse 2003, Nurse 2008). Logoori is extreme even among Bantu languages, with four future tense inflections as well as multiple periphrastic constructions to denote the future (Sarvasy 2016). The Logoori bridging constructions here involve a verb in the future tense or the "narrative" form in the reference clause, and a verb of the same lexical root in the Immediate Perfect inflection in the bridging clause.

2.1 Logoori bridging construction form

A typical sequence including bridging constructions from the procedural text *lunchtime food* (Chesi 2014) with the most such constructions (13 bridging constructions) is shown in the excerpt in (3), given in order from the text:

(3) a. *...aa-ɲɔr-e.*
         NARR-1SG.pick.leaves.from.stems-FV

         '...I pick the leaves from the stems.'

     b. *N-daka-ɲɔr-a,*   *a-m-bagar-e.*
         1SG-IMM.PF-pick.leaves.from.stems-FV NARR-1SG-lay.out.to.dry-FV

         'Once I have picked the leaves from the stems, I lay them out to dry.'

     c. *N-daka-vagar-a,*   *a-gu-ɲar-e.*
         1SG-IMM.PF-lay.out.to.dry-FV NARR-3-shrivel-FV

         'Once I have laid them out to dry, they shrivel.'

     d. *Gw-aka-ɲar-a...*
         3-IMM.PF-shrivel-FV

         'They having shriveled...'

Example (3) shows that Logoori bridging constructions in this text follow the pattern of "X does V1. X having done V1, Y does V2. Y having done V2...". The "having done V" in the bridging clause is framed in the Immediate Perfect inflection. More formally, the verbal inflections in such a sequence can be described as in (4):

(4) a. ... Reference1-*NARR*.

     b. Bridging1-*IMM.PF*, Reference2-*NARR*.

     c. Bridging2-*IMM.PF*, Reference3-*NARR*...

Hannah Sarvasy

A longer selection from Chesi (2014) can be found in the Appendix. Bridging, where it occurs in this text, almost always functions as in (3); the reference clause describes the last action of the preceding sentence and is either in the Narrative inflection, which lacks tense specification or, in two instances, a periphrastic Near Future tense (see Sarvasy 2016). Again, the bridging clause includes a verb that is lexically identical to that of the reference clause, but with different TAM, namely an inflection called here Immediate Perfect, meaning "just having done X".

Throughout Chesi (2014), the discourse units "bridged" by the bridging clauses extend back only as far as the reference clause, and forward only as far as the clause after the bridging clause. This is anticipated by Guérin & Aiton (2019 [this volume]); they note that procedural texts are a special genre in terms of discourse flow; every step in the procedure is equally significant, so that this genre does not lend itself to "paragraphs" longer than a single clause.

Incidentally, Guérin & Aiton (2019 [this volume]) suggest no term for the clause that follows the bridging clause. Building on Chapter 1, it is suggested here that we refer to this clause as the "succeeding clause", as in (5).

(5)   [... [reference clause]]$_{unit}$ [[bridging clause] [succeeding clause]...]$_{unit}$

The number of bridging constructions in a procedural text like Chesi (2014), comprising sequences of actions, can be quantified in terms of the number of actions. That is, the number of actions described in "reference clauses" that are followed by recapitulative bridging clauses can be expressed as a percentage of total "reference clauses", some of which are not followed by any recapitulation. This sort of quantification works for procedural texts here because of the equal weight of each action in the procedure, but would not serve in the same way for genres in other languages where bridging typically occurs only after multiple clauses. In such discourse, it would be harder to reckon the total number of bridging-eligible reference clauses. So, for the sequence in (3), bridging is at 100%, with each reference clause followed by a recapitulative bridging clause.

Bridging construction distribution is uneven even within Chesi (2014). This single text contains two procedural descriptions. The first explains how to make the *mutere* greens sauce that is served over a cornmeal paste. The cornmeal is mentioned within this description, just before the description concludes with the consumption of the meal by the speaker and children or guests. Then – perhaps as an afterthought – the speaker continues to explain the process of making the cornmeal paste itself, *vuchima*.

In Chesi (2014), the first procedural description, for *mutere*, includes 33 "reference" actions, of which 10 are repeated in bridging clauses as in example (3), which comes from this part of the text. The second description in Chesi (2014) includes 22 reference actions, of which only three are repeated in bridging clauses. The two procedural descriptions within Chesi (2014) thus differ from each other in having 30.3% recapitulative linkage versus only 13.6%. There is no apparent consistent stand-in construction for bridging constructions in this second description. Rather, as in the non-procedural texts in the corpus, one reference action simply follows another, *sans* any recapitulation.

The second procedural text in the small corpus consulted here was recorded from a different female speaker, Ms. Linette Mbone. In contrast to Chesi (2014), Linette Mbone's procedural text "Preparing Tea" (2014) contains only three recapitulative bridging clauses per 38 actions, or 7.9%. The most frequent verbal inflection in this text is morphologically identical to the Immediate Perfect form used by Chesi in bridging clauses, but in Mbone's text, this form is used with main clause prosody (see §2.2). The effect is a compressed version of the bridging constructions in Chesi: instead of the pattern [… [Reference1-*NARR*]] [[Bridging1-*IMM.PF*], [Reference2-*NARR*]] given in (5), Mbone's text shows the pattern:

[[Reference1-*IMM.PF*], [Reference2-*IMM.PF*], [Reference3-*IMM.PF*]…].

Sequentiality, a function of recapitulative bridging (see §2.3), is indicated solely through the Immediate Perfect inflection. In Chesi's text, Immediate Perfect forms are always lexical recapitulations of verbs introduced in the Narrative inflection first. In Mbone's text, in contrast, the main sequence of events is often described in consecutive Immediate Perfect forms, without any lexical repetition, as seen in (6):

(6) a. *N-daka-ŋor-a   ri-gɔkɛ,*
1SG-IMM.PF-gather.up-FV 5-ash

'I've just gathered up ash,'

b. *n-daka-vunaɲer-a   zi-ŋgu   jemo,*
1SG-IMM.PF-break-FV 10-wood in.here

'I've just broken the firewood in here,'

c. *m̩ ma-ʃiga ṇeṇ-aa   ko-fan-a   molo,*
in 6-oven 1SG.want-PRES.FV 15-start-FV fire

'in the hearth I want to start fire,'

d. *n-daka-vogor-a   ke-biridi,*
1SG-IMM.PF-take-FV 7-match

'I've just taken a match,'

e. *n-daka-fan-a   molo.*
   1SG-IMM.PF-start-FV fire
   'I've just started a fire.'

Here, there are no bridging constructions. The verbs in (6a), (6b), (6d), and (6e) are in Immediate Perfect form, just like the verbs in the bridging clauses in (3b–3d). But while the Immediate Perfect forms in (3b–3d) were lexical recapitulations of verbs in immediately preceding reference clauses, there is no such recapitulation here. The discourse style in (6) could be interpreted as a more laconic, compressed version of that in (3). Instead of the two-clause bridging constructions of (3), the inflection used in the bridging clause of such constructions occurs on its own in (6a), (6b), (6d), and (6e). The Immediate Perfect inflection has inherent relationality: it can be described as a relative, rather than absolute, tense. The Immediate Perfect forms in (6a), (6b), (6d), and (6e) are thus, in a sense, reference clauses with inherent bridging function!

Sequences like that in example (6) are more common than recapitulative linkage in Mbone (2014), where I identified only three actual bridging constructions. These three do all have the same form as in Chesi (2014), as exemplified in (7) from Mbone (2014):

(7) a. ...*ma m-ba-sav-iz-e.*
         then 1SG-2-wash-APPL-FV
         '...then I wash their hands.'

     b. *N-daka-va-sav-iz-a...*
         1SG-IMM.PF-2-wash-APPL-FV
         'Once I have washed their hands,...'

Note that the forms beginning with Narrative *a-* in Chesi's dialect are equivalent to *ma* 'then' followed by the tense-less Irrealis form with final vowel *-e* in Mbone's dialect (Mwabeni Indire, p.c.).

2.2 Logoori bridging construction prosody

Logoori prosodic sentences can be defined by a final relative pitch fall and pause after the final element. Sentence boundaries are represented in the translations of the examples with periods. In the preceding section, example (3a) is the end of a prosodic sentence, (3d) begins a prosodic sentence, and (3b) and (3c) are full, independent prosodic sentences. The verbs with the pre-root *aka* Immediate

Perfect element ([daka] after the 1SG nasal prefix) serve as bridges between a preceding prosodic sentence and the one beginning with the *aka* form.

Prosodically, Logoori bridging clauses follow a cross-linguistic pattern of non-final prosody (de Vries 2005). As stated above, Logoori declarative intonation features a final fall. Reference clauses follow this pattern. In contrast, bridging clauses feature a final intonational rise. Figure 1 shows the pitch contour for the excerpt including (3). Note that Chesi tends to exhale audibly after each verb, just before each pause.

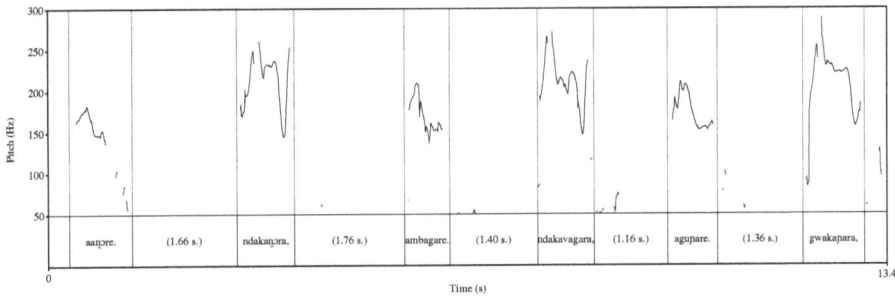

Figure 1: Intonation contour produced with PRAAT for six-clause reference-bridging sequence in (3).

Thus, Logoori bridging clauses are both morphologically finite and prosodically dependent, as in Oceanic languages and Jingulu (Australia; see Guérin & Aiton 2019 [this volume]).

2.3 Logoori bridging construction semantics

Semantically, Logoori bridging clauses in these two procedural texts uniformly accompany temporal sequentiality: the bridging clause makes it clear that the action described in the succeeding clause (the clause after the bridging clause) temporally follows the action described in the reference clause. This is facilitated by the omnipresence of the Immediate Perfect inflection, meaning "once X has V-ed…" or "X having just V-ed…" in the bridging clause. Beyond simple sequentiality, the semantics of the Immediate Perfect inflection also mean that there is a close temporal connection between the two actions: they are never distant in time.

The characteristics of Logoori recapitulative bridging constructions in procedural texts are summarized in Table 1.

Table 1: Characteristics of bridging constructions in Logoori procedural texts

	Reference clause	Bridging clause
Tense	Narrative, or periphrastic Near Future	Immediate Perfect
Subject person/number	Free	As in the reference clause
Semantics	Introduction of a new action	Close temporal link between action in the reference clause and action in the succeeding clause
Prosody	Final	Non-final

2.4 Marginal bridging constructions

One of the bridging clauses in Chesi (2014), and four potential bridging clauses identified in non-procedural texts in the corpus, do not follow the pattern in (3) and (7). These clauses feature lexical repetition in the predicate from a previous clause, but it is unclear whether they should be considered bridging clauses.

For instance, the corpus includes another text by Mbone describing how women used to live in the olden days. The potential bridging clause occurs in the sequence given in (8). Here, the inflected Far Past tense verb *va-a-ragel-a* 'they used to eat *vuchima*' occurs near the end of the first prosodic sentence and also begins (in identical inflection) the second sentence.

(8) a. *Kaande, kare, va-kere   va-a-r-aŋge   ne   zi-sahane zja*
         again   old   2-woman 2-FP-exist-PROGR with 10-plate   10.REL
         va-a-ragel-a   ko   daave.
         2-FP-squeeze.*vuchima*-FV LOC NEG

    'Again, in olden days, women did not have plates on which they used to squeeze *vuchima*.'

   b. *Va-a-ragel-a,   vi-ndo vja   va-a-raŋg-a, ri-dero,*
       2-FP-squeeze.*vuchima*-FV 8-thing 8.REL 2-FP-call-FV 5-*dero*

    'They used to squeeze *vuchima* (on), things that they called *ridero*,'

   c. *vijo   vja   va-a-ragel-a,   kaande...*
       8.DEM 8.REL 2-FP-squeeze.*vuchima*-FV again

    'it was (on) those that they used to squeeze *vuchima*, again...'

The first clause in (8b) could be considered a bridging clause since the last verb in (8a), *va-a-ragel-a*, is repeated there. This would be similar to the bridging constructions in §2.1 in that the lexical verb root and subject person/number are the same in the reference clause and the (possible) bridging clause. But unlike the true bridging constructions introduced earlier, the recapitulation in the first clause of (8b) also has the same tense as the earlier instance: in fact, the form is exactly the same. In this case, since *va-a-ragel-a* is also repeated a second time later in (8c), its repetition at the beginning of (8b) may be interpretable as not a bridging clause, but simply as expansion of the theme in (8a), which then continues throughout.

Two other instances of lexical repetition that diverge from the bridging construction pattern in §2.1 come from a fairy tale told by Ms. Grace Otieno. Here, two clauses that begin new prosodic sentences feature lexical repetition of predicates from the preceding sentences. But in both cases, the word *ruwa* 'while, when' precedes the recapitulated verb. This would seem to be a different type of linkage than the simple recapitulation in §2.1. One of these examples is in (9):

(9) a. *...ne ji-i-ran-a   je-eŋgo.*
     and 1-FP-return-FV 1-home

     '...and he returned to his home.'

   b. *Ruwa ji-i-ran-a,   ja-a-ṇɔr-a...*
     when 1-FP-return-FV 1-FP-find-FV

     'When he returned, he found...'

Such examples are included in parentheses in the final counts of bridging constructions in Table 2, in the last section §4. Similarly, the only potential bridging clause in Chesi (2014) that does not follow the pattern in §2.1 may serve a different function from the bridging clauses there. This is seen in example (10) below:

(10) a. *...ko-taŋg-e ko-raag-ir-a.*   *Na-vo.*
     1PL-begin-FV 15-squeeze.*vuchima*-APPL-FV COMIT-2

     '...We (will) start to squeeze *vuchima*. With them.'

   b. *Ko-taŋg-e   ko-raag-ir-a*   *nɛɛndɛ va-geni va-aŋge...*
     1PL-begin-FV 15-squeeze.*vuchima*-APPL-FV COMIT 2-guest 2-1SG.POSS

     'We (will) start to squeeze *vuchima* along with my guests...'

Here, the speaker originally simply states in (10a) that 'we (will) begin to squeeze *vuchima*', without indicating who are included in 'we'. She begins to expand on this with the explanatory fragment *na-vo* 'with them', but explains even more precisely in (10b). This explanation includes a verbatim repetition of the phrase 'we (will) begin to squeeze *vuchima*'. But this repetition arguably functions more to explain and expand on the earlier instance than to foster discourse coherence; it is thus considered only marginal bridging here.

3 Alternatives to bridging clauses: nominal repetition

Most of the Logoori corpus examined is remarkably free of bridging constructions or any other repetition of verbal predicates (numbers are given in Table 2 in the last section, §4). In the Logoori texts that are organized thematically (Farr 1999), there is a different type of lexical repetition. Here, the final NP of a preceding prosodic sentence sometimes recurs in the beginning of the following sentence. This may be natural for languages with AVO constituent order; the O argument of the preceding clause can be the subject of the following clause. An example from a Grace Otieno text on games played in the olden days is in (11):

(11) a. *Mu-keno gw-oonde gw-a-raŋ-w-a   zi-seembe.*
        3-game 3-other   3-FP-call-PASS-FV 10-*seembe*
        'Another game was called *ziseembe*.'

    b. *Zi-seembe zj-a-kob-aŋ-w-a   hari ka-ɲiŋge.*
        10-*seembe* 10-FP-play-PROGR-PASS-FV time 12-many
        '*Ziseembe* used to be played many times.'

This sort of repetition could be considered a type of bridging involving NPs rather than verbal predicates. While bridging clauses promote event continuity in discourse, bridging NPs arguably maintain discourse coherence relating to NPs.

There is no apparent discourse context where bridging NPs are requisite. A common context is that of (11), where something is introduced at the end of one sentence and reiterated at the beginning of the second sentence. Another example is in (12), from a text by Mr. Benjamin Egadwe on the benefits of bovine husbandry:

(12) a. *...no o-ɲor-a   mo zi-seendi.*
        CONJ 2SG-find-FV LOC 10-money
        '...and you find in it money.'

    b. *Zi-seendi zi-ra, zi-ra-ko-koɲ-a   ko...*
        10-money 10-DEM 10-NF-2PL-help-FV with
        'That money, it will help you with...'

Not counted as "bridging NPs" here are lexical repetitions from earlier parts of preceding sentences. In some instances, such repetition features the same lexical root but a different noun class marker, as in the consecutive sentence fragments in (13), from a descriptive text by Grace Otieno on children's games of yore:

(13) a. *...neva mi-keno ʤe   ke-mwaamo ʤe-ṇar-a*
          if   4-game 4.GEN 7-black   4-be.able-FV
          ko-taŋg-iz-w-a   mo zi-skuru.
          15-begin-APPL-PASS-FV LOC 10-school
          '...if games of Africans can be introduced to schools.'

      b. *Vu-keno kore, sugudi, eŋgɔjɔ...*
          14-game like *sugudi eŋgɔjɔ*
          'Play like *sugudi, eŋgɔjɔ...*'

Here, *mi-keno* 'games' and *vu-keno* 'play' share a lexical root but differ in noun class, as seen in the noun class prefix: Class 4, indicated with *mi-* here, is the usual plural of Class 3 nouns such as *mu-keno* 'game' in (11a). The *vu-* class, Class 14, includes some abstract conceptual nouns and some other collective nouns. While all lexical repetition surely enhances discourse coherence, NPs such as *vu-keno* in (13b) are not considered bridging NPs here, since the reference NP occurs much earlier in the preceding sentence.

Rampant in Logoori discourse, and much more widespread than bridging constructions involving either verbs or NPs, are anaphoric demonstratives that promote discourse coherence across clauses in terms of reference. Three different noun-modifying demonstratives "this" and "that" encode three relational distances between speaker and the referent. These take the form of suffixes (or roots, depending on the analysis) to which noun class prefixes are added, as seen in examples (8c) and (12b). In addition to these, there is a fourth nominal modifier usually translated "(that) particular" by Mr. Indire that modifies elements that have been previously introduced. At least one adverbial demonstrative *ndijo* 'like that' is also used. Counts of all of these are given in Table 2 in the next section.

4 Conclusion

A summary of bridging and related construction counts in the small corpus consulted for this chapter is in Table 2. "Corpus 1" refers to the Diercks corpus, "corpus 2" to texts recorded in the UCLA Field Methods class, and "corpus 3" to excerpts from the film Maragoli (Nichols & Ssenyonga 1976).

Table 2: Summary of bridging-related constructions in Logoori sample corpus. Counts for the marginal bridging constructions described in §2.4 are given in parentheses.

Text name	Speaker	Corpus	Genre	Bridging NP	Bridging construction	Nominal anaphor	Adverbial anaphor	Length in min.
Games for children	G. Otieno	1	Descriptive	8	0	11	4	7:51
Old flour	L. Mbone	1	Descriptive	0	(1)	4	0	2:04
Girls who wanted luck	G. Otieno	1	Fairy tale	0	(2)	11	3	5:42
Woman and the hen	G. Otieno	1	Fairy tale	0	0	5	3	4:56
On Murogooli	S. Magono	1	Narrative	2	0	4	1	3:07
How to care for cows	B. Egadwe	1	Descriptive	4	0	23	6	5:47
Preparing tea	L. Mbone	1	Process	0	3	2	0	1:20
Lunchtime food	C. Chesi	1	Process	0	13 (1)	4	1	2:42
Childhood games	M. Indire	2	Descriptive	0	0	1	0	0:52
Future wishes	M. Indire	2	Narrative	0	0	1	0	0:48
Monkey and dog	M. Indire	2	Narrative	0	(1)	1	1	1:30
Yesterday, today, and tomorrow	M. Indire	2	Narrative	0	0	0	0	3:23
Women on barns and hunger	various	3	Conversation	1	0	0	0	1:18
Men on many children	various	3	Descriptive	0	0	0	0	0:28

Table 2 shows that of the narratives and conversations sampled, only two have more than one non-marginal bridging construction involving verbs. Both of these are procedural descriptions. But these procedural descriptions differ in degree to which they employ recapitulative constructions. As seen in Table 2, "bridging NPs" – NPs that employ lexical repetition with the effect of correlating a preceding sentence with the following one – occur in three of the texts that lack verb-based bridging constructions entirely. But by far the most common device to link concepts in a sentence to earlier sentences is use of anaphors, either NP modifiers or predicate anaphors.

Guérin & Aiton (2019 [this volume]) define recapitulative bridging as involving clauses – a reference and a bridging clause, and, by implication, a clause after the bridging clause that might be called the "succeeding" clause. In the small corpus consulted for this chapter, Logoori recapitulative bridging is highly genre-specific, limited to procedural texts. Even within these texts, recapitulative bridging has uneven distribution. Although both procedural texts include them, this is in greatly differing proportions – even across two different sections of the same text – so there seems to be no genre-related requirement of bridging. The two texts also differ in that Mbone (2014) uses a kind of abridged bridge with no recapitulation: many of that speaker's independent clauses feature the same inflection as bridging clauses, seemingly eliminating the need for bridging.

Logoori recapitulative bridging constructions seem to scaffold a tightly sequential interpretation of actions. As anticipated by Guérin & Aiton (2019 [this volume]), the discourse units in Logoori procedural texts are short; the bridging clause serves as a bridge between single-clause units.

Another type of recapitulation that arguably serves to bridge two sentences involves "bridging NPs" rather than clauses. In the Logoori corpus here, recapitulation in the vessel of NPs uniformly occurs in descriptive texts, where concepts, rather than actions or events, are central. But both bridging NPs and bridging clauses are largely absent from narratives, where Logoori speakers seem to prefer a streamlined, non-repetitive discourse flow. Seifart (2010) argued that bridging in Bora occurs in the form of pronouns because of the prevalence of NPs over predicates in Bora discourse. While Seifart (2010) justifies the use of "bridging pronouns" in Bora through a general preference that supercedes discourse genre, in Logoori it is apparently the text genre that determines which type of recapitulation – predicative or NP – is primary in promoting discourse coherence.

The absence of bridging constructions from most of the Logoori corpus sampled here shows that clause chaining and agglutinative, complex verbal morphology are not necessarily conducive to bridging construction use in discourse.

Since recapitulative bridging constructions are present in some parts of the corpus, however, there is no structural incompatibility with their use. Mbone's application of the Immediate Perfect inflection for a similar effect to recapitulative bridging hints at a possible factor in their absence from most of the corpus: the rich Logoori inventory of highly-specific TAM inflections. This could combine with a possible stylistic dispreference for recapitulation by Logoori orators to limit use of bridging constructions, either nominal or clausal.

Appendix

The text here is excerpted from a procedural text recorded by Ms. Carolyn Chesi in 2014 as part of the Logoori corpus commissioned by Michael Diercks.

(A1) *Ko-meet-a va-naaŋg-a,* *Kaarɔlini, ʧeesi,*
15-start-FV 2-1SG.call.PROGR-FV Carolyn   Chesi
'To begin [n.d., idiomatic] they call me Carolyn, Chesi,'

(A2) *na-ṇeṇ-aa,* *n-zah-e,* *o-mo-tera, gwa-aŋge,*
NARR-1SG.want-PRES.FV 1SG-uproot-FV PRE-3-*tera* 3-1SG.POSS
'and I want to uproot my *mutere*,'

(A3) *gwa maṇ-e* *n-dug-er-e,* *lanstaim.*
3.REL 1SG.want-FV 1SG-prepare.cornmeal-APPL-FV lunchtime
'which I will prepare, at "lunchtime".'

(A4) *Maṇ-a* *n-zj-e* *ɱ-mo-rɛmɛ,*
1SG.want-FV 1SG-go-FV LOC-3-land
'I will go to the farm,'

(A5) *n-zj-e* *kw-ah-a* *i-ri-kove,*
1SG-go-FV 15-uproot-FV PRE-5-*kove*
'I go uproot *rikove*, [n.d., green "cowpea leaves"]'

(A6) *aa-n-zah-e* *nɛɛndɛ mo-tere,*
NARR-1SG-uproot-fv COMIT 3-*tera*
'I uproot it along with *omotera*,'

(A7) *aa-ɲɔr-e.*
NARR-1SG.pick.leaves.from.stems-FV
'I pick the leaves from the stems.'

(A8) **N-daka-ɲɔr-a,**   *a-m-bagar-e.*
1SG-IMM.PF-pick.leaves.from.stems-FV NARR-1SG-lay.out.to.dry-FV
'Once I have picked the leaves from the stems, I lay them out to dry.'

(A9) **N-daka-vagar-a,**   *a-gu-ɲar-e.*
1SG-IMM.PF-lay.out.to.dry-FV NARR-3-shrivel-FV
'Once I have laid them out to dry, they shrivel.'

(A10) **Gw-aka-ɲar-a,**
3-IMM.PF-shrivel-FV
'They having shriveled,'

(A11) *e-maɲ-a   e-dook-e   e-saa,*
9-want-FV 9-arrive-FV 9-hour
'it will arrive at the hour,'

(A12) *ʃimbe saa   tanɔ,*
about 9.hour five
'near eleven o'clock,'

(A13) *saa   siita, a-m-bek-e   ko ma-higa.*
9.hour six   NARR-1SG-put-FV LOC 6-stove
'twelve o'clock, then I will put (it) on the stove.'

(A14) **N-daka-vek-a   ko ma-higa,**
1SG-IMM.PERF-put-FV LOC 6-stove
'Once I have put it on the stove,'

(A15) *na   ŋ-gerek-el-a   muɲu.*
then 1SG-leach-APPL-FV 3.soup
'then I leach soup.'

(A16) **N-daka-mor-a   gw-a-kerek-el-a   muɲu,**
1SG-IMM.PF-finish-FV 3-PAST?-leach-APPL-FV 3.soup
'Once I have leached soup,'

(A17) *maṇ-a   m-bogor-e   n-zog-iz-e,*
1SG.want-FV 1SG-take-FV 1SG-wash-APPL-FV
'I will take it and wash it,'

(A18) *a-ŋ-gamor-e,*
NARR-1SG-wring-FV
'then I will wring it,'

(A19) *a-m-bogor-e   muɲu m-bek-e   mu i-ɲiŋgu,*
NARR-1SG-take-FV 3.soup 1SG-put-FV LOC 9-earthen.pot
'I will take the soup and put it in an earthen pot,'

(A20) *a-m-bek-e   ɱ   to-ze   ki-dɔɔkɔ.*
NARR-1SG-put LOC 13-water 7-little
'then I will put in it a little water a bit.'

(A21) *A-m-bek-e   ko   ma-ʃiga.*
NARR-1SG-put-FV LOC 6-stove
'And I will put it on the stove.'

(A22) *A-go-ʃj-e,*
NARR-3-cook-FV
'It will cook,'

(A23) *A-n-ʤokaɲ-e   ɱ.*
NARR-1SG-stir-FV LOC
'then I stir in it.'

Abbreviations

1SG, 2SG, 1PL, etc.	person/number	NEG	negation
1, 2, 3, ..., 15	noun class	NF	near future
APPL	applicative	NSG	non-singular
CONJ	conjunction	O	object
DEM	demonstrative	PASS	passive
DEP	dependent	POSS	possessive
FP	far past	PRE	pre-prefix
FV	final vowel	PRES	present
IMM.PF	immediate perfect	PROGR	progressive
LOC	locative	REL	relative
MV	medial verb	RP	remote past
NARR	narrative		

Acknowledgements

Many thanks to Mwabeni Indire, Michael Diercks, Sandra Nichols, the UCLA Field Methods PhD students, Valérie Guérin, two anonymous reviewers, and the speakers from Michael Diercks's corpus.

References

Albert, Ethel M. 1964. Culture patterning of speech behavior in Burundi. In John J. Gumperz & Dell Hymes (eds.), *Directions in sociolinguistics: The ethnography of communication*, 72–105. New York: Holt, Rinehart & Winston.

Appleby, L. L. 1961. *A first Luyia grammar, with exercises.* 3rd edn. Dar es Salaam: The East African Literature Bureau.

Boersma, Paul & David Weenink. 2019. *Praat: Doing phonetics by computer. Computer program, version 6.0.46.* http://www.praat.org, accessed 2019-1-3.

Botne, Robert & Tiffany L. Kershner. 2008. Tense and cognitive space: On the organization of tense/aspect systems in Bantu languages and beyond. *Cognitive Linguistics* 19. 145–218.

Chesi, Carolyn. 2014. Lunchtime food. In Michael Diercks (ed.), *Logoori corpus*. Unpublished audio recording & transcript.

Dalgish, Gerard. 1979. The syntax and semantics of the morpheme *ni* in Kivunju (Chaga). *Studies in African Linguistics* 10(1). 41–63.

de Vries, Lourens. 2005. Towards a typology of tail-head linkage in Papuan languages. *Studies in Language* 29(2). 363–384.

Emlen, Nicholas Q. 2019. The poetics of recapitulative linkage in Matsigenka and mixed Matsigenka-Spanish myth narrations. In Valérie Guérin (ed.), *Bridging constructions*, 45–77. Berlin: Language Science Press. DOI:10.5281/zenodo.2563680

Farr, Cynthia J. M. 1999. *The interface between syntax and discourse in Korafe, a Papuan language of Papua New Guinea* (Pacific Linguistics 148). Canberra: Australian National Universtity.

Guérin, Valérie & Grant Aiton. 2019. Bridging constructions in typological perspective. In Valérie Guérin (ed.), *Bridging constructions*, 1–44. Berlin: Language Science Press. DOI:10.5281/zenodo.2563678

Haspelmath, Martin. 1995. The converb as a cross-linguistically valid category. In Martin Haspelmath & Ekkehard König (eds.), *Converbs in cross-linguistic perspective*, 1–55. Berlin: Mouton de Gruyter.

Leung, Elizabeth Woon-Yi. 1991. *The tonal phonology of Llogoori: A study of Llogoori verbs* (Working Papers of the Cornell Phonetics Laboratory 6). Ithaca: Cornell University.

Marlo, Michael R. 2008. Tura verbal tonology. *Studies in African Linguistics* 37. 153–243.

Mbone, Linette. 2014. Preparing tea. In Michael Diercks (ed.), *Logoori corpus*. Unpublished audio recording & transcript.

Mould, Martin. 1981. Greater Luyia. In Thomas H. Hinnebusch, Derek Nurse & Martin Mould (eds.), *Studies in the classification of Eastern Bantu languages*, 181–256. Hamburg: Helmut Buske Verlag.

Nichols, Sandra & Joseph Ssenyonga. 1976. *Maragoli*. Berkeley: University of California Media Center.

Nurse, Derek. 2003. Aspect and tense in Bantu languages. In Derek Nurse & Gérard Philippson (eds.), *The Bantu languages*, 90–102. New York: Routledge.

Nurse, Derek. 2008. *Tense and aspect in Bantu*. Oxford: Oxford University Press.

Sarvasy, Hannah. Forthcoming. *A typology of clause chains*.

Sarvasy, Hannah. 2016. The future in Logoori oral texts. In Doris L. Payne, Sara Pachiarotti & Mokaya Bosire (eds.), *Diversity in African languages: Selected papers from the 46ᵗʰ annual conference on African linguistics*, 201–218. Berlin: Language Science Press.

Sarvasy, Hannah. 2017. *A grammar of Nungon: A Papuan language of Northeast New Guinea*. Leiden: Brill.

Seifart, Frank. 2010. The Bora connector pronoun and tail-head linkage: A study in language-specific grammaticalization. *Linguistics* 48(2). 893–918.

Chapter 4

Bridging constructions in Tsezic languages

Diana Forker
University of Jena

Felix Anker
University of Bamberg

This paper treats bridging constructions in the Tsezic languages (Bezhta, Hunzib, Khwarshi, Hinuq, and Tsez) of the Nakh-Daghestanian language family. We describe the syntactic and semantic properties of bridging constructions based on corpus data from all five Tsezic languages. Bridging constructions are defined as bipartite constructions that consist of a finite reference clause, which is followed by a non-main adverbial clause that functions as the bridging clause. The adverbial clause contains a variety of temporal converbs with general perfective converbs being more common than other types of temporal converbs. Reference and bridging clauses are both a target for additions, omissions, modifications and substitutions. Bridging constructions are primarily found in traditional oral narratives such as fairy tales where they index the genre and function as stylistic devices to express parallelism. Within the narratives they are often used to indicate episode changes and can be accompanied by switches of subject referents or locations.

1 Introduction

The Tsezic languages form one branch of the Nakh-Daghestanian (or North-East Caucasian) language family and are traditionally grouped into two sub-families, the East Tsezic languages comprising Bezhta and Hunzib and the West Tsezic languages comprising Hinuq, Khwarshi and Tsez. Tsezic languages are mainly spoken in the northern part of the Caucasus in the Republic of Daghestan in

Diana Forker & Felix Anker. 2019. Bridging constructions in Tsezic languages. In Valérie Guérin (ed.), *Bridging constructions*, 99–128. Berlin: Language Science Press. DOI:10.5281/zenodo.2563684 the Russian Federation. Tsezic languages are dependent marking and morphologically ergative. They are famous for their rich case systems, especially in the spatial domain, and their gender systems. For most of the Tsezic languages there are grammatical descriptions or at least sketch grammars (see Forker 2013a for Hinuq; Khalilova 2009 for Khwarshi; van den Berg 1995 for Hunzib; Comrie et al. 2015 for Bezhta; Kibrik & Testelec 2004 for a sketch grammar of Bezhta and Alekseev & Radžabov 2004 for a sketch grammar of Tsez). Further syntactic descriptions of Tsez are Radžabov (1999) and Polinsky (forthcoming).

We assume that bridging constructions can be found in all Nakh-Daghestanian languages. We will, however, concentrate on the Tsezic languages in this paper because for this subgroup we have more data at our disposal than for any of the other subgroups. The most common type of bridging construction in Tsezic is recapitulative linkage, while summary linkage is only used rarely and mixed linkage is not found at all (for a definition and classification of the three possible bridging constructions see the introductory chapter to this volume and §3 below).

The paper is structured as follows: in §2 we will outline formal properties of bridging constructions in Tsezic languages, i.e., syntactic properties of the reference clause and the bridging clause. §3 deals with the two types of bridging constructions, recapitulative linkage and summary linkage. In §4 we discuss the discourse functions of bridging constructions, and in §5 we look at further strategies of bridging constructions in other languages of the Nakh-Daghestanian language family.

Because bridging constructions are a strategy of natural discourse they cannot be easily elicited. The data analyzed in this paper originate from texts gathered by various researchers. For Tsez, Hunzib and Khwarshi published corpora exist (van den Berg 1995; Abdulaev & Abdullaev 2010; Karimova 2014). Around 42,500 words of the Tsez corpus have been glossed by André Müller, and have been employed for this paper. Most of the Khwarshi examples cited in this paper originate from texts gathered, glossed and translated by Zaira Khalilova. The Hinuq corpus is currently unpublished. It has been gathered by Forker and contains around 43,000 words. The Bezhta corpus (around 38,000 tokens) consists of the memories of Šeyx Ramazan, written down by himself at the end of the 20th century (thus they were composed in the written medium), translated and edited by Madžid Khalilov and glossed by Forker. In sum, all data used in this paper originate from written corpora, but the majority of them were oral narrations originally. Only for some of the Hinuq texts we have audio recordings at our disposal. For the Tsez, Khwarshi and Hunzib texts we do not have the relevant recordings and therefore cannot judge how much the texts have been edited and changed when the written versions were prepared.

2 Formal characteristics

Bridging constructions consist of two parts, the reference clause and the bridging clause. Reference clauses are main clauses that express an action or an event. The bridging clause immediately follows the reference clause and recapitulates the events given in the reference clause while being syntactically dependent on the following clause, i.e., bridging clauses are non-main clauses. An example for this kind of construction is given in (1) from Hunzib. Note that the bridging clause in (1b) contains the postposition *muyaλ*, which follows the converb. We are not in the position to judge whether the postposition functions as a complementizer in this example; its use in combination with the converb is optional.

(1) Hunzib (van den Berg 1995: 234)

   a. *uhu-n   lo   αbu*
       die-CVB be.PRS.I father(I)

       'Father died.'

   b. *αbu   uhu-n   muyaλ biššu iq'q'u is   ẽλe-n   lo   q'arawulɬi*
       father die-CVB after   very big   sibling go-CVB be.PRS.I guard(V)
       r-uw-a   diya
       V-do-INF BEN

       'After father died, the eldest son went to guard the grave.'

It is also possible for another clause to intervene between the reference clause and the bridging clause but this does not seem to be very common, see example (2).

(2) Hinuq (Forker, unpublished data)

   a. *hoboži y-iq-no   obu-zo   baru-s   ked.*
       now   II-become-PST.UW father-GEN2 wife-GEN1 daughter(II)
       hayɬu   kede-s   iyo   y-uh-en   zoq'e-n
       this.OBL girl.OBL-GEN1 mother(II) II-die-CVB be-PST.UW

       'Then the daughter of the stepmother was born. The mother of this girl had died.'

   b. *obu-zo   baru-s   ked   y-iq-no,   haw idu*
       father-GEN2 wife-GEN1 daughter(II) II-become-CVB she   home
       y-iči-r-ho   zoq'e-n
       II-be-CAUS-ICVB be-PST.UW

       'After the daughter of the stepmother was born, the (other) girl had to stay at home.'

2.1 Syntactic properties of the reference clause

Reference clauses are always main clauses and the majority of them are in the declarative mood. Theoretically, there are no restrictions concerning tense, aspect, modality and negation but since bridging constructions are very frequent in narratives, the most common strategy is the use of the unwitnessed past tense (3), the present tense (13) and the perfect tense as illustrated in (1) above, since those are the preferred tenses found in Tsezic narratives [1].

(3)　Khwarshi (Z. Khalilova, p.c.)

    a.　*k'ut'idin ãq'ˤwa=n*　　　*b-oq-un,*　　*l-ek'-x-un*
       suddenly mouse(III)=ADD III-catch-CVB IV-fall-CAUS-PST.UW
       'He took the mouse quickly and made her throw it (the ring).'

    b.　***l-ek'-x-uč***　　　　　*l-oq-un*　　　　*ise*
       IV-fall-CAUS-IMM.ANT IV-catch-PST.UW 3SG.ERG
       'When he made her drop it, he took it (the ring).'

Occasionally, the reference clause is a non-declarative clause. The reference clause in example (4) from Hunzib is an interrogative clause, marked by the interrogative marker *-i* and as opposed to the typical use of the perfect tense it is in the simple future tense. The interrogative clause in (4), however, is a kind of rhetorical question that the speaker asks after implying that somebody tried to frighten the cock by shooing it and the speaker immediately gives the answer by recapitulating the verbal predicate of the interrogative clause. It therefore rather functions as a declarative clause within the narrative. The form of the clause as a question has probably been chosen to raise the interest of the addressee in the continuation of the story and to involve her/him more intensively in the narration.

(4)　Hunzib (van den Berg 1995: 157)

    a.　*bed ħeleku deno m-uq'-oys-i?*
       then cock(IV) back IV-turn-FUT.NEG-INT
       'Would not the cock then turn around?'

    b.　***bed deno m-uq'e-n*** *ʕali-ł-do*　　*nuu-n*　*lo*
       then back IV-turn-CVB Ali-CONT-DIR come-CVB be.PRS.IV
       'Then having turned, it went to Ali.'

---

[1]Hinuq, Tsez and Khwarshi formally and semantically distinguish between the unwitnessed past and the perfect. By contrast, in Hunzib and Bezhta (with some restrictions) there is only one such tense-aspect form that functions as indirect evidential (unwitnessed past) or as perfect depending on the context (Khalilova 2011).

Examples of this kind, i.e., non-declarative reference clauses, are scarce in our data and therefore won't be treated further.

Since our data stem from written corpora, it is not possible to determine any prosodic differences between the reference clause and the bridging clause and therefore the prosodic properties of Tsezic bridging constructions must be left for future research.

2.2 Syntactic properties of the bridging clause

The only possible strategy to express bridging clauses in Tsezic languages is the use of converbs. Converbs are defined as a "nonfinite verb form whose main function is to mark adverbial subordination" (Haspelmath 1995: 3). Converbs are the main strategy to express subordinate clauses with adverbial function in Tsezic languages (for in-depth analyses of converbs see Comrie et al. 2012 and Forker 2013b). From a syntactic point of view the adverbial clauses in bridging constructions do not differ from other adverbial clauses.

Tsezic languages have a large number of converbs that can be divided into the following groups based on their semantics and their morphosyntactic properties (Comrie et al. 2012):

- general converbs

- specialized temporal converbs

- non-temporal converbs

- local converb/participle

General converbs can be characterized as contextual converbs that are semantically vague, in contrast to all other converbs that express particular semantic links. All Tsezic languages have at least two general temporal converbs: a perfective converb and an imperfective converb. They can be used together with copulas as auxiliaries for the formation of periphrastic verb forms that head main clauses. In this case, they form a single predicate together with a copula-auxiliary. In particular, in all Tsezic languages perfective converbs are used in periphrastic verb forms with the meaning of perfect or indirect evidential past (see footnote 1 in Section §2.1 above) as in (1a) and (2a). In Hunzib and Khwarshi, the imperfective converbs are identical to the simple present. In Hinuq and Tsez, they are used for the formation of periphrastic present tenses (by adding the copula as finite auxiliary) as in (2b).

The specialized temporal converbs express the major temporal meanings of posteriority, simultaneity, and anteriority. Each language in the Tsezic subgroup has several simultaneous and anterior converbs, but only one posterior converb. Non-temporal converbs form the largest group and include local, causal, conditional (realis and irrealis), concessive, and purposive converbs. In addition, all Tsezic languages have some local participle or converb that denotes locations where actions or situations take place.

Converbal clauses do not express their own absolute time reference, evidentiality, or illocutionary force. For these features, they are dependent on the form of the main clause. Applying Bickel's 2010 terminology we can describe them as "non-finite" and "asymmetrical" because they express fewer categories than main clauses. Temporal converbs express relative temporal reference whereby the event or situation referred to in the main clause serves as temporal anchor. Illocutionary force markers, i.e., imperative and interrogative suffixes, exclusively occur in main clauses. Their scope can be restricted to the main clause or extended to the converbal clause, depending on the construction in question. Evidentiality is only expressed in main clauses with past time reference and the scope of the evidential markers always extends to converbal clauses.

There are hardly any strict requirements of coreferentiality between converbal and main clauses. The most common way of expressing coreferential arguments between converbal clause and main clause is through zero arguments in at least one of the clauses. Coreferential overt nouns and pronouns are possible, but rather uncommon, and the precise restrictions are not fully understood.

Tsezic languages are predominantly head-final and converbal clauses commonly precede the main clause. However, center-embedding or a position after the main clause are also allowed. A few converbs such as posterior converbs or purposive converbs have a stronger tendency to occur after the main clause, which can be explained by their semantics and iconicity. Perfective converbs, anterior converbs, and to a somewhat smaller degree simultaneous converbs occur in the vast majority of examples before the main clause. This also has a semantic explanation: anterior converb clauses and most perfective converb clauses refer to situations that happened before the situation in the main clause. Therefore, if they precede the main clause their linear ordering reflects the temporal ordering of the situations, and the opposite ordering would sound rather unnatural. In the bridging constructions discussed in this paper the converbal clauses always precede the main clauses.

Table 1 shows the converbs that we found so far in our data. When we compare the range of converbs used in bridging constructions in the texts at our disposal, Tsezic languages differ to some extent. Because we did not elicit bridging constructions we cannot judge if more converbs can be used (although this is very likely). The converbs listed in Table 1 belong to the general and specialized temporal converbs. Non-temporal converbs and the local converb/participle are not found in our data, although such constructions seem theoretically possible. All converbs in Table 1 express temporal simultaneity ('when, while') or anteriority/immediate anteriority ('after, immediately after'). Anterior converbs are used when the event expressed in the bridging clause takes place before the event in the following main clause. The immediate anterior converb serves the same purpose although the time span between the two events is shorter ('immediately after'). The simultaneous converb is used to express that the two events, the one in the bridging clause and the one in the following main clause, happen at the same time. The reason why predominantly (or exclusively) simultaneous and anterior converbs are used lies in their semantics, i.e., the iconicity of linear order of the clauses and temporal order of the events as explained above. The bridging clause is a converbal clause that normally precedes the main clause, and this syntactic ordering fits well the simultaneous and anterior semantics of the converbs given in Table 1.

Table 1: Converbs in Tsezic bridging constructions

	Hinuq	Khwarshi	Tsez	Bezhta	Hunzib
PFV.CVB	-n(o)	-un	-n(o)	-na	-(V)n
SIM.CVB	-(y/o)λ'o	-q'arλ'u	-λ'orey		
ANT.CVB	-nos		-nosi		
ANT.CVB	-aɬi	-aλa			-oɬ
IMM.SIM		-uč	-run		

As can be seen in Table 1, the only converb that is found in bridging constructions in all Tsezic languages is the perfective converb. This converb is also used for the formation of complex finite verb forms (e.g., perfect, pluperfect). The general meaning of the perfective converb is anteriority, but it can also express simultaneity and occasionally manner of action. It is typically found in narrative sequences in chaining constructions as can be illustrated by means of examples (4) and (5a) (see also 24). In (5a), the main clause (containing the verb *b-ac'-* 'eat') is preceded by two adverbial clauses which contain perfective converbs (*k'oλ-* 'jump' and *λux-* 'remain') that refer to events that took place before the event described in the main clause.

In addition to the converbal suffixes, the dependent clauses often contain some argument or modifier marked with an additive enclitic enhancing cohesion in a narrative sequence, e.g., *lači=n* 'clothes(v)=ADD' and *hõgo-li-i-n* 'coat-OBL-IN=ADD' in (24). The additive enclitic also occurs in the converbal clauses in bridging constructions that are formed with the perfective converb, e.g., (5b), (13), and (18). In example (5) from Khwarshi the action expressed in the reference clause is almost identically repeated in the bridging construction and the only expressed argument in the bridging clause bears the additive enclitic (*kad-ba=n* 'girl-PL=ADD').

(5)   Khwarshi (Z. Khalilova, p.c.)

   a. *c'odora-y bala-l   k'oλ-un,   y-ac'-bič   λux-un*
      clever-II corner-LAT jump-CVB, II-eat-PROH remain-CVB
      λux-u-so   golluč kad-ba b-ac'-un
      stay-PST.PTCP-DEF all   girl-PL HPL-eat-PST.UW
      'In order not to be eaten the clever one jumped into the wooden trunk, (the wolf) ate the rest of girls.'

   b. ***kad-ba=n b-ac'-un,   m-ok'-še   b-eč-un   boc'o***
      girl-PL=ADD HPL-eat-CVB, III-go-ICVB III-be-PST.UW wolf(III)
      yon-o-ł-yul
      forest-OBL-INTER-ALL
      'Having eaten the girls, the wolf went to the woods.'

If we take a look at the reference clause in (5) we notice that the unwitnessed past and the perfective converb are formally identical (-*un*). Despite the homophony, they are functionally different, e.g., the perfective converb is not used to express evidentiality. The same homophony applies to Hinuq, Tsez, and partially to Bezhta (cf. Forker 2013a: 244; Khalilova 2009: 391; Khalilova 2011; Comrie et al. 2016).

3 Types of bridging constructions

In Tsezic languages we find two types of bridging constructions. The first and most common construction is recapitulative linkage that will be discussed in §3.1. In these constructions, the action expressed in the reference clause is repeated immediately in the bridging clause. Strictly verbatim repetition is rare and bridging constructions are frequently a target for modification, i.e., we have omissions, additions and substitutions that distinguish the bridging clause from the reference clause.

The second possibility is summary linkage, i.e., the use of a dedicated verb to recapitulate the events expressed in the reference clause. This strategy is commonly used to summarize the content of direct speech. It will be treated in §3.2.

3.1 Recapitulative linkage

(Almost) verbatim repetition is occasionally found and (3) provides an example. Generally, reference clauses and bridging clauses slightly differ in terms of formal make-up and consequently usually also in content. As mentioned in §1, there are four subtypes of recapitulative linkage. All four are found in Tsezic languages:

Modifications: reference clause and bridging clause contain the same information, i.e., there are no omissions or additions but word order might be changed or lexical NPs can be replaced by corresponding pronouns in either the reference clause or the bridging clause

Omissions: reference clause and bridging clause differ in terms of content, i.e., the bridging clause contains less information than the reference clause

Additions: reference clause and bridging clause differ in terms of content, i.e., the reference clause withholds information which is then provided in the bridging clause

Substitutions: information given in the reference clause is substituted in the bridging clause by (near) synonyms in order to broaden or narrow the semantics of the verbal predicate or in order to change the point of view

3.1.1 Modifications

Modifications are not as common as omissions and additions and are often accompanied by those. Possible modifications are different word order or replacement of lexical NPs by pronouns in the bridging clause and vice versa. The reference clause in (6) differs from the bridging clause in some aspects. The subject of the reference clause is encoded by a pronoun *iƛe* in the ergative case whose referent, *ɣʷade* 'raven' was introduced by a lexical NP in the preceding clause. In the bridging clause, the subject is repeated as a lexical NP. Furthermore, reference clause and bridging clause differ in their constituent order due to the diverging position of the verb: VOS (verb-initial reference clause) vs. OSV (verb-final bridging clause). A similar example with changed constituent order from verb-initial to verb-final is (1). The constituent order in the clause preceding the reference clause

(VS) and in the reference clause itself (VOS) is typical for introducing new referents into the discourse in the position of subject and object respectively. Both noun phrases denoting new referents ('raven' and 'chicken') occur after the verb. In the bridging clause the constituent order has been changed to verb-final since the clause does not serve to introduce a new referent.

(6) Khwarshi (Z. Khalilova, p.c.)

    a. *šari   coλ-še   idu eč-u-q'arλ'a,   b-ot'q'-un   ɣʷade*
       butter stir-ICVB this be-PST.PTCP-SIM.CVB III-come-PST.UW raven(III)

       y-ez-un   hos huho   iłe
       v-take-PST.UW one chicken(V) 3SG.ERG

       'When he was sitting and stirring the butter, a raven came and took one chicken.'

    b. ***hos huho   ɣʷad-i   y-ez-aλa,***   *l-oc-un*
       one chicken(V) raven.OBL-ERG v-take-ANT.CVB NPL-tie-PST.UW

       oč'e-č   huho   õču-lo   k'ak'a-qa-l
       nine-INTS chicken hen-GEN2 leg-CONT-LAT

       'When the raven took one chicken, he tied all nine chickens to the leg of the hen.'

The opposite can be observed as well, i.e., the reference clause contains a lexical NP that is pronominally repeated in the bridging clause as in (7). As mentioned above, modifications regularly go hand in hand with additions, omissions and substitutions. Thus, in (7) not only the linguistic form of the subject differs, but the goal expression in the referent clause has been omitted in the bridging clause.

(7) Hunzib (van den Berg 1995: 164)

    a. *bəda: eče-r-α-α   koro   r-oχ-on=no,   č'eq*
       so   stay-PST.PTCP-OBL-IN hand(V) v-take-CVB=ADD bird(IV)

       gič'-en   lo   kα-λ'o
       sit.down-CVB be.PRS.IV hand.OBL-SPR

       'While he was sitting, holding his hand out like this, a bird alighted in his hand.'

    b. ***ogu   gič'-oł,***   *rara-a=n   gul-un, ẽλ'e-n lo*
       that(IV) sit.down-ANT.CVB bosom-IN=ADD put-CVB go-CVB be.PRS.I

       humutkura-α hobolłi-la-α
       Garbutli-IN hospitality-OBL-IN

       'When it alighted, he put it in his bosom and went to Garbutli as a guest.'

The repetition of a lexical NP as pronoun in the bridging clause is only rarely found in Tsezic languages. The preferred strategy is to leave the referent unexpressed in the bridging clause. This is not surprising because in clause linkage coreferent arguments are usually omitted in adverbial clauses. More generally, in Tsezic languages arguments that are retrievable from the context are often not overtly expressed, not even in main clauses.

3.1.2 Omissions

Omissions are found in a vast amount of recapitulative linkage constructions. Typical targets for omission are lexical NPs and adjectives as in (5) and (8), numerals in (10), pronouns, adverbs, locative arguments in (11) and other verbal complements like purposive clauses in (9) or infinitival clauses.

(8) Hunzib (van den Berg 1995: 207)

　　a. *əg*　*buλii loder*　　*i?er*　*ože*　*iq'lə-n*　　*lo*
　　　　that.I home be.PRS.PTCP small boy(I) grow.up-CVB be.PRS.I

　　　　'Now, that little boy who was at home had grown up.'

　　b. *iq'l-oł*　　　　*iyu-g*　*nisə-n*　*li*　　"*diye*　*abu*　*niyo*
　　　　grow.up-ANT.CVB mother-AD say-CVB be.PRS.V 1SG.GEN father where

　　　　êλ'e-r?"
　　　　go-PST

　　　　'When he had grown up, he said to his mother, "Where did my father go?"'

The example in (8) displays the most radical type of omission, i.e., only the most important information given in the reference clause is repeated in the bridging clause, namely the verbal predicate, and all other information expressed by the lexical argument and the modifying adjective in the reference clause have been omitted. Example (9) from Tsez shows further possibilities of omission. Almost all information of the reference clause (adverb, lexical NPs and the purposive clause) has been left out in the bridging clause.

(9) Tsez (Abdulaev & Abdullaev 2010: 211)

　　a. *nełλ'osi*　　*kʷaxa=tow*　*habihan=n*　*ziru=n*　*xan-s*　　*kid*
　　　　of.that.time soon=EMPH miller=ADD fox=ADD khan-GEN1 daughter

　　　　esir-anix　　*b-ik'i-n*
　　　　ask-PURP.CVB HPL-go-PST.UW

　　　　'Soon after that, the miller and the fox went to ask for the king's daughter.'

b. ***ele-ayor   b-ik'i-λ'orey*** *ziru-de   dandir   ixiw*
there-IN.VERS HPL-go-SIM.CVB fox-APUD together big
bˤeλ'e-s   reqen=no žeda-ɬ   teɬ=gon
flock.of.sheep-GEN1 herd=ADD DEM.OBL-CONT inside=CNTR
b-ik'i-x   ixiw ɣˤʷay=no   keze b-oq-no
III-go-ICVB big   dog(III)=ADD meet III-become-PST.UW
'When they went there, the fox met a big flock of sheep and a large dog walking among them.'

Omission of subject-like arguments is common. In example (10), not only the ergative pronoun is absent from the bridging clause but also the numeral 'three'. Note that this changes the gender agreement prefix in the bridging clause; the omission of the numeral requires the P argument to be marked by the plural and thus the verb bears the neuter plural agreement prefix.

(10)   Tsez (Abdulaev & Abdullaev 2010: 92)

a. *zaman-λ'ay* <u>*neɬa*</u>   *ɬˤono* <u>*xexoy*</u>   <u>*b-oɣ-no*</u>
time-SPR.ABL it.OBL.ERG three young.animal(III) III-hatch-PST.UW
'After a while, it hatched three nestlings.'

b. ***xexoy-bi***   ***r-oɣ-no***   *kʷaxa=tow yun-xor=no*
young.animal-PL NPL-hatch-CVB soon=EMPH tree-AD.LAT=ADD
b-aɣ-n   ziru-a aɣi-qor   qˤaλi-n
III-come-CVB fox-ERG bird-POSS.LAT shout-PST.UW
'Very soon after the nestlings hatched, a fox came to the tree and shouted to the bird.'

In Hunzib, the copula, which forms together with the perfective converb the periphrastic perfect tense as in (1), (7), and (8), is dropped in many bridging clauses and although this looks formally like an omission such constructions are morphosyntactically substitutions and will be treated in §3.1.4.

3.1.3 Additions

Sometimes the bridging clause in recapitulative linkage expresses more information than the reference clause. Additional information that is given in the bridging clause is not new or doesn't crucially alter the event described in the reference clause but rather provides additional background information in the form of adverbs or spatial arguments. The bridging construction in (11) contains more information about the manner of movement of the group ('happily') and adds a locative argument ('on their way'), but there are also some omissions like the deletion of the locative adverb that expresses the place of origin. Furthermore, the bridging clause is introduced by the clause-initial manner adverb *hemedur* 'so'. Manner adverbials of this and similar types as well as temporal adverbials with a very general meaning are frequently used in narrative discourse to establish boundaries between individual episodes and at the same time link the episodes together. It comes thus naturally to add them in bringing constructions (see also 4).

(11) Tsez (Abdulaev & Abdullaev 2010: 138)

    a. *ža=n   hemedur=tow ešur-no   yizi-a*
       DEM.SG=ADD SO=EMPH   take.along-CVB DEM.PL.OBL-ERG

       yizi-ł   r-oq-no   ele-ay   bitor uyno=n
       DEM.PL.OBL-CONT PL-become-CVB there-IN.ABL thither four=ADD

       sadaq   r-ik'i-n
       together PL-go-PST.UW

       'So they took him along with them as well and from there the four went further together.'

    b. **hemedur uyno=n   rok'uɣʷey-ƛ' huni-x r-ik'i-ƛ'orey**
       SO   four=ADD fun-SPR   way-AD PL-go-SIM.CVB

       žeda-r   b-exur-asi   boc'i b-esu-n
       DEM.OBL-IN.LAT III-kill-RES.PTCP wolf III-find-PST.UW

       'So when the four of them went on their way happily, they found a wolf who was killed.'

In the bridging clause in (12) there are no omissions but only additions that slightly alter the content. The predicate in the reference clause is a causative verb that expresses an action carried out by the fox. In the bridging clause the predicate occurs in its bare intransitive form and consequently there is no agentive argument. Instead, the result of the action is described and the predicate is further modified by an adverbial phrase expressing quality/evaluation.

(12) Khwarshi (Z. Khalilova, p.c.)

    a. *zor-i   ło   gut'-un,   łuy-k'-un   boc'o bolo-qa-l*
       fox-ERG water pour-CVB, stick-CAUS-PST.UW wolf ice-CONT-LAT

       'The fox poured out the water and the wolf froze to the ice.'

b. ***b-og   b-oƚu   bolo-qa-l   boc'o   ƚuɣ-aλa,***   *goλ'-un*
   III-well III-alike ice-CONT-LAT wolf(III) stick-ANT.CVB call-PST.UW
   zor-i
   fox-ERG
   'When the wolf was good frozen to the ice, the fox called (the witch).'

3.1.4 Substitutions

Substitutions in bridging clauses can be formal and/or semantic. The most common kind of substitution concerns the verbal predicate of the reference clauses. Bridging clauses in Tsezic languages are generally subordinate clauses and therefore require different marking than the preceding reference clause. Verbs in reference clauses occur in "finite verb forms", most commonly present tense or unwitnessed past/perfect in our data (§2.1) and are replaced by a suitable converb in the bridging clause. The most frequent substitution strategy found in all Tsezic languages involves the verb form in the main clause being replaced by the perfective converb, indicating temporal anteriority with respect to the situation in the following main clause. In most examples presented so far in this paper, the verb form in the main clause is the unwitnessed past (4–12). This is due to the fact that the vast majority of texts analyzed for this paper are traditional fairy tales and legends that are almost exclusively narrated in the unwitnessed past. By contrast, example (13) from Bezhta belongs to an autobiographical narration that also contains other tenses such as the present (used as historical present in the example) or the witnessed past. In (13) it is the present tense that occurs in the main clause (reference clause). Regardless, (13) still illustrates the common substitution strategy within the bridging clause.

(13)   Bezhta (unpublished data, courtesy of M. Khalilov)

a. *holƚo-s*   *k'et'o gemo=na y-iq'e-na*   *holco huli y-ūq-ča*
   DEM.OBL-GEN1 good taste=ADD IV-know-CVB he.ERG DEM IV-eat-PRS
   'Knowing its good taste, he eats it.'

b. ***huli=na y-ūq-na***   *saala ničdiya   box-a-λ'a   ãko   ēλ'e-š*
   DEM=ADD IV-eat-CVB one   green.OBL gras-OBL-SPR release go-PRS
   huli
   DEM
   'Having eaten it he lays down on the green grass.'

Besides the perfective converb, we find the anterior converb (as in 7, 8, and 12), the immediate anterior converb in (3) and the simultaneous converb in (9) in bridging clauses.

Sometimes we find substitution by means of (near) synonymy, i.e., one of the verbs in either the reference clause or the bridging clause has a more general meaning than the other one. The verb -*ŭče* 'run' that is used in the reference clause in (14) provides a more precise description of the kind of movement that is used to return home (namely fast movement by foot), while the more general verb -*ĕλe* 'go' used in the bridging clause is a default verb to express movement. Note also that the locative adverb *deno* 'back' is substituted by *buλii* 'home' which provides, in contrast to *deno*, a more specific description of the goal of the motion.

(14) Hunzib (van den Berg 1995: 234)

    a. *ĕλe-n=no*   "*r-uwo-r q'arawulλi*" *λe*   *nisə-n* *šima-λ'o=n*
        go-CVB=ADD V-do-PST guard(V)   QUOT say-CVB grave-SPR=ADD

        λ'-it'o   <u>*deno ŭče-n*</u> <u>*lo*</u>   <u>*bəd*</u>
        go-CVB.NEG back run-CVB be.PRS.I 3SG.I

        'He went and without having gone to the grave, he said "I have guarded it" and he ran back (home).'

    b. **ĕλe-n buλii** *ut'-un*   *lo*   *łanα wədə*
        go-CVB home sleep-CVB be.PRS.I three day

        'Having gone home he slept for three days.'

Another kind of substitution we find regularly is the replacement of one verb of motion by another one with a different deictic meaning, e.g., 'go' is replaced by 'come' in (15). The reference clause contains a verb of motion that expresses movement away from the deictic center ('go') where previous events took place while the verb in the following bridging clause changes the perspective and expresses movement to the new deictic center ('come'). This strategy is almost always used when the event expressed in the following main clause takes place at a new location. Additionally, in example (15) the goal of the movement, namely the king's whereabouts, is replaced by the spatial adverb *elo* 'there', similar to example (9).

(15) Tsez (Abdulaev & Abdullaev 2010: 74)

    a. *aɣi=n*   *b-is-no*   *adäz=gon*   *b-oc'-no*
        bird(III)=ADD III-take-CVB ahead=CNTR III-drive-CVB

        t'eka=n   <u>*kid*</u> <u>*xan-däyor*</u>   <u>*y-ik'i-n*</u>
        he.goat(III)=ADD girl(II) khan-APUD.VERS II-go-PST.UW

        'Having taken a bird and chased a goat ahead, the girl went to the king.'

    b. ***elo-r***   ***y-ay-nosi***   *yiɫa*   *xan-qor*   *aɣi teλ-xo*
        there-LAT II-come-ANT.CVB she.OBL.ERG khan-AT.LAT bird give-ICVB
        zow-no
        be-PST.UW
        'After she arrived there, she wanted to give the bird to the king.'

Further substitution can be found in the nominal domain, i.e., a lexical NP can be replaced by another lexical NP with a similar meaning. In (16) one word to express 'time', *meχ*, is replaced in the bridging clause by another word *zaban* expressing roughly the same meaning. Note again that gender agreement on the verb *-ēλe* 'go' changes because the two words belong to different genders.

(16)   Hunzib (van den Berg 1995: 202)

    a. *ãq'-oɫ*   *boɫu-l* *lač'i*   *n-iza:-n*   *li,*   *həs=no*
        come-ANT.CVB this-ERG clothes(v) v-wash-CVB be.PRS.V one=ADD
        q'am *n-iza:-n*   *li*   *həs=no bəʔi-d* *əgi-d*
        head(v) v-wash-CVB be.PRS.V one=ADD here-DIR there-DIR
        tiq-en   <u>*meχ*</u>   <u>*m-eλ'e-n*</u> <u>*lo*</u>
        be.busy-CVB time(IV) IV-go-CVB be.PRS.IV
        'After he had come, time passed while she washed clothes, washed her head, keeping busy with this and that.'

    b. ***zaban n-eλ'-oɫ,***   *b-u<wɑ>t'-a*   *anta*
        time(v) v-go-ANT.CVB HPL-sleep<PL>-INF moment(IV)
        m-aq'-oɫ   *nisə-n* *li*   "*b-u<wɑ>t'-a*"   *λe*   *nisə-n*
        IV-come-ANT.CVB say-CVB be.PRS.V HPL-<PL>sleep-INF QUOT say-CVB
        li   *yurdelo-l*
        be.PRS.V mullah-ERG
        'And when the time had passed, when the moment came to go to bed, the mullah said "Let's go to bed."'

3.2 Summary linkage

In summary linkage the reference clause is replaced by a dedicated verb which summarizes its content. This kind of bridging construction is not very common in Tsezic languages since recapitulative linkage is the preferred bridging construction, but nevertheless can occasionally be found. In example (17) from Hunzib summary linkage is achieved by using the dedicated verb *-ɑq* 'happen'. In this example, the verb 'happen' has scope over two reference clauses and is used to summarize both events.

(17) Hunzib (van den Berg 1995: 160)

    a. *ẽλ'e-n lo   oɫu-dər   k'arλe-n   lo   oɫu-γur*
    go-CVB be.PRS.I 3SG.OBL-ALL wander-CVB be.PRS.I 3SG.OBL-COM
    'And he went down to her and went for a walk with her.'

    b. **αq-oɫ**   *bəd λ'i ũχe-n   χoχ-λ'o ẽλ'e-n lo   bəd*
    happen-ANT.CVB 3SG.I back turn-CVB tree-SPR go-CVB be.PRS.I 3SG.I
    'Having done this, he returned and went back into the tree.'

Another type of summary linkage that is relatively common is given in (18) and (19). The reference clauses in (18) and (19) consist of quotes whose contents are summarized by a demonstrative pronoun that is used together with a verb of speech.

(18) Tsez (Abdulaev & Abdullaev 2010: 87)

    a. "*di mi γuro-x   egir-an=λin   odä-si zow-č'u   ži*
    1SG 2SG COWS-AD send-FUT.DEF=QUOT do-RES be-NEG.PST.WIT now

    r-od-a   šebin anu=λin"
    IV-do-INF thing be.NEG=QUOT
    '"I didn't give birth to you to have you pasture the cows but now there is nothing to do."'

    b. *ža=n   **eλi-n**   hemedur=tow ozuri-λay   gugi-n*
    this=ADD say-CVB so=EMPH   eye-SUB.ABL escape-PST.UW
    'Having said this, he flew out of sight.'

(19) Hinuq (Forker, unpublished data)

    a. *hibayɫu minut-ma b-aq'-a   goɫ dew-de   aldoγo-r*
    that.OBL minute-IN III-come-INF be you.SG.OBL-ALOC in.front-LAT

    debe   goɫa   murad t'ubazi b-uw-ayaz
    you.SG.GEN1 be.PTCP wish(III) fulfill III-do-PURP
    '(The horse said:) In that minute I will be in front of you to fulfill your wish.'

    b. **hag=no** *eλi-n   gulu   k'oλe-n   hawa-λ'o b-iλ'i-yo*
    that=ADD say-CVB horse(III) jump-CVB air-SPR   III-go-PRS
    'Having said that the horse goes away jumping through the air.'

4 Functions of bridging constructions

4.1 Discourse functions

Cross-linguistically, bridging constructions are used to keep the discourse cohesive and ease tracking of characters and events. Therefore, bridging constructions are regularly found in languages that employ switch reference. Although there are no switch reference constructions in Tsezic languages, bridging constructions, or to be more precise recapitulative linkage, can sometimes be found when the subject of the clause that follows the bridging clause deviates from the one in the reference and bridging clause. In (20), the reference clause contains a lexical NP that is omitted in the following bridging clause but still serves as subject. The main clause that follows the bridging clause switches the subject to another character of the narrative.

(20) Hunzib (van den Berg 1995: 209)

    a. <u>*ẽdu*</u>   <u>*m-aq'e-n*</u>   *lo*   *ʕaždah*
       inside IV-come-CVB be.PRS.IV dragon(IV)

       'The dragon went inside.'

    b. **ẽdu** **m-aq'-oɬ**   *boɬu-l*   *bodu*   *ʕaždah*   *b-iƛ'e-n*
       inside IV-come-ANT.CVB 3SG.I-ERG this(IV) dragon(IV) IV-kill-CVB
       gač'
       be.PRS.NEG

       'When it went inside, the boy did not kill the dragon.'

Example (21) is another instance of subject switching. The reference clause and the following bridging clause share the subject 'girl', but the following clause changes to another subject (see also (22) below).

(21) Khwarshi (Z. Khalilova, p.c.)

    a. *akal-un*   *gollu*   *kad zamana-č*   *m-ok'-šehol*
       be.tired-CVB be.PRS.PTCP girl time(III)-INTS III-go-POST.CVB
       <u>*ƛus-un*</u>
       sleep-PST.UW

       'The girl who has been tired fell asleep as some time passed.'

    b. **kad ƛus-uč,**   *abaxar-i*   *m-oc-un*   *iɬe-s*
       girl sleep-IMM.ANT neighbour-ERG III-tie-PST.UW 3SG.OBL-GEN1
       kode=n   *ɣon-o-qo-l*
       hair(III)=ADD tree-OBL-CONT-LAT

       'As soon as the girl fell asleep the neighbor tied her hair to the tree.'

In many instances the switched subject occurs in the immediately preceding discourse. For instance, in example (6) above the clause preceding the reference clause has a demonstrative pronoun 'he' as subject, referring to a male human being. The reference clause and the bridging clause share the subject 'raven'. The next clause after the bridging clause switches back to the previous subject 'he'. Other examples of this type are (7) and (12).

However, in most of the examples the clause following the bridging construction describes a new episode. An episode is a brief unit of action in a narrative. Consecutive episodes in narratives can but need not share some or all of the characters. They can take place in the same or in distinct locations. Therefore, a new episode can be accompanied by a change of the subject referent in comparison to the previous episode. This can mean that an entirely new referent is introduced in the clause after the referent clause as in (9), (10) and (11), or the previous subject-referent is taken up again as in (6), (7), or (12). It is also possible to switch back to a protagonist who was not a subject referent in the bridging clause, but is not entirely new to the narration as in (1) and (21). Similarly, in a number of the examples the utterance following the reference clause moves the string of narration to a new spatial goal or location. For instance, in (5a) the situation takes place at the home of the protagonist. In (5b) the clause following the bridging construction describes that the place of the action has changed from inside the house to outside. Comparable examples are (18) and (19) in which the clause after the bridging construction describes how one of the protagonists disappears from the scene.

A change of the protagonists or location more clearly indicates that a new episode follows and thus the bridging construction helps to structure the narration by demarcating episodes. As mentioned above, new episodes do not necessarily have new protagonists or new locations, but are defined by new actions. Therefore, the bridging construction can also mark the end of an episode and thus the beginning of a new episode in which the subject referent is just the same such that we have subject/topic continuity as in (11), (14), and (15). More specifically, in (11), the episode in the bridging construction describes the joint walk of the protagonists. The new episode refers to how the protagonists found a dead wolf. The bridging construction in (14) describes the walk back home of the protagonist and the following clause his lying down to sleep.

Similarly, a change in the location is not obligatory, e.g., (16), (20), and (21). For example, in (20) the bridging construction narrates that the girl fell asleep. This episode is followed by a new one in which the neighbor tied her hair to a tree.

Furthermore, bridging constructions may be used to express the chaining of events, i.e., consecutive events can be recapitulated. The reference clause in (22) actually consists of two clauses that express consecutive events, the drinking and the sleeping afterwards. Both events are recapitulated in the bridging clause that consists of two converbal clauses.

(22) Hunzib (van den Berg 1995: 216)

    a. *wedra*   *γino*   *χuλ-un*   *lo,*   <u>*χura:-n*</u>   <u>*lo,*</u>
       bucket(IV) wine(IV) drink-CVB be.PRS.I get.drunk-CVB be.PRS.I
       <u>*ut'-un*</u>   <u>*lo*</u>   <u>*bəd*</u>
       sleep-CVB be.PRS.I 3SG.I

       'He drank a bucket of wine, got drunk and went to bed.'

    b. *χura:-n*   *ut'-oɬ*   *bəd eže-n*   *lo*   *boɬu-l*
       get.drunk-CVB sleep-ANT.CVB 3SG.I take-CVB be.PRS.I this.OBL-ERG

       'When he got drunk and went to bed, the dragon took him outside.'

4.2 Genre

In the corpora of Tsezic languages, bridging constructions are primarily found in fictional narratives, that is, fairy tales, sagas and legends. We do not have examples of bridging constructions from historical narratives except for a single instance in the autobiographical narration in (13). In procedural texts, we also find occasional occurrences of bridging constructions, but they cannot often be unambiguously separated from repetitions (see Section §4.3 for a discussion).

Therefore, it seems that bridging constructions are stylistic devices of traditional narrations together with other stylistic markers such as unwitnessed past tenses and narrative formulae. For instance, traditional narratives are characterized by use of special introductory formulae which index the genre. In Tsezic languages as well as in many other languages of the wider area the introductory formulae consist of a repetition of the verb 'be', i.e., 'There was, there was not...'

Bridging constructions in Tsezic represent a particular instance of parallelism. Parallelism, i.e., recurring patterns in successive sections of the text, is one of the most common framing devices of ritual language, to which the genre of traditional narratives belongs (see Frog & Tarkka 2017 for a short introduction). Parallelism has extensively been studied in poetry, including songs, epics, proverbs and other forms of ritual language, where it is used to express emphasis, and to provide authority or significance (e.g., Jakobson 1966; Fox 2014; among many others). Formulaic parallelism as instantiated by the bridging constructions in Tsezic help the narrator buy time while s/he mentally prepares the next sentences, and are a hallmark of oral performance (Fabb 2015).

Another criterion for the occurrence of bridging constructions seems to be the medium, i.e., if texts are written or originate from oral narrations. Oral narrations seem to have more bridging constructions than written texts (though, as in §1 explained, we do not know how much the Tsez, Khwarshi and Hunzib texts have been edited). The Bezhta texts used for this paper have been written down and no oral versions exist. This might explain why we have only relatively few examples from Bezhta in which the perfective converb always occurs in the bridging clause.

4.3 Bridging constructions, repetition, and predicate doubling

A problem we encountered when analyzing bridging constructions is keeping them apart from simple repetition of clauses. For instance, (23) has been uttered in a procedural text that describes the preparation of the Daghestanian national dish khinkal (a type of dumplings). The speaker repeats verbatim one clause with a short break between the two utterances. The example resembles (25) below, but in contrast to (25), both clauses in (23) are main clauses containing imperative verb forms as all other main clauses in the texts. It is probable that the speaker who uttered (23) repeated the sentence because she was concentrating on narrating all individual actions in the correct order and the repetition of the clause gave her a little bit more time to prepare the next utterances. As can be seen in (23b), she also repeats a preposition.

(23) Hinuq (Forker, unpublished data)
   a. *xok'o   b-uw-a   b-aq'e-yo   at'=no   r-ux!*
       khinkal(ɪɪ) ɪɪɪ-make-ɪɴꜰ ɪɪɪ-must-ᴄᴏɴᴅ flour=ᴀᴅᴅ v-take
       'If you have to prepare khinkal, take flour!'
   b. *at'=no   r-ux!   k'ot'o-ma tełer, tełer čiyo=n   kur!   soda=n*
       flour=ᴀᴅᴅ v-take plate-ɪɴ into into salt=ᴀᴅᴅ throw soda=ᴀᴅᴅ
       kur!
       throw
       'Take flour! Pour (lit. throw) salt into, into a plate! Pour soda!'

Example (24) contains another repetition of a main clause that could have been used by the speaker as a stylistic device to indicate intensity. Again the clauses resemble bridging constructions, but without the morphosyntactic structure of main clause followed by converbal clause that we have identified in §2.

Diana Forker & Felix Anker

(24) Hunzib (van den Berg 1995: 257)
ēλ'e-n lo   bəd wazir,   ēλ'e-n lo   əgi-do   ãq'-oɬ
go-CVB be.PRS.I this advisor(I) go-CVB be.PRS.I there-DIR come-ANT.CVB
m-ɨqə-k'-ən   gudo   m-uχe-n,   lači=n   r-αhu-n
IV-catch-CAUS-CVB hen(IV) IV-slaughter-CVB clothes(V)=ADD V-take-CVB
λ'odo-s, hə̃s b-ɨq:'u hõgo   b-oχče-n,   hõgo-li-i=n   ẽdu
above-ABL one IV-big coat(IV) IV-take-CVB coat-OBL-IN=ADD inside
k'arλe-k'-en   hadeʔeče-n sɨd   bač-do raʕal-li-λ'   gəl-ən
twirl-CAUS-CVB be.slow-CVB one.OBL rock-INS edge-OBL-SPR put-CVB
lo
be.PRS.I
'The advisor went and he went and when he arrived there, he caught a
hen and killed it, he took the (boy's) outer clothes off and took a furcoat
and he wrapped the boy in the coat and put him on the edge of the rock.'

In example (25) the first clause is a converbal clause with the reduplicated
perfective converb. It is followed by another clause with the same predicate inflected as narrative converb. The construction looks similar to bridging constructions because of the identical predicates, but the two clauses slightly differ. The
first converbal clause lacks any arguments, contains only a temporal adjunct and
is verb-final. The second converbal clause, by contrast, contains the object and
the verb occurs in the clause-initial position. However, because both clauses are
converbal clauses, the example does not adhere to our definition of bridging constructions in Tsezic and is therefore analyzed as repetition.

(25) Hinuq (Forker, unpublished data)
[oc'era oc'era ɬera   minut-ma r-exir-an   r-exir-no], [b-exir-no
ten.OBL ten.OBL five.OBL minute-IN V-cook-RED V-cook-CVB III-cook-CVB
haw pulaw],   hoboy hezodoy k'ot'o-ma got'-no q'idi=n   b-iči-n,
this pilaw(III) then then   plate-IN pour-CVB down=ADD HPL-sit-CVB
ga
drink.IMP
'Cooking it for 10–15 minutes, and having cooked the pilaw, then pour it
into plates, sit down and eat (lit. drink) it.'

Hinuq, Khwarshi and Bezhta also have constructions in which the predicate
is doubled. The first occurrence of the predicate occurs in the infinitive or perfective converb followed by the additive particle or another particle. The second
occurrence of the predicate can also have the form of the perfective converb or it

is used as finite verb and inflected for the appropriate tense. These constructions can express intensity, prolonged duration, emphasis, predicate topicalization and sometimes polarity focus (Maisak 2010; Forker 2015). The Bezhta example in (26) can be paraphrased with 'As for coming, people do not come here'. Another instance of predicate doubling is the first converb clause in (25).

(26)   Bezhta (unpublished data, courtesy of M. Khalilov)
       bekela-a-qa   hiyabač'e-na hoλoʔ ädäm   õq'-an=na   õq'-aʔa-s
       snake-PL-POSS fear.PL-CVB   here   person come-INF=ADD come-NEG-PRS
       'Because of fear for snakes people do not come here.'

5 Bridging constructions in other Nakh-Daghestanian languages

Not only Tsezic languages but also other languages of the Nakh-Daghestanian language family use bridging constructions. One of those languages is Chirag Dargwa, a member of the Dargwa (or Dargi) sub-branch. (27) illustrates that Chirag Dargwa uses the same strategy that we already saw in Tsezic languages. The reference clause is a main clause in the past resultative tense while the bridging construction is again a non-main converbal clause. Additionally, there is a change in the word order. The reference clause has VS constituent order because it introduces new referents (as it was explained for the Khwarshi example in (6)). The bridging clause is verb-final because this is the preferred order for adverbial clauses and for clauses with neutral information structure.

(27)   Chirag Dargwa (D. Ganenkov, p.c.)
       a.   *k'aˤ   q'ilae ʔaši-l-i   ag-ur-re   niš=ra*
            DEM.UP Qilae caraway-OBL-SPR go.PFV-AOR-RES.3 mother=ADD
            rus:i=ra
            girl=ADD
            'A mother and a daughter went there to Qilae for caraway.'
       b.   *niš=ra   rus:i=ra ʔaši-l-i   ag-ur-s:aħ,   [...]*
            mother=ADD girl=ADD caraway-OBL-SPR go.PF-AOR-TEMP
            q'ʷala   d-arq'-ib-le   it:-a-d   ʔaše
            <collect> N.PL-do.PFV-AOR-RES.3 DEM.DIST-PL-ERG caraway
            'When the mother and the daughter went for caraway, [...] they collected the caraway.'

Diana Forker & Felix Anker

In example (28) from Agul, a language of the Lezgic sub-branch, the main verb of the bridging clause is marked by a temporal converb while the verb in the reference clause is finite and bears the aorist suffix.

(28) Agul (Maisak 2014: 134)

   a. *aχira χ.i-s   qaχ.i-naw   mi   bäʕž*
       finally leave.INF-INF start.PFV-AOR DEM.M friend

       'The friend was about to go.'

   b. *χ.i-s   qaχ.a-gana mi   ruš.a-s   raqq.u-naw*
       leave.INF-INF start.PFV-TEMP DEM.M daughter-DAT see.PFV-AOR

       p.u-naw
       say-AOR

       'When he started to go, the girl saw him and said...'

In Tsova-Tush, one of the three Nakh languages, the use of converbs is the primary strategy to express recapitulative linkage. Bridging constructions can also be found regularly in Chechen (Molochieva, p.c.).

(29) Tsova-Tush (ECLING)

   a. *d-ax-en, xi   meł-or=e*
       II-go-AOR, water drink.IPFV-PST=ADD

       'They went off and drank water.'

   b. *xi   meł-oš   o   maq'vlen   oqar   c'omal*
       water drink.IPFV-SIM.CVB that Makvala.DAT 3PL.ERG drug(v)

       eg-b-iẽ   ču, me ču-toħ-y-it-ra-lŏ
       mix-v-do.PFV.AOR in COMP PVB-sleep-II-CAUS-PST-EVID

       'While drinking they mixed drugs for that Makvala to make her fall asleep.'

Due to the lack of data we cannot judge if some sub-branches of the Nakh-Daghestanian language family such as Tsezic show a larger preference for bridging constructions than others (e.g., Lak). Furthermore, except for the Tsezic languages we do not have examples of summary linkage or mixed linkage, and all examples (27)–(29) contain specialized temporal converbs in the bridging clause and not general converbs. It seems reasonable to assume that narrative traditions and genres largely overlap among the Nakh-Daghestanian peoples such that from a functional perspective we would expect to find bridging constructions across the same types of narrations (traditional fictional narratives) and within the same types of (oral) performance (as suggested in Matsigenka, see Emlen 2019 [this volume]).

6 Conclusion

Bridging constructions are a common feature in narratives of Nakh-Daghestanian languages. In this paper, we focused on the Tsezic languages, but bridging constructions seem to exist in most, if not all, branches of the Nakh-Daghestanian language family.

We defined bridging constructions as bipartite consisting of a main reference clause followed by a subordinate bridging clause. The bridging clause expresses adverbial subordination and is marked by a variety of general or specialized temporal converbs. In Tsezic, bridging constructions instantiate recapitulative linkage as well as summary linkage, although the latter is not very frequent. The main functions are stylistic rather than grammatical. They are stylistic devices of traditional narratives and represent a specific type of parallelism, which is characteristic of oral performances. In addition, Tsezic bridging constructions are repeatedly used to indicate episode changes in narration, which can but need not be accompanied by switches of subject referents or locations. More research is required in order to explore how bridging constructions relate to other forms of repetition and parallelism such as predicate doubling.

Appendix

A Hunzib story told by Džamaludin Atranaliev from Stal'skoe (van den Berg 1995: 154–157) about a mother and a father who were frequently ill, both of them claiming to want to die first so the other one could take care of the son. The excerpt sets in right after the parents discuss the probable looks of Malakulmawt, the angel of death, to which their son replies that he looks like a plucked cock.

(A1) *əg-ra   bowaž-er   m-ac'-oɫ,   əg-ra*
that-PL believe.PL-PST.PTCP HPL-see-ANT.CVB that-PL

m-učaχ-ašun   bed   ože   gišo-ke-n   ẽλ'e-n
HPL-slumber-IMM.ANT then boy(I) outside-INCH-CVB go.I-CVB

m-iqə-k'-en   žide-s   b-iʔer   ɦeleku=n   ogu
IV-find-CAUS-CVB self.OBL.PL-GEN IV-small cock(IV)=ADD that

m-oλ'ak'-en lo
IV-pluck-CVB be.PRS.IV

'When he saw that they believed him, the boy went out, as soon as they fell asleep, caught their own little cock and plucked it.'

(A2) **m-oλ'ak'-en** *hĭja-do=n*　　　*b-əc'-əru*　　　　*səsəq'an*
　　　IV-pluck-CVB blood.OBL-INS=ADD IV-be.filled-PST.PTCP some
　　　pode=n=žun　　　*hade<b>eče-n*　*ẽdu*　*m-ije-n*　　　*lo*
　　　feather(IV)=ADD=with be.slow<IV>-CVB inside IV-send-CVB be.PRS.IV
　　　oɬu-l　　　*ogu buλii*
　　　that.OBL-ERG that home
　　　'Having plucked it, covered with blood, some feathers left, he let it
　　　carefully into the house.'

(A3) *bed-do ogu k'ok'ol-eru*　*m-oλ'ak'-eru*　*taχ-li-λ*　　　*λirə*
　　　then-DIR that hurt-PST.PTCP IV-pluck-PST.PTCP ottoman-OBL-SUB under
　　　m-eλ'e-n b-eče-n　　*lo*
　　　IV-go-CVB IV-stay-CVB be.PRS.IV
　　　'Then it, being mauled and plucked, went and sat under the ottoman.'

(A4) *sɨd*　　*zaban-li-i*　*əgi-s*　　*bed gišo-ke-n*　　　*lo*
　　　one.OBL time-OBL-IN there-ABL then outside-INCH-CVB be.PRS.IV
　　　'At one point, it came out from there.'

(A5) **gišo-ke-n**　　　*b-αλλe*　*m-aq'e-n*　　*zuq'u-n lo*　　*qoqo-o*
　　　outside-INCH-CVB IV-middle IV-come-CVB be-CVB be.PRS.IV house-IN
　　　ħeleku
　　　cock(IV)
　　　'It came out, the cock came into the middle of the room.'

(A6) *deno t'uwαt'-en*　*lo*　　　*q'anu=n əg-ra oɬu-l*　　　*qoqoqo*
　　　back throw.PL-CVB be.PRS.HPL two=ADD that-PL that.OBL-ERG INTERJ
　　　λe　　*nɨs-oɬ*
　　　QUOT say-ANT.CVB
　　　'They woke up when it crowed.'

(A7) **deno t'uwαt'-oɬ**　　　*ogu bed tišo,*　　*ʕali-ɬ-do-s*
　　　back throw.PL-ANT.CVB that then over.there Ali-CONT-DIR-ABL
　　　beddo=n　*m-uχe-n*　*ʕajšat-i-ɬ-do*　　　*m-eλ'e-n lo*
　　　back=ADD IV-turn-CVB Ayshat(II)-OBL-CONT-DIR IV-go-CVB be.PRS.IV

ogu, art'o j-uh-a   j-at'ə-r-o-ɬ-do
that before II-die-INF II-want-PST.PTCP-OBL-CONT-DIR

'When they woke up, the cock went across (the room) from Ali, having turned to Ayshat, to her who wanted to die first.'

(A8) *žini-ɬ-do   m-aq'e-č   m-ac'-oɬ   ħeleku, "bodu*
self.OBL-CONT-DIR IV-come-ICVB IV-see-ANT.CVB cock(IV) this
ħeleku Malakulmawt lo"   ƛe   gič'-en,   ħič'e-ru
cock(IV) Malakulmawt be.PRS.IV QUOT think-CVB fear-PST.PTCP
oɬu-l,   ʕali-ɬ-do   "kiš" ƛe   n-ac'əj   nisə-n,
that.OBL-ERG Ali-CONT-DIR INTERJ QUOT V-appear say-CVB
ʕali-ɬ-do   "kiš" ʕali-ɬ-do   "kiš"
Ali-CONT-DIR INTERJ Ali-CONT-DIR INTERJ

'When she saw it coming, thinking that the cock was Malakulmawt, she said, frightened, "Shoo!" to Ali.'

(A9) *bed ħeleku   deno m-uq'-oys-i?*
then cock(IV) back IV-turn-FUT.NEG-INT

'Would not the cock then turn around?'

(A10) **bed deno m-uq'e-n** *ʕali-ɬ-do   nuu-n   lo*
then back IV-turn-CVB Ali-CONT-DIR come-CVB be.PRS.IV

'Then having turned, it went to Ali.'

(A11) **ʕali-ɬ-do   nuw-oɬ,**   *"ʕajšat-i-ɬ-do   kiš,*
Ali-CONT-DIR come-ANT.CVB Ayshat-OBL-CONT-DIR INTERJ
ʕajšat-i-ɬ-do   kiš" ƛe   nisə-n ʕali-lo-n   b-oc'-on
Ayshat-OBL-CONT-DIR INTERJ QUOT say-CVB Ali-ERG=ADD IV-chase-CVB
lo   ogu
be.PRS.IV that

'When it came to Ali, Ali chased it away, saying "Shoo!" to Ayshat.'

(A12) *deno m-eλ'e-n beddo m-eλ'e-n maha-a-λ'*
back IV-go-CVB back IV-go-CVB courtyard-IN-TRANS
žoʁ-i-i-λ'　　　　　　*tuwɑc'ə-n　ože=n　maduhanɬi=n　zuq'un*
window-OBL-IN-TRANS look.PL-CVB boy=ADD neighbours=ADD be.CVB
lo
be.PRS.HPL
'While it went back and forth, the boy and the neighbours were looking at them from the courtyard through the window.'

(A13) *ʕadam-la zuq'un lo　　　ɬejaʔe-č　　əg-ra-λ'*
person-PL be.CVB be.PRS.HPL laugh.PL-ICVB that-PL-SPR
'The people were laughing at them.'

(A14) *əgaa-s žo　　r-ɑqu-n　　li*
so-GEN thing(v) v-happen-CVB be.PRS.V
'Such a thing happened.'

Abbreviations

1SG	first person singular	DAT	dative
2SG	second person singular	DEF	definiteness
3SG	third person singular	DEM	demonstrative
I-V	gender	DIR	directional
ABL	ablative case	DIST	distal
AD	adessive case	EMPH	emphatic enclitic
ADD	coordinating enclitic	ERG	ergative
ALL	allative case	EVID	evidentiality
ANT.CVB	anterior converb	FUT	future tense
AOR	aorist	GEN	genitive
APUD	apudessive case	GEN1	first genitive
CAUS	causative	GEN2	second genitive
CNTR	contrastive	HPL	human plural
COM	comitative	IMM.ANT	immediate anterior converb
COMP	complementizer	IMP	imperative
COND	conditional converb	IN	in case
CONT	contact case	INCH	inchoative
CVB	perfective/narrative converb	INF	infinitive

INS	instrumental	PST.UW	unwitnessed past tense
INT	interrogative particle	PST.WIT	witnessed past tense
INTER	inter case	PTCP	participle
INTERJ	interjection	PURP.CVB	purposive converb
INTS	intensifier	QUOT	quotative
ICVB	imperfective converb	RED	reduplication
LAT	lative case	RES	resultative
N	neuter singular	SG	singular
NEG	negation	SIM.CVB	simultaneous converb
NPL	non-human plural	SPR	super case
OBL	oblique stem marker	SUB	sub case
PFV	perfective	TEMP	temporal converb
PL	plural	TRANS	translative
POSS	possessive	UP	located above speaker
PROH	prohibitive	VERS	versative
PRS	present tense		

References

Abdulaev, Arsen K. & I. K. Abdullaev. 2010. *Didojskij (cezskij) fol'klor.* Makhachkala: Lotos.

Alekseev, Mikhail E. & Ramazan N. Radžabov. 2004. Tsez. In Michael Job (ed.), *The indigenous languages of the Caucasus, vol. 3: The North East Caucasian languages, part 1*, 115–168. Ann Arbor: Caravan Books.

Bickel, Balthasar. 2010. Capturing particulars and universals in clause linkage: A multivariate analysis. In Isabelle Bril (ed.), *Clause linking and clause hierarchy: Syntax and pragmatics*, 51–101. Amsterdam: Benjamins.

Comrie, Bernard, Diana Forker & Zaira Khalilova. 2012. Adverbial clauses in the Tsezic languages. In Holger Diessel & Volker Gast (eds.), *Clause-combining in cross-linguistic perspective*, 157–190. Berlin: de Gruyter.

Comrie, Bernard, Diana Forker & Zaira Khalilova. 2016. Insubordination in the Tsezic languages. In N. J. Evans & Honoré Watanabe (eds.), *The dynamics of insubordination*, 171–182. Amsterdam: John Benjamins.

Comrie, Bernard, Madzhid Khalilov & Zaira Khalilova. 2015. *Grammatika bežtinskogo jazyka*. Makhachkala: Aleph.

ECLING. 2016. *Corpus, tsova-tush language documentation within ecling-project.* https://hdl.handle.net/1839/00-0000-0000-000A-3ED7-8, accessed 2018-9-13.

Emlen, Nicholas Q. 2019. The poetics of recapitulative linkage in Matsigenka and mixed Matsigenka-Spanish myth narrations. In Valérie Guérin (ed.), *Bridging constructions*, 45–77. Berlin: Language Science Press. DOI:10.5281/zenodo.2563680

Fabb, Nigel. 2015. *What is poetry? Language and memory in the poems of the world*. Cambridge: Cambridge University Press.

Forker, Diana. 2013a. *A grammar of Hinuq*. Berlin: de Gruyter.

Forker, Diana. 2013b. Microtypology and the Tsezic languages: A case study of syntactic properties of converbal clauses. *SKY Journal of Linguistics* 26. 21–40.

Forker, Diana. 2015. Towards a semantic map for intensifying particles: Evidence from Avar. *Language Typology and Universals* 68. 485–513.

Fox, James J. 2014. *Explorations in semantic parallelism*. Canberra: ANU Press.

Frog & Lotte Tarkka. 2017. Parallelism in verbal art and performance: An introduction. *Oral Tradition* 31. 203–232.

Haspelmath, Martin. 1995. The converb as a cross-linguistically valid category. In Martin Haspelmath & Ekkehard König (eds.), *Converbs in cross-linguistic perspective*, 1–55. Berlin: Mouton de Gruyter.

Jakobson, Robert. 1966. Grammatical parallelism and its Russian facet. *Language* 42. 398–429.

Karimova, Raisat Sh. 2014. *Xwarshinskij folklor*. Leipzig: MPI EVA.

Khalilova, Zaira. 2009. *A grammar of Khwarshi*. Utrecht: LOT.

Khalilova, Zaira. 2011. Evidentiality in Tsezic languages. *Linguistic Discovery* 9. 30–48.

Kibrik, Aleksandr E. & Jakov G. Testelec. 2004. Bezhta. In Michael Job (ed.), *The indigenous languages of the Caucasus, vol. 3: The North East Caucasian languages, part 1*, 217–295. Ann Arbor: Caravan Books.

Maisak, Timur. 2010. *Predicate topicalization in East Caucasian languages*. Presentation at the SWL 4 Conference, Lyon, 23–26 September 2010.

Maisak, Timur. 2014. *Agul'skie teksty 1900-1960-x godov*. Moscow: Academia.

Polinsky, Maria. Forthcoming. Tsez syntax. Ms. Harward University.

Radžabov, Ramazan N. 1999. *Sintaksis cezskogo jazyka*. Moscow: MGLU.

van den Berg, Helma. 1995. *A grammar of Hunzib: With texts and lexicon*. Munich: Lincom.

Chapter 5

Bridging constructions in narrative texts in White Hmong (Hmong-Mien)

Nerida Jarkey

School of Languages and Cultures, University of Sydney

This chapter examines bridging constructions in narrative texts in White Hmong (Hmong-Mien, Laos). Bridging constructions occur in all the texts examined for the study, with frequency and type of construction varying according to narrator and text type. Recapitulative linkage is far more common than either summary linkage, which is limited to first-person narratives and reported speech, or mixed linkage, which serves to summarize direct quotations in oral and written texts with a more literary character. In terms of function, the analysis shows that bridging constructions in White Hmong narrative texts work cohesively, linking one unit in the event line of the narrative to the next and thus serving to progress the main sequence of events. The event described by the bridging construction is constructed as a salient point in the event line, and becomes the base from which the next unit in the event line of the narrative proceeds.

1 Introduction

1.1 White Hmong language

White Hmong (ISO code: mww) is a language of the Hmong-Mien (Miao-Yao) family, mainly spoken in the mountainous regions of northern Vietnam, Laos, and Thailand, and of southern China, as well as in some diasporic communities. White Hmong is an analytic, isolating language; most words are monosyllabic, although compounding and borrowing result in some multisyllabic words. Syllable structure is basically open and every syllable carries one of seven phonemic tones, represented by syllable-final consonant letters in the orthography used

Nerida Jarkey. 2019. Bridging constructions in narrative texts in White Hmong (Hmong-Mien). In Valérie Guérin (ed.), *Bridging constructions*, 129–156. Berlin: Language Science Press. DOI:10.5281/zenodo.2563686 here. Some consonants are quite complex, including combinations of features such as pre-nasalisation with both lateral and aspirated release.

Alignment in White Hmong is nominative-accusative, and the syntactic function of core arguments is coded by constituent order: generally AVO for transitive clauses and SV for intransitive clauses. Presentative existentials are verb initial and copula clauses are CS copula CC. Topical elements can be fronted and ellipsis of arguments can occur when referents can easily be retrieved through the linguistic or extra-linguistic context. While head modifier order is most common, within the noun phrase some elements, including possessives, numerals and numeral classifiers, precede the head.

Like many other languages of Mainland Southeast Asia, White Hmong is rich in serial verb constructions (SVCs). These involve two or more distinct verbs, linked together in a single clause by virtue of the fact that they share one or more core arguments as well as all grammatical categories. Thus it is very common in White Hmong for a single event to be expressed by multiple verbs, none of which is subordinate to any other (Jarkey 2015: 76–110). This phenomenon, along with the ellipsis of arguments, mentioned above, is illustrated in many of the examples in this chapter, such as in the sequence of verbs in (1):

(1) *muab coj   mus los   tas*
    take   take.along go   bury finish
    'after (they) took (him) (and) carried (him) away (and) buried (him),...'

1.2 Chapter overview

This chapter examines bridging constructions in White Hmong narrative discourse. In accordance with Guérin & Aiton (2019 [this volume]), a bridging construction is viewed here as a discourse cohesion strategy linking two discourse units, often though not always immediately adjacent to one another. The final clause of the first unit is referred to as the "reference clause" (underlined throughout) and initial clause of the second unit, as the "bridging clause" (bolded throughout). The bridging clause refers back to the reference clause by recapitulation or anaphora.

The corpus for this study, comprising six narrative texts (approximately 15,000 words in total), is presented in §1.3. §2 deals with the topics of the frequency (§2.1), position (§2.2), form (§2.3), and types of linkage (§2.4) that occur in bridging constructions in this corpus. §3 examines their function. All bridging constructions in the data work cohesively, linking one unit in the event line of the narrative to the next (Longacre 1983: 14–17). This often involves a change in aspect between the reference clause and the bridging clause, which contributes to constructing that point as a salient one in the narrative progression and highlights its function as a pivot between the preceding and following discourse units (§3.1). In other cases, the bridging construction simply serves to bring the narrative back to the event line after a brief digression (§3.2).

1.3 Data sources

All of the six narrative texts examined for this study are in linear narrative form – four transcribed from recordings of oral narratives (Fuller 1985; Johnson 1992) and two produced in written form from the outset (Vang et al. 1990). The texts and text types are shown in Table 1.

Table 1: Texts and text types

Mode	Person	Narrative type	Source text
Oral	First	Personal account	*Kee's story* (Fuller 1985: Appendix B)
	Third	Traditional myth	*The beginning of the world* (Johnson 1992: Chapter 1) *The story of Ms Fine Flower I* (Johnson 1992: Chapter 5) *The story of Ms Fine Flower II* (Johnson 1992: Chapter 6)
Written		Semi-historical account with legendary elements	*The beginning* (Vang et al. 1990: Chapter 1) *God sends the Pahawh* (Vang et al. 1990: Chapter 2)

The first text shown in Table 1 – *Kee's Story* – is a first-person oral account of the narrator's escape from Laos in 1975, after the end of the war (Fuller 1985: 225–235). The next three – *The beginning of the world* and two versions of *The story of Ms Fine Flower* told by two different narrators – are traditional White Hmong myths (Johnson 1992: 3–13, 120–140, 161–168). These stories are told in the third person, but contain some first-person components in reported speech. The final two texts are also in the third person with some first-person, reported speech components. These are accounts of the life and teachings of a messianic figure, Shong Lue Yang, who was active in northern Laos from 1959 until his assassination in 1971. The story was written by two of his disciples using the Hmong writing system Shong Lue Yang himself had developed (Vang et al. 1990: 11–37).

2 Characteristics of bridging constructions in narrative texts

Having introduced the language and data in §1 above, this section discusses the frequency, position, form, and types of bridging constructions found in the texts examined.

2.1 Frequency

On average, across all the texts used as data for this study, one bridging construction occurs roughly every 37 clauses. Although this gives a general idea of frequency, it must be noted that this figure is not particularly robust. This is due not only to the limited amount of data examined, but also to the fact that it is often quite challenging to determine the boundaries of a single clause in White Hmong. A number of factors contribute to this challenge, including the range of paratactic strategies involving simple juxtaposition that occur (in addition to verb serialisation), as well as the frequent linkage of multiple serial verb constructions (Jarkey 2015: 183–186, 237–241).

One of the texts examined – *The legend of Ms Fine Flower I* – stands out from the others in that very few bridging constructions appear in it: only one in approximately 174 clauses. A second version of this same traditional myth, told by a different narrator, was also examined, and was found to use bridging constructions far more frequently: around one in every 28 clauses. This shows that the low frequency in some texts cannot be attributed to narrative mode, person, or type, and probably relates simply to the style of the narrator.

2.2 Position

To understand more about the functions of bridging constructions in narrative texts, it will help to begin by looking at the positions in which they predominantly occur. Bridging constructions in the texts examined occur most commonly at the boundary between discourse episodes, at what might be thought of as major boundaries ("chapters") or minor boundaries ("paragraphs") (see Guérin & Aiton 2019 [this volume]). The only cases in which they appear other than at the junction of discourse episodes is where they are used simply to bring the narrative back to the event line after a diversion containing supportive material. This minor type will be discussed later, in (§3.2). Here the focus is on their most common position, at the boundary of discourse episodes.

The extract below from *The Story of Ms Fine Flower I* comes at the end of a series of paragraphs describing a plot to kill the character Mr Sultry Toad by having a snake bite him. We pick up the story in clause (2a), just after the snake has bitten his foot four times:

(2) a. *Ces   Nraug.Kub.Kaws mob~mob   ko.taw*
         and.then Mr.Sultry.Toad   REDUP~be.hurt foot
         'And then Mr Sultry Toad's foot really hurt.'

     b. *ces   Nraug.Kub.Kaws tuag lawm lau.*
         and.then Mr.Sutry.Toad   die PRF IP
         'and then Mr Sultry Toad died.'

     c. ***Nraug.Kub.Kaws tuag tas,*** ...
         Mr.Sultry.Toad   die finish
         'After Mr Sultry Toad died, ...'

     d. *muab coj   mus los   tas,*
         take take.along go   bury finish,
         '(and) after (they) took (him) away (and) buried (him),'

     e. *ces   Txiv.Nrau.Ntsuag thiaj.li mus coj*
         and.then The.Young.Orphan so.then go   take.along
         Niam.Nkauj.Zuag.Paj rov   los.
         Ms.Fine.Flower   return come.home
         'then The Young Orphan came back home, bringing Ms Fine Flower along.' (Johnson 1992: 140)

The major episode concerning the murderous plot culminates in the death of Mr Sultry Toad, described in the reference clause (2b). The bridging clause (2c) then serves to pivot the narrative to the final episode of the story, introducing the events after Mr Sultry Toad's death, as the plotters bury him (2d), return home (2e), subsequently taking up their life together.

In example (2), the bridging construction brings a relatively lengthy discourse episode, a whole series of paragraphs or a "chapter", to a close and creates a link to the next episode. In other cases, however, a bridging construction serves to introduce what might be thought of as simply a new minor episode, or "paragraph". In the myth of *The beginning of the world*, the first man and woman on earth have suffered the loss of their first crop, swept away by a windstorm. A new major episode begins:

(3)   a. *Txiv.Nraug.Luj.Tub thiab Niam.Nkauj.Ntxhi.Chiv nyob~nyob*
        Master.Lu.Tu   and Ms.Ntxi.Chi   REDUP~live

         'Master Lu Tu and Ms Ntxi Chi lived on'

     b. *ces   ua.ciav ya mus poob rau puag   nram   kwj.ha*
        and.then how.is.it fly go   fall to yonder place.down valley

        'and then – how can it be! – (the grains) flew way off (and) fell in yonder valley'

     c. *ces   pob.kws xya nplooj laus   txaus*
        and.then corn   seven leaf be(come).old be.sufficient

        'and then the seven-leaf corn became fully matured'

     d. *ces   nws <u>xub</u>   <u>taug</u> <u>kev</u> <u>los</u>.*
        and.then 3SG initiate follow way come.home

        'and then it was the first to follow the path home.'

     e. **Nws taug kev los   txog**
        3SG follow way come.home arrive

        'It followed the path right back home'

     f. *ces   nws hu hais tias, "Niam thiab txiv,   quib qhov.rooj."*
        and.then 3SG call say COMP mother and   father open door

        'and then it called out, "Mother and Father, open the door!"' (Johnson 1992: 4)

After just three clauses of this new major episode (3a–3c), a bridging construction (3d–3e) is used to draw to a close the minor episode of what happened way off yonder, and to focus in again on the home scene. Here the bridging construction works to link two minor episodes (or "paragraphs") within a much longer major episode.

2.3 Form

The reference clause in a bridging construction in White Hmong is always a main clause. It can exhibit all the properties of a main clause, including the expression of illocutionary force, as shown by the final illocutionary particle *lau* in example (2b), and exclamatory topicalizers, such as *ov* 'oh!' in example (9). Another sign of the status of the reference clause as a main clause is its ability to be preceded by a coordinating conjunction. By far the most common coordinating conjunction used, not only before reference clauses but in general throughout narrative texts, is *ces* 'and then'.[1] As shown in example (4), this conjunction often appears both immediately before the reference clause and immediately after the bridging clause, bracketing the construction as it links one unit to the next in the narrative sequence.

(4)   a.   *Mus txog   tom   kev,*
           go   arrive place.over.there road

           '(She) got to the road,'

      b.   CES   *txawm mus ntsib nraug zaj.*
           and.then then   go   meet young dragon

           'and then (she) went (and) met a young dragon.'

      c.   *Ntsib nraug zaj,*
           meet young dragon

           '(She) met the young dragon'

      d.   CES   *nraug zaj   txawm hais tias, ...*
           and.then young dragon then   say COMP

           'and then the young dragon said, ...' (Johnson 1992: 163)

Example (4) also illustrates the fact that the coordinating conjunction *ces* is very often accompanied by another type of conjunction indicating temporal sequence in relation to the preceding event, such as *txawm* 'then', as in (4b) and (4d), *thiaj (li)* 'so then', and *mam (li)* 'then next'. These sequential conjunctions appear not before the whole clause, as the coordinating conjunctions do, but rather clause internally, after the subject (if it appears). In (5), we see both the clause external *ces* 'and then' and the clause internal *mam li* 'then next' in clauses (5a) and (5c).

(5)   a.   CES   *nws* MAM.LI   *tho   theem hauv   no.*
           and.then 3SG then.next pierce layer place.underneath this

           'And then next he pierced the layer underneath this.'

      b.   *Luj.Tub tho   theem hauv   no to*
           Lu.Tu   pierce layer   place.underneath this make.hole

           'Lu Tu pierced the layer underneath right through'

---

[1] Another two coordinating conjunctions that appear occasionally before reference clauses in the corpus are *es* 'so' in (13) and *tab sis* 'but'.

    c.   CES   *ib   co*   *coob~coob*   MAM.LI   *tawm*
       and.then one CLF:COLL REDUP~be.many then.next emerge

       hauv   *los.*
       place.underneath come

       'and then next a great many (people) came out (from) underneath.'
       (Johnson 1992: 12)

While the reference clause is always a full main clause, the bridging clause never is. It can be, first, a somewhat reduced main clause or, second, a temporal subordinate clause. Both of these clause types freely occur sentence-initially in other contexts in White Hmong; they are not restricted to bridging constructions. The bridging clauses in examples (4) and (5) are both cases of the first type: reduced main clauses. Clauses like this are reduced in that they cannot contain topic markers or outer operators such as illocutionary force, nor the clause-external coordinating conjunctions or clause-internal sequential conjunctions such as those so commonly occurring with the clauses that both precede and follow them. The bridging clause in example (6) exemplifies the second type: a temporal subordinate clause, that is, one that indicates the temporal relationship (*when*, *after*, etc.) between the event described by the bridging construction and that described by the following main clause. The bridging clause in (6b) is introduced by the subordinating conjunction *thaum* 'when'.

(6)   a.   *ces*   <u>*nws*</u> <u>*poj.niam*</u> *thiaj*   <u>*xauv.xeeb*</u> <u>*tau*</u> <u>*ob*</u> <u>*leeg*</u> <u>*tub*</u> <u>*ntxaib.*</u>
       and.then 3SG woman so.then give.birth get two CLF son twin

       '...and so then his wife gave birth to twin boys.'

     b.   **Thaum xauv.xeeb tau nkawd...**
       when   give.birth get 3DU

       'When she had given birth to them...' (Vang et al. 1990: 31)

Whether in the form of a reduced main clause or a subordinate clause, bridging clauses cannot stand alone as independent sentences, and so are never followed by a sentence-final pause (indicated by a full stop in the orthography). No more than a brief, comma-like pause separates them from the following main clause, which functions to introduce the next event in the event line. Within the bridging construction itself the sentence-final break after the reference clause functions iconically as a signal of a momentary break in the temporal flow of the narrative. The repetition in the bridging clause reinforces this sense that the sequential flow of events has halted briefly, before it takes off again with no more than a minor pause after the bridging clause.

2.4 Types of linkage

With only a small number of exceptions, bridging constructions in the narrative data examined involve recapitulative linkage. Exact recapitulation seems rare; in fact, considerable variation between the reference clause and the bridging clause is the norm. This is discussed and exemplified in §2.4.1.

Examples of summary linkage are limited to the first-person text (*Kee's Story*) and to reported speech components within third-person narratives, shown in §2.4.2. A mixed linkage type occurs with speech verbs introducing direct quotations. This is discussed in §2.4.3.

2.4.1 Recapitulative linkage

Most examples of recapitulative linkage found in the data involve one or more than one of the types of variation identified by Guérin & Aiton (2019 [this volume]): modification, omission, addition, and substitution. Below, each type of simple variation is illustrated in turn.

The high frequency of variation between the reference clause and the bridging clause relates to one of the key features of bridging constructions in this language: variation of the aspectual construal of the event described so that it can function as a pivot between the preceding and following discourse units. This is discussed in detail in §3.1. In addition to change in aspect, the examples in the next subsections show a range of other kinds of variation.

2.4.1.1 Almost exact recapitulation

No example of exact recapitulation, in which the reference clause is simply repeated word-for-word in the bridging clause, occurs in the data. Example (7) came closest.

(7) a. *ces*   *Txiv.Nraug.Ntsuag txawm mus pom nkawd.*
      and.then The.Young.Orphan then   go   see   3DU

      '... and The Young Orphan then went to see them.'

   b. ***Txiv.Nraug.Ntsuag mus pom nkawd.***
      The.Young.Orphan   go   see   3DU

      'The Young Orphan went to see them'

   c. *ces*   *Txiv.Nraug.Ntsuag hais tias,...*
      and.then The.Young.Orphan say   COMP

      'and The Young Orphan said,...' (Johnson 1992: 161)

Here the only difference is the sequential conjunction *txawm* 'then', which appears in the reference clause (7a), supporting the preceding coordinating conjunction *ces* 'and then' in anchoring the reference clause in the sequential flow of events. As noted above (§2.3) and as seen in (7b), sequential conjunctions do not appear in bridging clauses, which offer a momentary break in this sequential flow.

2.4.1.2 Modification

Example (8), illustrating modification, is from a story about the first man and woman on the earth, who emerged from a rock fissure and initially survived by cooking the seeds of a magic flower.

(8)   a.   *ces   nws rauv zeb.ntsuam   xwb.*
           and.then 3SG burn pieces.of.coal only

           '... and he burned only pieces of coal.'

   b.   ***Luj.Tub nkawd ob.niam.txiv rauv cov   ntawd.***
        Lu.Tu   3DU   couple   burn CLF:COLL that

        'Lu Tu and his wife burned those'

   c.   *kib lub paj   ntawd cov   noob noj xwb.*
        fry CLF flower that   CLF:COLL seed eat only

        '(to) fry the seeds of that flower to eat.' (Johnson 1992: 3)

In (8a), the reference clause refers to the protagonist, *Lu Tu*, with the third singular pronoun *nws*, and to the pieces of coal with the full NP *zeb ntsuam*. These nouns appear in modified form in the bridging clause (8b), as the full NP *Luj Tub nkawd ob niam txiv* 'the Lu Tu couple' and the pronominal phrase *cov ntawd* 'those', respectively.

2.4.1.3 Omission

The bridging clause may represent a considerably reduced recapitulation of the reference clause by virtue of the omission of one or more elements.

(9)   a.   *ces   cua-daj-cua-dub   ov txawm nplawm puag*
           and.then wind-yellow-wind-black EX then   beat   long.way

           tim   qab   ntug   tuaj.
           place.beyond behind boundary come

           '... and then a storm [lit. wind yellow wind black] oh! (it) then came whipping (from) way over the horizon.'

b. ***Cua   nplawm tuaj*** *ces,...*
wind beat   come and.then

'The wind came whipping and then,...' (Johnson 1992: 4)

Here the locative phrase *puag tim qab ntug* '(from) way over the horizon', which appears in the reference clause (9a), is completely omitted from the bridging clause (9b), as are the sequential conjunction *txawm* 'then' and the exclamatory particle *ov* (which functions in (9a) as a topicaliser). Substitution also occurs to further reduce the length of the bridging clause, with the simple noun *cua* 'wind' replacing the four-part elaborate expression *cua-daj-cua-dub* (wind-yellow-wind-black) 'storm' (Jarkey 2015: 233–237, Johns & Strecker 1982; Mortensen 2003).

2.4.1.4 Addition

While a locative phrase that occurs in the reference clause is omitted in the bridging clause in example (9), a temporal phrase is added in (10).

(10)   a. *ces   thiaj   mam   xeeb   nws tus poj.niam rau*
           and.then so.then then.next be.born 3SG CLF wife   to

ntawm   nws qhov.chaw.
place.nearby 3SG place

'... and so then next his wife was born into his place [i.e., into the rock fissure from which the first man, Lu Tu, had emerged].'

b. *xeeb   nws tus poj.niam rau ntawm   nws qhov.chaw*
       be.born 3SG CLF wife   to   place.nearby 3SG place

puv-hnub-puv-nyoog   ces...
be.filled-day-be.filled-age and.then

'His wife was born into his place (until her) time was fulfilled and then...' (Johnson 1992: 3)

The elaborate expression *puv-hnub-puv-hnoog* 'fulfil one's days', not found in the reference clause (10a), appears in the bridging clause (10b) to indicate the length of time that the protagonist's wife remained behind before she followed her husband out to the earth.

2.4.1.5 Substitution

In some cases, rather than modification, omission, or addition in the bridging clause, an element of the reference clause is substituted by an alternative in the bridging clause. Example (11) shows this kind of variation:

(11) a. *thiab <u>tau</u> <u>nyob</u> <u>tos</u>,*
          and PFV stay wait

          '...and (he) stayed (there and) waited,'

      b. **thaum nws tab.tom mus nyob tos** ces...
          when 3SG just   go stay wait and.then

          '(and) when he had just gone to stay (there) and wait, then...' (Vang
          et al. 1990: 28)

The morpheme *tau*, marking perfective aspect, in the reference clause (11a) is
substituted by the morpheme *tab tom* 'just (begin to)', functioning here to mark
immediate inceptive aspect, in the bridging clause (11b). Inceptive aspect is rein-
forced by the addition of the verb *mus*, here meaning 'go to do something'.

2.4.2 Summary linkage

As explained by Guérin & Aiton (2019 [this volume]), summary linkage involves
the use of a summarizing verb (such as a light verb) in the bridging clause, which
links anaphorically to the reference clause without lexical recapitulation. This
kind of linkage occurs in the first-person text, *Kee's Story*, where it is roughly as
frequent as recapitulative linkage. In the third-person texts, on the other hand,
it appears only occasionally, and then only in reported speech (both direct and
indirect). This suggests that summary linkage may be associated more with unplanned personal narrative and conversation than with more literary style, third-
person narration (the narrative parts of the myths and written accounts examined).

   Summary linkage is expressed in these texts with the copula verb *yog* 'be'
followed by the adverbial *li* 'like, as' and, optionally, by a demonstrative pronoun,
no 'this' or *ntawd* 'that'. This is illustrated from *Kee's Story* in example (12):

(12) a. *<u>Lub</u> sij.hawm ntawm neeg   khiav coob   heev mas.*
          CLF time   that   person run   be.many very IP

          '(At) that time there were very many people fleeing.'

      b. **Yog li   ntawd,**
          COP like that

          'That being the case,'

c. *lawv thiaj hais tias   ua peb puas yog neeg   nyob nram*
3PL   then say COMP do 1PL Q   COP person live   place.down
tiag.
level.place
'they then asked whether we were people (who) lived down (in Vientiane).' (Fuller 1985: 227)

The expression *yog li ntawd* 'that being the case' in (12b) summarizes the information in the reference clause – that there were many people fleeing at the time – to explain why the officials asked the travellers where they came from. The narrator goes on to explain that only travellers who lived in Vientiane were allowed to go there.

In (13), a similar expression, *yog li no* 'this being the case', is used in an indirect speech report from *The legend of Ms Fine Flower II*:

(13)   a. *Niam.Nkauj.Zuag.Paj teb   tias   Txiv.Nraug.Ntsuag tsis yuav*
Ms.Fine.Flower   reply COMP The.Young.Orphan NEG marry
Niam.Nkauj.Zuag.Paj es Niam.Nkauj.Zuag.Paj los   mus.
Ms.Fine.Flower   so Ms.Fine.Flower   come go
'Ms Fine Flower replied that The Young Orphan (would) not marry her so she (had) left.'

b. *Ces   nraug zaj   txawm tias   yog li   no ces   nraug*
and.then young dragon then   COMP COP like this and.then young
zaj   yuav nws no   ces   ...
dragon marry 3SG this and.then
'And then the young dragon said that, this being the case, then he (would) marry her, and then ...' (Johnson 1992: 163)

In this example the expression, *yog li no* 'this being the case' is attributed to the dragon, summarizing the heroine's explanation of her plight as the basis for his marriage proposal. Here the reference clause and the bridging clause function as a bridging construction within the reported conversation, rather than in the narrative text that reports it.

2.4.3 Mixed linkage

There are other examples in the third-person narrative parts of the more literary texts (both written and oral) which do not qualify as summary linkage, but which are quite similar. They are characterized here as mixed linkage because, while the verb of the reference clause is recapitulated in the bridging clause, the remainder of the bridging clause consists only of summarizing, anaphoric elements.

All examples found involve verbs of speech introducing a direct quotation in the reference clause, and it is the quotation only, not the whole of the reference clause, that is summarized anaphorically in the bridging clause. This is exemplified in (14).

(14) a. *Ces   Luj.Tub thiaj.li hais tias   "Yog tsaug~tsaug.zog thiab*
         and.then Lu.Tu   so.then say COMP COP REDUP~be.sleepy and
         nqhis~nqhis nqaij mas yuav.tau rov   mus..."
         REDUP~crave   meat TOP must   return go
         'And so then Lu Tu said, "If (you) are very sleepy and are really craving meat, (I) must go back"...'

      b. ***Hais li   ntawd tag   ces...***
          say   like that   finish and.then
          'After saying that, then...' (Johnson 1992: 8)

Rather than a copula or light verb appearing in the bridging clause, as in summary linkage, the speech verb of the reference clause, *hais* 'say', is repeated. It is accompanied by the adverb *li* 'thus, like' and the demonstrative *ntawd* 'that, there', which serve to summarize the direct quotation.[2]

In other examples of this mixed type of linkage, substitution is also involved:

(15) a. *Vaj.Leej.Txi tau teb   tias   "tsis tau txog   caij,   koj kav.tsij*
          God   PFV reply COMP NEG PFV arrive season 2SG hurry.to
          rov   qab mus dua."
          return back go   again
          'God replied, "The season has not come; you hurry back again".'

      b. ***Vaj.Leej.Txi tau txhib li   ces...***
          God   PFV urge like and.then
          'God urged (him) like (that) and then...' (Vang et al. 1990: 17)

Here the narrator substitutes the speech verb *teb* 'reply' in the reference clause with a semantically more specific speech verb *txhib* 'urge', which describes the nature of God's reply.

---

[2]This is somewhat similar to the type of linkage reported by Guillaume (2011: 128–129) for Cavineña (Tacanan, northern Bolivia), except that there is no restriction on the speech verbs that can be used in Hmong, while in Cavineña the verbs used are limited to two summarizing verbs, which literally mean 'be' and 'affect'.

3 Functions of bridging constructions in White Hmong narratives

As shown in §2.2, bridging constructions in White Hmong all play a role in enhancing discourse cohesion, serving to progress the main event line. Furthermore, the occurrence of a bridging construction often contributes to constructing a particularly salient point of progression – a point at which the narrative moves forward to a new event, a new scene, a new episode, or a new "chapter". Kress & van Leeuwen (2006: 210) describe the notion of salience as "the degree to which an element draws attention to itself due to its size, its place in the foreground or its overlapping of other elements, its colour, its tonal values, its sharpness or definition and other features."

The salience of the event described by the bridging construction is signaled linguistically in all cases by virtue of the simple fact that the clause describing that event is repeated in some way, whether by recapitulative, summary, or mixed linkage. However, as will be shown in §3.1, in many cases of recapitulative linkage in White Hmong, the salience of the event described is further enhanced by variation, not only due to the features of modification, omission, addition, substitution, and summary (§2.4), but also involving a change in aspect between the reference clause and the bridging clause. This change allows the narrator to shift from a "bird's eye" view of the event to a more engaged construal, as if pausing momentarily to observe the event as it is realized. This event then becomes a base from which the event line of the narrative moves forward. This aspectual variation is the first main way in which bridging constructions serve to progress the narrative sequence.

The second way in which a bridging construction can facilitate the narrative progression is where supportive material temporarily interrupts the flow of the event line. This is discussed in §3.2. In this case the bridging clause serves to pick up the action exactly where it was left off, bringing the focus back to the main event line and allowing it to proceed. These two ways in which bridging constructions are used to progress the narrative sequence are not necessarily distinct; a single construction can serve to bring the narrative back to the main event line and also facilitate a change in aspectual construal.

3.1 Change in aspect; change in construal

In the clear majority of cases of recapitulative linkage in the narrative texts examined, there is a change in aspect between the reference clause and the bridging clause. This not only enhances the salience of the event by adding to its temporal texture but also results in a change in its construal. It often allows the narrator to move from a more removed, "bird's eye" perspective on the event to a more involved stance – to zoom in on the event and describe it as it unfolds. The narrator then uses this revised construal of the event as a point of departure, from which to move on to the next event in the narrative sequence.

Aspectual meaning is conveyed in White Hmong in a variety of ways beyond the inherent aspectual meaning of the verb itself, including the use of pre-verbal aspectual morphemes, time adverbs, verbal reduplication, and some types of serial verb constructions (SVCs). The use of pre-verbal aspectual morphemes to change the way in which the same event is depicted between the reference clause and the bridging clause has been illustrated in example (11). Aspectual change from a simple verb in the reference clause to a SVC in the bridging clause occurs in example (2), while the opposite occurs in (4), which starts with verbs in series and changes to a simple verb. Variation in the type of SVC resulting in aspectual change is shown in examples (3) and (5). The use of time adverbs in combination with reduplication is illustrated in example (16), and that of reduplication with SVCs in (17).

Example (16) comes from the *Legend of Ms Fine Flower II*. Ms Fine Flower and her companion, Ms Sultry Toad, are introduced as being very poor. There follows a brief word picture that captures their poverty, describing how they go out every day to scavenge for wild nuts:

(16) a. <u>nkawd niaj</u>   hnub <u>mus khaws txiv.ntseej txiv.qhib noj.</u>
        3DU   every day go pick chestnut acorn   eat
        'Every day the two of them went to pick chestnuts (and) acorns to eat.'

    b. **Nkawd mus khaws~khaws txiv.ntseej txiv.quib noj,**
        3DU   go REDUP~pick chestnut   acorn   eat
        '[One day] they went along picking (and) picking chestnuts (and) acorns to eat,'

    c. *ces*   *Txiv.Nraug.Ntsuag txawm mus pom nkawd.*
        and.then The.Young.Orphan then   go see 3DU
        'and then The Young Orphan went to see them.' (Johnson 1992: 161)

The young women's action is explicitly indicated as habitual with the use of the time adverb *niaj hnub* 'every day' in the reference clause (16a). The bridging clause (16b) then switches to continuous aspect, using the reduplicated verb *khaws˜khaws* ('(be) picking (and) picking'). With this aspectual change, the narrator zooms in from an initial overview of their life circumstances to focus on a particular moment when, as they were busily engaged with their daily task, The Young Orphan entered their life (16c), and changed their fortunes completely.

The next example of aspectual change is from later in the same story, by which time the heroine, Ms Fine Flower, has married The Young Orphan. Her companion Ms Sultry Toad, enraged and jealous, devises a scheme to shame Ms Fine Flower.

(17) a. *es Niam.Nkauj.Kub.Kaws txawm muab Niam.Nkauj.Kub.Kaws*
      so Ms.Sultry.Toad   then take Ms.Sultry.Toad

      cov   niag ntshav pim   coj   mus pleev~pleev
      CLF:COLL great blood vagina take.along go REDUP~smear

      Niam.Nkauj.Zuag.Paj lub qhov.ncauj,
      Ms.Fine.Flower   CLF mouth

      'so then taking her own menstrual blood, Ms Sultry Toad took (it) over (to) smear (and) smear (on) Ms Fine Flower's mouth,'

    b. **muab pleev~pleev Niam.Nkauj.Zuag.Paj lub qhov.ncauj**
      take   REDUP~smear Ms.Fine.Flower   CLF mouth

      lo   ntshav liab-vog,
      be(come).plastered blood   red-speckled

      '(she) took (it) (and) smeared (and) smeared (it) (on) Ms Fine Flower's mouth (so that it) was plastered (with) red blood.' (Johnson 1992: 162)

The reference clause (17a) uses a serial verb construction, also involving reduplication, to focus on the process of Ms Sultry Toad's action – *muab ... coj mus pleev~pleev* (take ... take.along go REDUP~smear) – taking up the blood, carrying it over to her victim, and smearing it all over her mouth. The bridging clause (17b) retains some focus on this process – *muab ... pleev~pleev* (take ... REDUP~smear) – but adds another verb in the series – *lo* (become plastered with) – to also include the result of the action, Ms Fine Flower's mouth becoming plastered all over with blood. This is a point of great significance in the story, as Ms Sultry Toad then tells The Young Orphan that Ms Fine Flower's red mouth is a sign that she has been drinking sheep's blood, provoking him to drive his young wife out of their home.

In this section we have discussed the extremely common phenomenon of variation in aspect between the two clauses in a recapitulative linkage. This variation in aspect results in a change in the construal of the event, giving a sense that the narrator moves to a closer focus and pauses briefly as the event unfolds, before moving on with the main line and thus progressing the narrative sequence. In the next section we will look at the second way in which bridging constructions are used in White Hmong to achieve this same broad function of moving the event line of the narrative forward.

3.2 Return to the event line after supportive material

In White Hmong bridging constructions, the bridging clause generally follows the reference clause directly. Less commonly, one or more clauses intervene between the reference clause and the bridging clause. Their purpose is always to provide information that supports the narrative, but which is not part of the event line. The bridging clause then serves to bring the narration back to the event line, as the narrator picks up the main sequence of events again following this parenthetical digression. In example (18) the event line is describing the ceremonies associated with the birth of twins in the story of Shong Lue Yang.

(18) a. *lawv thiaj   muab ob   leej me.nyuam ntxaib hu plig   thiab tis*
       3PL so.then take two CLF child   twins call spirit and   assign

   npe.
   name

   '... so then they took the two children (and) called (their) spirits and gave (them) names.'

   b. *Leej hlob   muab hu.ua Tsab.Yaj,*
      CLF be.old take name Tsa.Ya

   'The older one (they) called Tsa Ya,'

   c. *leej yau   muab hu.ua Xab.Yaj.*
      CLF be.young take name Xa.Ya

   'the younger one (they) called Xa Ya.'

   d. **Tom.qab muab nkawd hu plig tis   npe tag,**
      after   take 3DU   call spirit assign name finish

   'After having taken those two, calling (their) spirits (and) giving (them) names,'

   e. *niam.tais   thiab yawm.txiv   tau rov   mus tsev lawm.*
      mother-in-law and   father-in-law PFV return go   home PRF

   'mother-in-law and father-in-law went back home.' (Vang et al. 1990: 33)

The reference clause (18a) introduces the ceremonies. The two juxtaposed main clauses in (18b) and (18c) follow, providing supportive information concerning the names given to the babies. The bridging clause (18d) then functions both to bring the narrative back to the main event line and to introduce the fact that the next event – (18e) the in-laws' return home – occurred after the ceremonies were concluded.

While the intervening clauses in example (18) are main clauses, in example (19) non-main clauses intervene. This excerpt also comes from the story of Shong Lue Yang, whom the narrators believed to be one of the twelve sons of *Vaj Leej Txi* 'Sovereign Father, God'.

(19)   a. *ces*   *<u>nws thiaj tau muab lub tsho Soob.Lwj</u>* *<u>hle</u>*
         and.then 3SG so   PFV take CLF shirt Shong.Lue remove

         <u>tseg</u>   *<u>cia</u>*
         leave.behind set.aside

         '...and so he took (his) Shong Lue garb, removed (it) (and) left (it) behind'

    b. *tso*   *rov*   *qab* *mus nug Vaj.Leej.Txi dua*
        release return back go   ask God   again

         'so (he) could go back [to heaven] to ask God again,'

    c. *seb*   *tim.li.cas nkawd thiaj tsis lawv qab los.*
        find.out why   3DU   so   NEG follow back come

         'to find out why those two [his younger brothers] had not followed (him) back [to earth].'

    d. **Nws tau hle**   **lub tsho Soob.Lwj** **tseg**   *cia,*
        3SG PFV remove CLF shirt Shong.Lue leave.behind set.aside

         'He removed his Shong Lue garb (and) left (it) behind'

    e. *ces*   *nws rov*   *qab* *mus...*
        and.then 3SG return back go

         'and then he went back...' (Vang et al. 1990: 16)

The digression in the non-main clauses (19b) and (19c) in this case serves to explain the purpose of the action described in the reference clause (19a): the protagonist took off his human garb *in order to return to heaven*. The action of taking off his human garb is repeated in the bridging clause (19d), as the event line is resumed.

In example (20) from the first-person narrative text *Kee's Story*, we see quite a lengthy diversion occurring between the reference clause (a) and the subsequent bridging clause (f). The narrator, along with his father and younger brother, managed to buy a letter giving permission to travel to Vientiane, so that they could then cross the Mekong River and flee war-torn Laos.

(20)   a. *peb thiaj.li, peb txiv-tub, peb thiaj.li, aws, yuav lawv ib daig*
         1PL so.then 1PL father-son 1PL so.then HESIT obtain 3PL one CLF

         ntawv.
         letter

         'So then we – we father and sons – so then we – um – bought their letter.'

       b. *Lawv daim ntawv ntawm yog ua   Vientiane tuaj*
          3PL CLF letter that COP make Vientiane come

          'That letter of theirs came from Vientiane'

       c. *hais tias   tuaj xyuas kwv.tij nyob rau pem   Xieng.Khouang.*
          say COMP come visit relative live to place.up Xieng.Khouang

          '(and it) said (they would) come (to) visit relatives up in Xieng Khouang.'

       d. *Lawv muaj peb   leeg   thiab*
          3PL have three people also

          'They had three people too'

       e. *ces   peb muaj peb   leeg tab.tom phim lawv daim ntawv ntawd*
          and.then 1PL have three CLF just   match 3PL CLF letter that

          'and then we had three people just matching that letter of theirs'

       f. *ces   **peb thiaj   yuav lawv daim ntawv ntawm**, ces...*
          and.then 1PL so.then obtain 3PL   CLF   letter that   and.then

          'and then we bought that letter of theirs, and then...' (Fuller 1985: 227)

This long diversion involving multiple clauses clearly supports the main line events of the narrative – the story of flight from Laos – by explaining how the letter the travellers bought suited their needs and facilitated their journey. The length of this intervening material may be related to the informal, unplanned nature of this personal monologue.[3] When the event line is picked up again in

---

[3]This use of recapitulation following a lengthy gap seems quite similar to some examples of self-repetition used for cohesion in Greek conversations, given by Alvanoudi (2019 [this volume]). In the Greek examples, however, the repetition connects a speaker's previous and current turn, establishing contiguity after intervening turns by (an)other speaker(s).

(20f), it is introduced by the sequential conjunction *ces* 'and then', which normally does not occur again until after a bridging clause. This clearly serves to reinforce the return to the sequential event line of the story.

The use of bridging clauses described here, to pick up the event line after a parenthetical diversion, should not be thought of as completely separate from their use to modify the construal of the event (discussed in §3.1). In (18), for example, the bridging clause clearly serves both functions, not only returning the narrative to the event line but also shifting to completive aspect and thus explicitly asserting the ordered sequence of this event with the following one. Throughout the texts these two functions of bridging constructions can be seen to work together to progress the main event line and to facilitate discourse cohesion.

4 Conclusion

This chapter has examined the position, form, frequency, and types of bridging constructions in White Hmong narrative texts, along with their discourse functions.

Bridging constructions are commonly positioned at the boundary between discourse units that belong to the event line of the narrative. Here they serve to link both major episodes ("chapters") and minor episodes ("paragraphs"). They can also occur in the absence of a discourse boundary, simply to bring the narrative back to the event line after a brief digression.

In terms of form, reference clauses are all main clauses, and bridging clauses are either reduced main clauses, or temporal subordinate clauses serving to relate the event of the bridging construction to the next event in sequence (e.g., "after", "when", etc.). The construction as a whole is usually explicitly embedded in the sequential event line of the narrative with coordinating, sequential, or subordinating conjunctions.

The data show that the frequency and type of bridging constructions can vary in White Hmong depending on narrator and text type. Recapitulative linkage is far more common than summary linkage, which is limited to unplanned, spoken styles. A further mixed type of linkage involving a speech verb introducing a direct quotation occasionally occurs in more literary spoken and written texts.

The bridging constructions examined in this data from narrative texts in White Hmong serve to enhance the salience of the events they describe. This occurs in all cases by virtue of the fact that the clause describing that event "draws attention to itself" (Kress & van Leeuwen 2006: 210) through repetition. However, in White Hmong, this salience is further enhanced in most cases by variation between the reference and bridging clause, including modification, omission, addition, substitution, and summary. A particularly common kind of variation involves a change in aspect. This change allows the narrator to shift from a "bird's eye" view of the event concerned to a more engaged construal, as if pausing momentarily to observe the event as it unfolds. This momentary pause allows the narrator to use that event as a base from which the narrative then moves forward. In these multiple ways, bridging constructions in White Hmong work cohesively, linking one unit in the event line to the next and serving to progress the main sequence of events.

Appendix

The excerpt below is the beginning of the story of the first man and woman on earth (Johnson 1992: 3–4). There are five bridging constructions in this excerpt, each of which helps to move the story forward in some way. The first bridging construction takes the story from the depiction of the man alone on the dark, barren earth, to the time when his wife is ready to join him. The second introduces a complication: the man has brought a magic flower with him to earth, but there is no wood to use to cook its seeds to eat. This dilemma is resolved, as the third bridging construction explains how they manage to burn coal to cook the seeds. When the seeds begin to run out, we see two bridging constructions in succession: the first resolving this complication, as they plant the remaining seeds, and the second introducing a new complication, as only one plant comes forth.

This excerpt illustrates well how bridging constructions function in White Hmong as part of a wider phenomenon involving the strategy of repetition with variation, to build up elements in a narrative text as it moves forward in intricate, overlapping layers.

(A1) *Thaum ub   tsis muaj hnub tsis muaj hli,*
       time   yonder NEG have sun   NEG have moon,

       'Long ago, there was neither sun nor moon,'

(A2) *tsis muaj ib   tug neeg   nyob   hauv lub ntiaj.teb no li.*
       NEG have one CLF person be.located inside CLF earth   this at.all

       '(and) there were no people at all on this earth.'

(A3)   *Muaj ib hnub, ib   tug txiv.neej txawm tawm   ntawm   txoj*
            have one day, one CLF man   then   emerge place.nearby CLF
            sawv.toj   los.
            vein.in.hillside come
            'One day, a man emerged from a vein in the hillside.'[4]

(A4)   *Nws lub npe   hu.ua   Txiv.Nraug.Luj.Tub.*
            3SG CLF name be.called Master.Lu.Tu
            'His name was Master Lu Tu.'

(A5)   *Nws tawm   ntawm   txoj mem.toj   los   xwb.*
            3SG emerge place.nearby CLF fissure.in.hillside come only
            'He just emerged from a fissure in the hillside.'

(A6)   *Thaum nws tawm   los   txog   saum   yaj.ceeb no mas,*
            when   3SG emerge come arrive place.above earth   this IP
            'When he came out up onto the earth,'

(A7)   *ntuj tsaus   li   qhov.paj teb   tsaus   li   qhov.tsua.*
            sky be.dark like cavern   earth be.dark like cave
            'The sky was as dark as a cavern, the earth as dark as a cave.'[5]

(A8)   *Yeej   tsis muaj hnub tsis muaj hli.*
            originally NEG have sun   NEG have moon
            'There was no sun (and) no moon.'

(A9)   *Nws cev   tes   xuas txawm tau ntuj nyob   ntawd   ntag.*
            3SG raise.up hand touch then   get sky be.located place.nearby IP
            'He raised up his hand (and) was able to touch the sky there!'[6]

---

[4] The terms *sawv toj* and (a few lines further on) *mem toj* both mean 'vein/fissure in the hillside', and are related to the Hmong practices of geomancy.

[5] The expression *qhov paj* (lit: 'hole flower') does not, by itself, mean 'cavern'. However here, in combination with *qhov tsua* 'cave' (lit: 'hole rock'), it is probably functioning poetically to refer to limestone caves characterized by flower-like stalactite formations, more generally referred to as *qhov tsua tawg paj* (lit: 'hole rock bloom flower') or *qhov tsua paj kaub* (lit: 'hole rock flower crust') in Hmong.

[6] In Hmong myths, the sky is often presented as a hemisphere that meets the earth at the horizon (Johnson 1992: 14, fn.2).

(A10) *Nws tawm   ib.leeg ua.ntej los   rau nraum   yaj.ceeb no*
3SG emerge alone first   come to place.outside earth   this
'He came out first, all alone, to this earth'

(A11) *ces   thiaj   mam   xeeb   nws tus poj.niam rau ntawm*
and.then so.then then.next be.born 3SG CLF wife   to place.nearby
nws qhov.chaw.
3SG place
'and so then next his wife was born in his place [i.e., in the fissure from which he had emerged].'

(A12) **Xeeb   nws tus poj.niam rau ntawm   nws qhov.chaw**
be.born 3SG CLF wife   to place.nearby 3SG place
puv-hnub-puv-nyoog
be.filled-day-be.filled-age
'His wife was born into his place (until her) time was fulfilled'

(A13) *ces   nws tus poj.niam thiaj   mam   tawm   lawv qab*
and.then 3SG CLF wife   so.then then.next emerge follow behind
los.
come
'and so then next his wife came out after (him).'

(A14) *Nws tus poj.niam mas hu.ua   Niam.Nkauj.Ntxhi.Chiv no.*
3SG CLF wife   TOP be.called Ms.Ntxi.Chi   this
'His wife, (she) was called Ms Ntxi Chi.'

(A15) *Ces   nkawd ob   tug niam.txiv thiaj   los   nyob ua.neej.*
and.then 3DU   two CLF couple   so.then come live   prosper
'And then the two of them came [to earth] to live and prosper.'

(A16) *Tsis muaj hnub tsis muaj hli;*
NEG have sun   NEG have moon
'There was no sun (and) no moon;'

(A17) ntuj tsaus   li   qhov.paj teb   tsaus   li   qhov.tsua xwb.
       sky be.dark like cavern   earth be.dark like cave   only
       'the sky was as dark as a cavern, the earth as dark as a cave.'

(A18) Thaum Txiv.Nraug.Luj.Tub tawm   los
       time   Master.Lu.Tu   emerge come
       'When Master Lu Tu came out'

(A19) ces   nws txawm tau ib   lub paj   Caus Ci uas nyob
       and.then 3SG then   get one CLF flower Cau Ci REL be.located
       ntawm   nws qhov.chaw nrog   nws los.
       place.nearby 3SG place   be.with 3SG come
       'then he got a Cau Ci flower, which had been in his place [i.e., in the
       fissure] with him.'

(A20) Nws nqa   tau lub paj   tawm   los   rau nraum yaj.ceeb no.
       3SG carry get CLF flower emerge come to outside world   this
       'He brought the flower out to this world.'

(A21) Coj   los
       take.along come
       '[He] brought [it] along'

(A22) ces   tsis muaj xyoob   muaj ntoo, tsis muaj hluav.taws li
       and.then NEG have bamboo have tree, NEG have fire   at.all
       'and then (he) had neither bamboo [nor] trees, [so] (he) had no fire at
       all.'

(A23) Thaum ntawd nws txawm los   nyob;
       time   that 3SG then   come live
       'At that time he came to live (here);'

(A24) ces   nws rauv zeb.ntsuam xwb.
       and.then 3SG burn coal   only
       'and then he burned only (pieces of) coal.'

(A25) *Luj Tub nkawd ob.niam.txiv rauv cov   ntawd*
      Lu Tu 3DU   couple   burn CLF:COLL that
      'Lu Tu and his wife burned those'

(A26) *kib lub paj   ntawd cov   noob noj xwb.*
      fry CLF flower that   CLF:COLL seed eat only
      '(to) fry the seeds of that flower to eat.'

(A27) *Nkawd nyob ces   nyob~nyob,*
      3DU   live and.then REDUP~live
      'The two of them lived on and on,'

(A28) *kib~kib   cov   noob ntawm lub paj   ntawd noj yuav tag;*
      REDUP~fry CLF:COLL seed that   CLF flower that   eat will finish
      '(and) kept frying the seeds of that flower to eat (until) (they) were
      going to run out;'

(A29) <u>*ces*</u>   *nkawd* <u>*thiaj*</u>   *muab* <u>*coj*</u>   <u>*mus*</u> <u>*cog*</u>.
      and.then 3DU   so.then take   take.along go   plant
      'So then they took (the seeds) and went to plant (them).'

(A30) *Cog tas   na*
      plant finish IP
      '(They) finished planting (them), don't you know,'

(A31) <u>*tuaj*</u> <u>*ib*</u> <u>*tsob xwb.*</u>
      come one CLF only
      '(and) there came forth only one plant.'

(A32) *Tuaj tau...*
      come get
      'There came forth (one plant)...'

Abbreviations

1	first person	IP	illocutionary particle
2	second person	NEG	negation
3	third person	O	transitive object
A	transitive subject	PFV	perfective
CC	copula complement	PL	plural
CLF	classifier	PRF	perfect
CLF:COLL	collective classifier	Q	question particle
COMP	complementizer	REDUP	reduplicated
COP	copula	REL	relativizer
CS	copula subject	SG	singular
DU	dual	SVC	serial verb construction
EX	exclamative	TOP	topic
HESIT	hesitation	V	verb

Acknowledgements

I wish to express my sincere thanks to Valérie Guérin for inviting me to contribute to this volume, and for her wonderful support as I prepared this chapter. Many thanks also to Sasha Aikhenvald, Grant Aiton, and two anonymous reviewers for very helpful comments on earlier versions. Although the data for the chapter come from published sources, my analysis would not have been possible without the help of my dear Hmong teachers and friends. Particular thanks go to Cua Lis, Thaiv Thoj, and Zoo Lis.

References

Alvanoudi, Angeliki. 2019. Clause repetition as a tying technique in Greek conversation. In Valérie Guérin (ed.), *Bridging constructions*, 239–267. Berlin: Language Science Press. DOI:10.5281/zenodo.2563694

Fuller, Judith Wheaton. 1985. *Topic and comment in Hmong*. Minneapolis, USA: The University of Minnesota PhD Dissertation.

Guérin, Valérie & Grant Aiton. 2019. Bridging constructions in typological perspective. In Valérie Guérin (ed.), *Bridging constructions*, 1–44. Berlin: Language Science Press. DOI:10.5281/zenodo.2563678

Guillaume, Antoine. 2011. Subordinate clauses, switch-reference, and tail-head linkage in Cavineña narratives. In Rik van Gijn, Katharina Haude & Pieter Muysken (eds.), *Subordination in native South American languages*, 109–140. Amsterdam: John Benjamins.

Jarkey, Nerida. 2015. *Serial verbs in White Hmong*. Leiden: Brill.

Johns, Brenda & David Strecker. 1982. Aesthetic language in White Hmong. In Bruce T. Downing & Douglas P. Olney (eds.), *The Hmong in the West: Observations and reports*, 160–169. Minneapolis: Center for Urban & Regional Affairs, University of Minnesota.

Johnson, Charles. 1992. *Dab neeg Hmoob: Myths, legends and folk tales from the Hmong of Laos*. St Paul, MN: Macalester College.

Kress, Gunther & Theo van Leeuwen. 2006. *Reading images: The grammar of visual design*. 2nd edn. London: Routledge.

Longacre, Robert E. 1983. *The grammar of discourse*. New York: Plenum Press.

Mortensen, David R. 2003. *Hmong elaborate expressions are coordinate compounds*. http://www.davidmortensen.org/papers.html, accessed 2018-7-31. Unpublished manuscript.

Vang, Chia Koua, Gnia Yee Yang & William A. Smalley. 1990. *The life of Shong Lue Yang: Hmong 'Mother of Writing'; Keeb kwm Soob Lwj Yaj: Hmoob 'Niam Ntawv'*. Minneapolis, MN: Center for Urban & Regional Affairs, University of Minnesota. English translation by Mitt Moua and See Yang.

Chapter 6

The form and function of bridging constructions in Eibela discourse

Grant Aiton

James Cook University

Discourse in Eibela utilizes extensive repetition and summarization of events as a means of bridging discourse episodes. These bridging constructions consist of a main reference clause at the end of a unit of discourse, which is immediately referenced by a non-main bridging clause at the commencement of the following unit of discourse. Bridging clauses may be formed by medial clauses initiating a clause chain, and topic clauses that are embedded within another medial or final clause. Differing units of discourse are often accompanied by differing forms of bridging construction, with clause chain boundaries featuring verbatim repetition of clauses, and larger paragraphs being bound by bridging clauses utilizing anaphoric predicates. Bridging constructions have been previously shown to serve various functions in Papuan languages, including thematic continuity, reference tracking, and event sequencing, which will also be illustrated in the current discussion of bridging constructions in Eibela.

1 Introduction and background

Eibela, also referred to as Aimele (Ethnologue code: AIL), has approximately 300 speakers living primarily in Lake Campbell, Western Province, Papua New Guinea. The genetic affiliation of Eibela has not been thoroughly investigated, but it is likely that it belongs to the proposed Trans-New Guinea Phylum, of the central and South New Guinea stock, since this is the classification given to the closely related language Kaluli by Wurm (1978) and Voorhoeve (1968). A lower level classification is given as the Bosavi language family in Shaw (1986). The data for this paper is drawn from a corpus of approximately 17 hours of transcribed speech from a variety of genres, including narratives, procedurals, myths,

Grant Aiton. 2019. The form and function of bridging constructions in Eibela discourse. In Valérie Guérin (ed.), *Bridging constructions*, 157–184. Berlin: Language Science Press. DOI:10.5281/zenodo.2563688 sermons, discourse, and songs, which is available online in the Endangered Languages Archive (Aiton 2016). This corpus is the result of approximately 13 months of immersive fieldwork in Lake Campbell and Wawoi Falls in Western Province, Papua New Guinea. Since bridging constructions are a phenomenon of discourse organization, they predominantly occur in long stretches of speech from a single speaker, and the examples in this chapter are therefore drawn from monologues, including narratives, myths, and procedural descriptions. An extended excerpt from a monologue is provided in the Appendix. The text chosen for the Appendix is considered by the author to be representative of personal narratives in terms of event structure and the usage of bridging constructions. Where possible claims made in the prose of this chapter are supported by examples from the Appendix so that the reader may view these clauses in the context of a larger discourse.

Discourse in Eibela utilizes frequent repetition and summarization of events as a means of bridging discourse episodes. These bridging constructions consist of a main reference clause at the end of a unit of discourse, which is immediately reiterated by a repetition in a non-main bridging clause at the commencement of the following unit of discourse. This paper offers an extensive description of this phenomenon in Eibela, but first a basic introduction to some aspects of Eibela is warranted. The canonical constituent order for Eibela is SV in intransitive clauses and AOV in transitive clauses, though other constituent orders are possible. Constituents which are prominent or topical are often omitted from clauses completely. Morphology is exclusively suffixing, with complex verbal morphology for tense, aspect, mood, and evidentiality, with optional ergative-absolutive case marking on noun phrases in core argument positions (see Aiton 2014). Word classes include open classes of nouns, verbs, and adverbs, and closed classes of adjectives, demonstratives, postpositions, verbal particles, and quantifiers.

Predicates in Eibela can be formed by lexical roots of nearly any word class, although only verbs may be inflected by the full range of tense, aspect, mood, and evidentiality suffixes. Complex inflectional classes of verbs feature various patterns of stem alternations and suppletive tense forms, as well as complex predicates consisting of multiple verbal roots forming a single predicate.

(1) [age ɸeɸe-jaː]$_s$ [ena]$_x$ [dobosuwɛ]$_x$ [tɛ   aːnɛ]$_{pred}$
     dog skinny-ABS there underneath go.down go;PST
     'The skinny dog went down underneath there.'

(2) [sobolo-wa]$_s$ [tɛbɛ do-wa]$_{pred}$
     plane-ABS   land STAT-PST
     'A plane has landed.'

These complex predicates may take the form of serial verb constructions as in (1), or auxiliary constructions, as in (2). In these constructions, only the final verbal root is inflected for predicate categories such as tense, aspect, mood, and evidentiality.

Eibela clauses may be linked together into clause chains, which include several medial clauses culminating in a fully inflected final clause. Clauses in examples will be labeled in subscript to show whether they are a final or a medial clause. In medial clauses, the different-subject marking suffix *-bi* may be used to show that the subject of the medial clause differs from the subject of the main clause, as seen in example (3).

(3) a. *[nɛ ɛja-jaː   mumunɛ ɛlɛbɛ la-bi]*~medial~
      1;SG father-ABS NAME   head be-DS

     'My father was at the head of Mulume creek, and...'

  b. *[saːgoi ɛjalɛ   motuwɛ ɛjalɛ   gɛdajoɸa   sɛdɛ hɛna*
      NAME COORD;DU NAME   COORD;DU tree.trunk;ABS hit   DUR

     mi-jaː]~final~
     come-PST

     'Sagoi and Motuwe came while beating tree trunks (so their approach would be heard).'

In this example, the subject of the medial clause in (3a) is *nɛ ɛjaja* 'my father', who is described as being at a location, whereas in the final clause (3b), the subject is the coordinated noun phrase *saːgoi ɛjalɛ motuwɛ ɛjalɛ* 'Saːgai and Motuwe', who are coming while hitting trees. Clauses and noun phrases may additionally be morphologically topicalized as can be seen in (4) where the verb in the topic clause is suffixed by *-bi* since its subject differs from that of the main predicate. In this case, the marking of different subjects functions in much the same way as in (3).

(4) a. *[[na   no-wa   ɛimɛ   ka agle-si]*~medial~   *kɛkɛkɛ]*~final~
      animal INDF-ABS quickly FOC laugh-MED;PFV laugh;IDEO

     'The other animals were already laughing.'

  b. *[no-wɛ-mi=jaː   ɛimɛ   ka agle-bi=jaː]*~topic~
      INDF-LOC-ASSOC=TOP already FOC laugh-DS=TOP

     'Another one was already laughing, then...'

c. [[*no wɛ a:gɛ kɛga=ja:*]*topic* *wɛ suwɛ da-li lɛ-ki wɛ dɛdɛ*
   CONTR this dog bony=TOP   this inside lie-SIM be-CONT this hear
   la:-bi]*final*
   be-DS

   'This one, this bony dog who was still inside was listening to this.'

A direct contrast between these two usages of the suffix *-bi* is shown in example (4). In (4b) topic clause has a different subject from the following main clause, and therefore bears the different-subject marker. The subject of the topic clause is a pig, who is laughing at the dogs in a folk tale, while the subject of the main clause is one of the dogs, who is covertly listening. In (4c) the different-subject marker appears in the main clause as well, specifying an unexpected or non-topical subject for this clause, where the dog is an unexpected introduction into the story. This use of the different-subject marker in a main clause may be interpreted as a kind of desubordination, in which a clause with the morphological form of a non-main clause is functionally and syntactically independent (Evans 2012).

With this introduction to Eibela morphosyntax in mind, the bridging clauses described in subsequent sections may be formed from two types of non-main clause, namely medial clauses initiating a clause chain, and topic clauses which are embedded within another medial or final clause. Bridging constructions have been previously shown to serve various functions in Papuan languages, including thematic continuity, reference tracking, and event sequencing, which will also be illustrated in the current discussion of bridging constructions in Eibela. The morphosyntax of clause-chaining and clause topicalization strategies will be further discussed in §2 below. The use of these clause linking devices in bridging constructions will be shown in §3, and finally, the semantics and function of bridging constructions will be explored in §4, including discourse organization, temporal anchoring, causation, and argument tracking.

2 Clause linking and topic clauses

Two clause linking strategies are relevant to the current discussion of bridging constructions in Eibela: clause chaining and topicalization. A clause will be assumed to include a predicate and all arguments of that predicate, although topical or given arguments may often be elided. Clause chaining consists of a series of at least two clauses, which describe a series of related events. A clause chain will be an important unit of Eibela discourse throughout this paper. Topicalization is a feature of a complex clause whereby a single non-main clause or noun phrase appears immediately before a clause and functions as the topic or reference point of the following clause.

2.1 Clause linking

Clause chaining is a form of clause linking where one or more non-main clauses with limited inflection appear in a sequence, or chain, and the full inflection of tense aspect and mood is expressed on the final main clause of the chain (Longacre 2007: 374–376). For example, in the short clause chain shown in examples (A3) and (A4) of the Appendix, the first medial non-main clause includes the predicate *hɛna: disi*, which is not specified for tense, and is suffixed by the perfective clause chaining morpheme *-si*. Tense specification is only provided on the verb of the final main clause, *mu:du:* 'washed' in (4). Clause chaining structures have previously been described as something intermediate between coordinate and subordinate clause linking, or labeled as "coordinate but dependent" (Haiman 1983) or "cosubordinate" (Van Valin Jr 1984).

The two clause linkers *=nɛgɛ:* and *-si* are more or less synonymous and have no obvious distributional differences. The aspectual difference represented by the glossing as imperfective for *=nɛgɛ:*, and perfective for *-si*, reflects a tendency rather than a strict correspondence. The enclitic *=nɛgɛ:* is seen more frequently with ongoing events that will still be co-occurring alongside the subsequently described events, whereas the suffix *-si* is seem more often with perfective events which are completed and then followed by a consecutive event.

An additional chaining enclitic *=ki* may be used for ongoing or persisting events, as in (5) and (6). This is used for ongoing imperfective events which continue up until the occurrence of the following clause. The continuous enclitic *=ki* is aspectually similar to the imperfective enclitic *=nɛgɛ:*, but differs in usage primarily in that *=ki* represents stative, repetitive, or unchanging event structures, whereas *=nɛgɛ:* is often used for processes or telic events. Non-verbal predicates may be used in clause chaining constructions, but must be accompanied by a verbal auxiliary in non-main clauses as seen in (6).

(5) *[sɛnɛ=**ki**]ₘₑₔᵢₐₗ [a:mi   makiso-wa ɛ-sa:-bi]ᶠᵢₙₐₗ*
     stay=CONT   DEM;ASSOC visitor-ABS do-3;VIS-DS
     'We were living there and a visitor did that (came).'

(6) a. *[ɛja:gɛ   dɛmɛ di-sɛnɛ   wa:lɛ-mɛna]ᶠᵢₙₐₗ*
         butterfly do   do-NMLZ tell-FUT;NON.3
         'I will tell about what butterflies do.'

b. *[ɛjaːgɛ   do-si=ki]*~medial~   *[uʃu]*~final~

butterfly STAT-MED;PFV=CONT egg

'There being a butterfly then there is an egg.'

c. **[uʃu do-si=ki]**~medial~   *[kɛkɛbeaːnɛ]*~final~

egg STAT-MED;PFV=CONT caterpillar

'There being an egg then there is a caterpillar.'

d. **[kɛkɛbeaːnɛ do-si=ki]**~medial~   *[kokoːno]*~final~

caterpillar   STAT-MED;PFV=CONT pupa

'There being caterpillar then there is a pupa.'

e. **[kokoːno do-si=ki]**~medial~   *[ɛjaːgɛ]*~final~

pupa   STAT-MED;PFV=CONT butterfly

'There being a pupa then there is a butterfly.'

f. *[ɛjaːgɛ   maːna   wa kam]*~final~

butterfly behavior;ABS DIR finish

'The (story of) butterfly behavior is finished.'

Every line given in (6) is a clause chain, and each of the main clauses (6c–6f) begin with a non-main medial clause (shown in bold) which repeats the proposition of the preceding main clause. When the nominal predicate is the predicate of a main clause, no auxiliary is needed, but in non-main clauses, the clause linking morphology may only appear with a verbal auxiliary being appended to the nominal predicate to for a complex predicate.

2.2 Topicalization

Topicalization is a general process of identifying some concept as the topic or theme of a clause. In Eibela, this is accomplished by means of left dislocated clause position and the enclitic *=jaː*. Aiton (2014) summarizes the use of topicalized noun phrases and clause arguments in Eibela argument structure, such as the example given in (7).

(7)   a. *[[seinaːbiː=jaː]*~topic~ *gomoːlo-wɛː hojɛ-kɛː   henaː-genɛː]*~medial~

tree.kangaroo=TOP NAME-ERG   hunt-ITER go-MED;IPFV

'Tree kangaroos, Gomoolo had gone hunting (for those animals)...'

b. *[olaː   ka laː]*~final~

shoot;PST FOC DEF

'...and (he) had shot one (a tree kangaroo).'

The current discussion will not further explore topical noun phrases, and will focus on the occurrence of clauses as the topic of a subsequent main clause. A clause is presented in the topic position to provide a conceptual point of reference for the event described in the main clause. When the topic is a clause, as in example (8), the clause is followed by the topic-marking enclitic *=ja:* and precedes the main clause.

(8) [[*nɛ ɛsɛ   no-wa   ogɛ   di=ja:*]topic *ɸili:-nɛ*]final
     1;SG string.bag INDF-ABS pick.up take=TOP ascend-PST
     'Taking another bag, I went up.'

The semantic relationship between the topic clause and main clause is rather vague. In (8), the intended meaning is that the speaker primarily intended to take his string bag somewhere, and in order to do this, he walked uphill. In future time contexts, a topic clause can produce a conditional reading, as in (9).

(9) [[*gɛ so:wa sugu:lu:-mɛna:=ja:*]topic *ɛ:lɛmɛ:ntɾi: ti:sa-ja:*   *kɛlɛ-ma:*]final
     2;SG child attend.school-FUT=TOP elementary teacher-ABS find-IMP
     'If your children are to go to school, then find a teacher!'

A conditional meaning as in (9) could simply be paraphrased as an intentional meaning, i.e., 'Find a teacher in order to ensure that your children attend school.' However, this intentional/conditional meaning cannot be taken for granted. Instead it seems to be an incidental result of the topic clause's role as a prominent and given piece of information (Haiman 1978). In both (8) and (9), the topic clause refers to previously mentioned information which is a prominent and ongoing topic of the narrative. The role of the main clause is then to expand upon the given topic and provide new information which has not yet been presented. For example, in clause (A6) of the Appendix, the events of the topic clause and main clause are sequential, with the topic clause clearly preceding the events of the main clause, and no intentional interpretation is possible. When a clause appears as a topic, the topicalized clause reiterates familiar or already mentioned information as a reference point for new information which is introduced in the following main clause. This results in the bridging constructions, which will be discussed in greater detail in §3.

2.3 Topicalized medial clauses

Interestingly, chaining and topicalization, the two strategies of clause linking, may co-occur. The perfective clause linking suffix *-si* may be used in a topicalized clause to provide specific aspectual information, as in example (10). In the example (10b), the clause *nɛ bɛdɛsijaː* is presented with both the clause linking suffix *-si* and the topicalizing enclitic *=jaː*.

(10) a. *[kosuwa-jaː   ja   gigɛ   di   bɛda-nɛ]*_{medial}
       cassowary-ABS come make.noise PFV hear;PST-MED;IPFV

       'I heard a cassowary come and make noise.'

    b. *[[nɛ bɛdɛ-si=jaː]*_{topic}   *ma bobo]*_{final}
       1;SG hear-MED;PFV=TOP NEG real

       'I heard that, and (I thought) it was not real (i.e., a spirit).'

In this construction, the clause linking suffix *-si* provides aspectual information regarding the timing of the topic with respect to the main clause. Specifically, the topic and main clause are consecutive events, where the topic clause is a perfective event occurring immediately prior to the main clause. In addition to these semantic and functional considerations, topical clauses containing an auxiliary within the predicate require the clause linking suffix *-si*. This is true even if the aspectual information provided by the suffix *-si* is redundant as in (11b).

(11) a. *[aːmi   dɛɸija-ɸɛi]*_{final}
       DEM;ASSOC measure-HYPOTH;COMP

       '(The other sleeping space being made like this,) measure there.'

    b. *[[ɛ di-si=jaː]*_{topic}   *henaː-nɛː]*_{medial} *[isi-jaː   kodu-mɛi]*_{final}
       do PFV-MED;PFV=TOP DUR-MED;IPFV post-ABS cut-HYPOTH

       'That being done, go and cut the posts.'

In example (11), the auxiliary *di* specifies a perfective aspect, and in this context, the aspectual overtones of the suffix *-si* are redundant. In contrast, the auxiliary *henaː* is used for continuing durative action, which is incompatible with the perfective aspect which often corresponds to the clause linker *-si*.

3 Formal aspects of bridging construction in Eibela

In this section the form of bridging constructions in Eibela will be examined and shown to fall into two types: Recapitulative linkage and summary linkage. The general notion of a bridging construction, along with these two sub-types of bridging construction, is thoroughly explained in Guérin & Aiton (2019 [this volume]), and this section will follow the same terminology and conventions except where noted. These notational conventions will include underlining the reference clause and displaying in bold the bridging clause in a bridging construction. This section will include the presentation and definition of key terms and concepts involved in the realization of bridging constructions in Eibela, and the ways in which clause chaining and topical clauses form linking structures in Eibela discourse.

3.1 Overview of bridging constructions

The type of bridging constructions examined in this paper is confined to non-main clauses, including medial and topical clauses, which repeat or summarize a previous element of the discourse (de Vries 2005; 2006; Dixon 2009; Thompson et al. 2007: 382–383). If example (11) is again considered, it is apparent that the topical clause in (11b) is a repetition of the main clause in (11a). In the discussion of these sorts of repetitions, it will be useful to refer to the original clause, as in (11a), as the reference clause, while the repetition, as in (11b), will be referred to as the bridging clause as presented in Chapter 1 of this volume. A reference clause is most often a final main clause, but as seen from the medial clause in (11a), this is not always the case. Additionally, a reference clause need not be a main clause with a verbal predicate, as evidenced by the nominal predicates involved in the bridging constructions in example (6). A bridging clause on the other hand may be either a medial non-main clause, or an embedded topic clause, as seen in the topic clause forming a bridging clause in (11b).

3.2 Recapitulative linkage

The form of the bridging clause may broadly be described as either recapitulation or summarizing. Recapitulative linkage refers to a bridging clause with a predicate which is synonymous or identical to the predicate of the reference clause. In contrast, summary linkage refers to a bridging clause with a generic or anaphoric verb which makes reference to the same event as the reference clause. All of the examples given thus far fall into the category of recapitulation. In these examples, much of the lexical content and argument structure from the reference clause is repeated in the bridging clause, as illustrated in clauses (A6) and (A7) of the Appendix where the predicate and object of the reference clause is repeated in the bridging clause, and only the case-marking and verbal inflection differ.

In addition to very close repetitions of vocabulary like the examples seen in (A6) and (A7) of the Appendix, recapitulative linkage may also include substitutions in the reference clause as described in Guérin & Aiton (2019 [this volume]). This may be due to differing word choices which may slightly alter the proposition by including more or less information than the reference clause, or to the inclusion or exclusion of clause constituents. Of course the bridging clause and the reference clause must by definition describe the same event, but the use of synonyms or the choice to include or exclude certain details may alter the information load of the bridging clause relative to the reference clause.

In instances where a synonym or near synonym is used, the predicates may differ in their precise meaning, and therefore offer differing perspectives on an event. For example, in example (12), the reference clause in (12a) and the bridging clause in (12b) both refer to the same event, namely the act of whittling a strip of vine so that it is thin and smooth and can be used as a fine cord in construction.

(12)   a.   [*sɛːli   gaːlɛ-mɛi*]*final*
             properly shave.thin-HYPOTH

             '(You) should shave it properly'

       b.   **[*sɛli   ɛmɛlɛ-si*]**medial
             properly make.flat-MED;PFV

             'Flatten it properly (by shaving) and then...'

       c.   [[*gaːjɛ-liːː   gaːlɛ   di=jaː*]topic *ɸogono   di-si*]medial
             shave.thin-SIM;DUR shave.thin PFV=TOP other.side PFV-MED;PFV

             'Keep shaving it thin, when it's shaved thin, take the other side, and then...'

       d.   [*mɛːgi ɛna gudɛː-kɛi   ɸiliː-mɛi*]final
             rope   DEM wrap-INST ascend-HYPOTH

             '(You) should wrap the rope going up.'

The reference clause and bridging clause use different verbs to predicate the event however, and in doing so, they each present a different aspect of the action being described. Initially, the verb *gaːlɛ* is used in (12a) and describes the act of whittling or shaving thin strips of material off of an item with a knife. The bridging clause in (12b) then describes the same action, but uses the predicate *ɛmɛlɛ* meaning 'to level' or 'to make flat'. This word choice describes the intention or goal of the event in the bridging clause and complements the description of the method described in the reference clause. In this way, the two clauses taken together present a more complete description of the event than either clause taken on its own. Elements of the reference clause are also routinely omitted in bridging clauses, as noted in Guérin & Aiton (2019 [this volume]). This is not particularly surprising in Eibela since backgrounded arguments are often elided in all Eibela clause types. A given argument is typically elided when it is readily predictable from the context. Additionally, a complex noun phrase in the reference clause may be repeated in a simplified form as in line (A2) of the Appendix where *baːkɛlɛ duna* 'bush turkey nest' is reduced to the simpler form *baːkɛlɛ* 'bush turkey (nest)' in the bridging clause seen in line (3). Elements of a bridging clause are obviously very predictable given their repetitive nature, and omitting arguments, or elements of complex arguments, is simply a means of back-grounding known information which has less prominence within the discourse.

In cases where the reference clause contains a topic, the topic is also omitted from the repetition in the bridging clause, as in examples (A28–A30) of the Appendix. The bridging clause makes reference to only the main clause of this final clause of the clause-chain, and does not repeat the embedded topic *hanɛ sɛja* 'river shore' or the preceding medial clause *henaːnɛgɛː* 'went and...'. In summary, recapitulative linkage is a repetition of lexical elements from the reference clause. These can be exact repetitions of the same lexical items, or may be semantically related terms with the same predicative or argument reference. The repeated bridging clauses are typically reduced relative to the previous reference clause and tend to include only the predicate and highlighted arguments, while less prominent elements are reduced or omitted. The function and motivation for choosing particular clause elements to be repeated in a bridging clause will be further explored in §4.

3.3 Summary linkage

Summary linkage differs from recapitulative linkage in that the predicate of the bridging clause utilizes a generic verb to refer to a preceding event rather than repeated lexical items. In Eibela, this can take several forms, including the light verb *ɛ* 'do', the demonstrative verb *wogu* 'do thus', or the durative auxiliary verb *henaː*. In contrast to recapitulative linkage, the bridging clause in summary linkage is always preceded by a final clause. In recapitulative bridging, the preceding reference clause may be either a final or medial clause. This means that summary linkage in Eibela is always the first part of a new clause chain or complex clause. As with recapitulative linkage, the bridging clause may take the form of either a medial clause or topic clause.

3.3.1 *ɛ* 'do'

The light verb *ɛ* is by far the most common summary linkage strategy. It occurs with a variety of aspectual and conjunctive enclitics, including switch reference, perfectivity, and completion, but without any tense morphology. The reference of ε 'do' is non-specific and general. In (A9) of the Appendix, the topic clause ɛbija 'do' makes reference to the preceding final clause, ɛimɛ o:ɸa a:nɛ 'The sun set'. Bridging clauses formed with ε are commonly medial clauses, as in (13), or topic clauses as in (14). In these cases, the bridging clause is an introductory dependent of a larger complex clause or clause chain. In (13), the summary bridging clause in (13b) forms the initial medial clause of a short chain of three clauses.

(13)   a.   [a:mi   ɛna   bɛ:-ɸɛi]$_{final}$
             DEM;ASSOC DEM;ABS put.on-HYPOTH;COMP

             'Then put it on there.'

       b.   [ɛ di-si]$_{medial}$
             do PFV-MED;PFV

             'Do that and then...'

       c.   [ɛna mɛgi ɛna   adlɛ-lɛ-si]$_{medial}$ [ta:lɛ=ta]$_{final}$
             DEM rope DEM;ABS tie.on-SIM-MED;PFV finish=ATEL

             '...then tie that rope on there and finish.'

Similarly, the non-main clause in (14b) is the topic of the following main clause.

(14)   a.   [usaja ka ja   di]$_{final}$
             NAME FOC came marry

             'Usaja came and married her.'

       b.   [[ɛ=ta-bi=ja:]$_{topic}$ ɛgɛ-ja: ugɛi ɛna   a:mi
             be-ATEL-DS=TOP someone-ABS NAME that;ABS DEM;ASSOC
             mi-ja:-bo]$_{final}$
             come-PST-INFER

             'He was doing that, so this guy, this Ugei came there.'

The main difference between the uses seen in (13b) and (14b) is the scope of the bridging clause's dependency, either as a constituent of a single following main clause, as with the topical function in (14), or a component in a series of medial clauses forming a clause chain as in (13).

3.3.2 wogu 'do thus'

The demonstrative verb wogu (commonly reduced to o or ogu) functions very similarly to the semantically light verb ε with regard to bridging constructions, except that the reference of the demonstrative verb must be a specific event. A reference event is either an exophoric reference (e.g., 'doing that' where the event is in progress and may be seen), or an event described immediately previously. In a bridging role, *wogu* does not present any tense, absolute aspect, mood, or evidentiality morphology, and is limited to clause-linking morphology such as relative aspect, topicalization, and switch reference. This results in a slightly more morphologically deficient predicate than *ɛ*. A prominent semantic difference is that *wogu* is more limited with regard to its scope of reference, whereas *ɛ* may reference an entire discourse episode or state of affairs. For example, in (15) there are multiple instances of *wogu* bridging clauses which specifically reference the immediately preceding clause. Bridging clauses with the demonstrative verb *wogu* may take the form of topic clauses as in (15b), and medial clauses as in (15d) and (15e).

(15) a. *[isa-ja: tila   bu-sa:-bi]ₐₙₐₗ*
        ground-ABS descend impact-VIS;3-DS
        'They continued struggling and fell to the ground.'

    b. *[[wogu-bi=ja:]topic bɛda=nɛgɛ:]medial [a:mi   kolu-wa*
        do.thus-DS=TOP   see=MED;IPFV   DEM;ASSOC man-ABS
        wɛlɛ-sa:-bi]ₐₙₐₗ
        shout-3;VIS-DS
        'They did that and then I saw (Hauwa) call to the men.'

    c. *[dobuwɛ-jo:: ɛ-sa:-bi]ₐₙₐₗ*
        NAME-VOC do-VIS;3-DS
        'He said, "Dubuwe!"'

    d. *[wogu-bi]medial [bɛda-lolu=wa   wa::]final*
        do.thus-DS   see;PST-COMP=TOP wah!
        'He did that and I saw them go "whaa!"'

    e. *[o-si=ki]medial   [ja-bi]final*
        do.thus-MED;PFV=CONT come-DS
        'I did that (saw them) and they came.'

As seen in (15e), and (16b), in topic and medial positions, the two reduced forms of *wogu* (*o* and *ogu*) are commonly used in free alternation.

(16) a. *[gɛ: hɛ:ga-ja: ɛ-sa:]final*
        2;SG how;PST-INTER;NON.PRS say-3;VIS
        'He said "What happened to you?".'

b. *[ogu   bɛda]ₘₑdᵢₐₗ [nɛ ɛnɛbɛ wɛ dɛːja   wɛ kɛi]fᵢₙₐₗ*
   do.thus CONS   1;SG leg   this swollen this ASSER

   'He did (said) that, so (I said) "My leg is swollen, this one."'

This reduction does not occur when *wogu* is used as the main predicate of the clause, and is a prominent feature of topical and medial bridging clauses formed with *wogu*.

3.3.3 *hɛnaː* 'durative'

The durative auxiliary *hɛnaː* may also be used as the predicate of a bridging clause, as shown in (17c). Like *wogu*, there is no tense, aspect, mood, or evidentiality inflection in topic or medial clauses predicated by durative *hɛnaː*. Additionally, the auxiliary *hɛnaː* cannot appear as the final predicate in a final clause.

(17) a. *[ɛimɛ   oga   ɛ   gɛ-mɛna=ta]ₘₑdᵢₐₗ [holo   anɛ-obo]fᵢₙₐₗ*
         already pandanus seedling plant-FUT=ATEL DEM;up go;PST-INFER

         'He had already gone up there to plant pandanus seeds.'

  b. *[[ogu-bi=jaː]ₜₒₚᵢ꜀ nɛ nɛ-ɸɛni   ena ja   di]fᵢₙₐₗ*
     do.thus-DS=TOP 1;SG 1;SG-alone still here PFV

     'He did that, I was still alone here.'

  c. *[[hɛnaː-si=jaː]ₜₒₚᵢ꜀ si-jaː]fᵢₙₐₗ*
     DUR-MED;PFV=TOP move.around-PST

     'That being the case, I was wandering around here.'

Other auxiliaries must be preceded by the dummy verb *ɛ* (e.g., 13b), and the independence of *hɛnaː* as a predicate is unique among auxiliaries. Semantically, *hɛnaː* specifies an ongoing action or continuing state, and originates from a verb meaning 'to go'.

Similarly to *wogu*, in medial clauses *hɛnaː* is often reduced, in this case to *naː*, as shown in (18a).

(18) a. *[ɛ-ɸɛija]ₘₑdᵢₐₗ [naː-si]ₘₑdᵢₐₗ*
     do-PRF   DUR-MED;PFV

     'That had happened and then...'

  b. *[nɛ ɛna hodosu-wɛ=mi]ₘₑdᵢₐₗ*
     1;SG still small-LOC=ASSOC

     'when I was still small...'

This reduction occurs only in bridging constructions such as the example in (18a). The primary difference between ε 'do', *wogu* 'do thus', and *hɛna:* 'continue doing' is a semantic contrast. ε 'do' has no substantive semantic content, and makes reference to an indefinite stretch of preceding discourse while providing a verb stem for clause-linking morphology. *wogu* 'do thus' on the other hand makes definite reference to a specific event which immediately precedes the bridging clause, or is clear from the extra-linguistic context. Finally, *hɛna:* 'continue doing', has a prominent aspectual meaning of durativity, and references a definite immediately preceding event. More on the discourse roles of bridging constructions follows in §4.

4 Discourse functions of bridging constructions

Bridging constructions are found to have several functions within a discourse, including frame-setting, argument tracking, showing temporal relations between clauses, and defining discourse episodes. Generally speaking, these functions revolve around establishing a given frame of reference, and then situating new information within this frame of reference. Prince (1981) presents a relevant discussion in which given entities may be thought of as "hooks" for new information. Thus, the given information therefore provides a sentential anchor for additional information. This anchor provided by the bridging clause may establish information such as a temporal setting, the participants involved, or the relevance of events to one another with regard to reasons, causes, and effects. This information then helps the hearer to integrate the subsequent new information in the broader discourse thereby promoting textual cohesion.

In this analysis, two levels of discourse organization become apparent. A larger series of related events is broken into episodes, while the entire series of related events forms a cohesive unit within a larger discourse. This larger unit will be referred to as the paragraph (corresponding to the idea of a paragraph in Thompson et al. 2007: 372), and the constituent parts will be referred to as episodes. Episodes are made up of one or more clause chains, and the formal realization of these discourse units is the preference for recapitulative linkage at episode boundaries, and summary linkage at paragraph boundaries. The use of bridging constructions in discourse organization to define two levels of discourse is discussed in greater detail in Aiton (2015).

4.1 Discourse organization

Bridging constructions occur at a boundary between discourse episodes. They are a way of reiterating and summarizing the conclusion of a series of events, and then highlighting the relationship of the following episode to the previous events (see de Vries's 2005 discussion of thematic continuity and discontinuity). In Eibela narratives, the identity of these two discourse units is often defined by the type of bridging clause that is used. Accordingly, these distinctions will result in different types of bridging constructions having differing discursive functions. Two representative examples will be discussed in the text below, and additional examples may be seen in the final Appendix of this chapter.

For example, in (19a–19c), there is a significant shift between a description of an event in the distant past, when the speaker burned himself as a child, and a description of the present state of affairs, when the speaker shows the scar that is currently present due to these past events. The summary linkage in (19c) appears at the end of a text, and marks the end of the final paragraph of the narrative, and the beginning of a metatextual commentary on the narrative as a whole rather than a single identifiable reference clause. This transition both marks a shift in temporal reference and highlights the semantic relationship between the paragraphs.

(19) a. *[gulu tila=nɛgɛ:]*$_{medial}$
          knee descend=MED;IPFV

          'This knee was down and then...'

      b. *[dɛ ɛna ka gɛ-ɸɛija]*$_{medial}$
          fire that FOC burn-PRF

          'It was burned on that fire.'

      c. *[ɛ-ɸɛija]*$_{medial}$ *[umoko wɛ da: ko]*$_{final}$
          do-PRF   scar   this exist DEM;PRED

          'That happened and this is the scar.'

      d. *[ɛ-ɸɛija]*$_{medial}$ *[nana la babalɛ do-wa]*$_{final}$
          do-PRF   1;SG;P DEF not.know STAT-PST

          'That happened and I didn't know (about it).'

      e. *[ɛ-ɸɛija]*$_{medial}$ *[ka nɛ ɛja ɛ wa:lɛ bɛda]*$_{medial}$
          do-PERF   FOC 1;SG father 3;SG tell CONS

          'That happened, and my father, he told (me about it) so...'

f. *[nɛ ɛna dɛda]ᶠᵢₙₐₗ*
    1;SG DEM understand;PST
    'I know about that (story).'

While the excerpt in example (19) is not long enough to show the individual episodes in the initial paragraph, a larger example drawn from the Appendix shows a long series of events broken into four discourse episodes which describe three stages of a narrative and a final episode marking the coda of the paragraph. In the first episode beginning line (A17) of the Appendix, the protagonists decide to attack a pig that was unexpectedly encountered. In the second episode, (A18) of the Appendix, the protagonists are attacking the pig without successfully killing it. Then in (A21–A23) of the Appendix the speaker steps into the assault and successfully kills the pig. The bridging clauses in (A18) and (A21) of the Appendix signal a transition between these three distinct episodes in the narrative. Finally, another instance of summary linkage in (A24) of the Appendix references the entire series of events and is followed by a finale of sorts which describes the final result of the entire narrative.

In the lines (A17–A23) of the Appendix, the entire sequence constitutes one paragraph. This paragraph is divided into four episodes in total, with the first three episodes describing the events that occurred, and the final episode providing a summary and result of the whole paragraph. Whereas the bridging constructions in (A18) and (A21) of the Appendix reference only the immediately preceding event, the final example of summary linkage references the entire series of events and comments on the result of the entire paragraph. This shows two levels of discourse organization, which are associated with different types of bridging construction. Individual events form episodes, which are linked to other episodes describing related events by means of recapitulative linkage. A series of episodes linked by recapitulative linkage may then form a paragraph. An instance of summary linkage at the termination of a paragraph may then present a conclusion or commentary, which is presented in relation to the entire series of linked episodes.

The same pattern can be seen in procedural texts, where a series of steps constitute a larger coherent stage in the project. Example (20) is a continuation of the process described in example (12) above in which the speaker is describing the process of making a headdress. The paragraph from (20a) to (20i) describes how to wrap the frame of the headdress in vine cord before inserting feathers into the cord. Each individual step is part of the larger task of wrapping the head dress and inserting feathers into the cord, and the paragraph is brought to a conclusion by the concluding episode in (20h) which is introduced by summary linkage.

(20) a. [*a:mi*   *kowɛ:gɛ-si*]_{medial}   [*ɸili:-mɛi*]_{final}
       PRO;ASSOC weave.together-MED;PFV ascend-HYPOTH
       'Then weave (the strands) going up.'

   b. [*a:nɛ-kɛi*   *go=ta:*]_{medial}
       two-INST meet=TEL
       'The two ends are joined together.'

   c. [[*kowɛ:gɛ-si*   *ɸili:=ja::*]_{topic}   *ta:lɛ=ta:*   *di-si*]_{medial}
       weave.together-MED;PFV ascend=TOP;DUR finish=TEL PFV-MED;PFV
       'Having woven (the strands) together, then that's finished.'

   d. [*a:mi*   *mɛgi no-wa*   *la*   *ga:lɛ-mɛi*]_{final}
       DEM;ASSOC rope another-ABS DEF;ABS shave.thin-HYPOTH
       'Then shave thin another piece of rope.'

   e. [[*mɛgi no=wa*]_{topic}   *abo bu*   *solu-mɛi*]_{final}
       rope   another=TOP bird quill put.in-HYPOTH
       'Then push bird quills into the other rope.'

   f. [[*mɛgi no=wa*   *ga:=ja:*]_{topic}   *la-bi-no*   *di-si*]_{medial}
       rope   another=ABS shave.thin=TOP exist-DS-IRR PFV-MED;PFV
       'The other shaved rope is there, so...'

   g. [*a:mi*   *ɛna*   *bɛ:ɸɛi*]_{final}
       DEM;ASSOC DEM;ABS put.on;HYPOTH
       'Then put it on there.'

   h. [*ɛ di-si*]_{medial} [*ɛna*   *mɛgi ɛna adlɛ-li-si*]_{medial}
       be   PFV-MED;PFV DEM rope DEM;ABS
       [*ta:lɛ=ta*]_{final}
       tie.on-SIM-MED;PFV finish=ATEL
       'That's done, and then tie that rope on there and finish.'

   i. [*no-wa*   *la*   *wogu-mɛi*]_{final}
       other-ABS DEF do.thus-HYPOTH
       'Do the other one like that.'

The final line in (20i) describes a new series of events in the discourse and constitutes a separate and distinct stage in the construction of the head dress. Another detail of note in the extract is that the instances of recapitulation bridging at episode boundaries within the paragraph are not contiguous with the reference clause that they refer to. Instead the bridging clauses seems to precede a paraphrase of the immediately preceding clause. It is possible that the speaker is self-correcting to repeat a clause with the addition of a bridging clause referring to the preceding event for clarity.

The concluding episode of a paragraph, such as (20h), is typically marked by a summary linkage clause utilizing the light verb ɛ, which references the events of the entire paragraph. In some cases, summary linkage can introduce commentary on a much larger discourse unit such as an entire narrative. In (19) a speaker is commenting on a story he has just completed which describes events from his childhood. He is explaining how he came to know the story and the lasting scar that resulted. In this example, the summary linkage clauses in (19c–19e) all reference the entire narrative and offer concluding remarks on the story. Bridging constructions are a way to signal a shift in an episode and perspective, while maintaining a clear sentential link between related episodes.

4.2 Temporal relations

One of the most straightforward functions of bridging constructions is to repeat the reference clause with the addition of a morpheme which specifies relative aspect. These morphemes specify the temporal relationships between the main clause and the bridging clause, and in so doing, specify the temporal relationship between two stretches of discourse. The first example is beginning a new clause chain with a bridging clause consisting of a medial clause using the perfective linker -si, either specifying a completed perfective event, or in conjunction with the simultaneous action suffix -li. When used to describe a completed perfective event, as in (20h), this represents an immediately preceding completed action followed by a subsequent action. When combined with the simultaneous event suffix -li, the bridging clause specifies that the preceding event is still in progress when the following events in the clause chain occur, as in solalisi 'peeling' in line (A7) of the Appendix. When describing an ongoing state rather than a telic event, a bridging clause may present the enclitic =ta, which specifies that the state continues during the following events of the following discourse episode, which is seen in ta: do:ta: 'having crossed' in line (A12) of the Appendix. A final example is the perfect aspect suffix -ɸɛija, which specifies a completed event, the result of which is still relevant to the ensuing discourse, as seen prominently in the bridging clauses in (19c–19e).

4.3 Causal relations

The consequential auxiliary bɛda specifies a consequential relationship rather that a temporal one. In a bridging clause utilizing bɛda, the events of the previous discourse episode are represented as the cause of the subsequent events. For example, in line (A30) of the Appendix, the final event of the previous series of events, i.e., the setting of the sun, is presented as the event which initiates the following series of events, i.e., the decision to leave. Similarly, in line (A21) of the Appendix the event preceding the reference clause, a failed attempt to kill a pig, is presented as the cause of the events following the bridging clause, i.e., another attempt to kill the pig. By adding a consequential auxiliary when making reference to previous summary-linked discourse, the relevance of the reference clause and the previous series of events to the subsequent series of events is made explicit.

4.4 Argument tracking

Another way that bridging constructions situate new information within an on-going discourse is to specify the participants involved. The different-subject morpheme *-bi*, introduced in §1, serves this function by displaying a change in subject. The usage of the different-subject marker differs in function between main clauses and non-main clauses. In main clauses, an unexpected or non-topical subject will also necessitate a different-subject marker, as in (15a) and (15c) where the different-subject marker is used on the predicate of a main clause. In non-main clauses, a different-subject marker specifies that the subject of the non-main clause differs from the following main clause. For example, in line (A9a) of the Appendix the anaphoric form *ɛbija:* also specifies a change in subject, from 'the sun' in the preceding reference clause 'the sun was setting' to the narrator in following clause '(I) finished peeling the *owa:lo* bark'. The excessive and perhaps redundant switch reference marking in (15) may be a way of emphasizing the shift in participant reference and further clarifying the relevant arguments for each clause. In (15), for example, four different participants are referenced, which might contribute to confusion regarding the roles that each person or group in playing in the individual clauses.

5 Summary

To conclude, bridging constructions in Eibela are formed through two syntactic clause-linking strategies, topicalization and clause chaining. These bridging constructions may be further described as either summary linkage, which utilizes one of three different anaphoric verbs to form the bridging clause, or recapitulative linkage, which repeats the lexical material of the reference clause.

Summary linkage using the verb *wogu* 'do thus' or the aspect-marking verb *hɛ-na:* 'continue doing' has definite reference to the immediately preceding reference clause, while the pro-verb *ɛ* 'do' makes indefinite reference to preceding discourse. Recapitulative linkage repeats elements of the reference clause as a non-main bridging clause, but may omit or substitute elements.

Discourse organization is also shown to feature two levels of discourse which coincide with the usage of recapitulative linkage and summary linkage. Individual events form smaller units of discourse, here referred to generically as episodes, which may be combined with related events by means of bridging constructions to form larger units of discourse, here referred to as paragraphs. These two discourse units are formally distinguished in Eibela. At episode boundaries, recapitulative linkage is used to show that a subsequent episode is related to the previous episode, while summary linkage at the end of a series of related episodes may assert that a proposition is relevant to the entire series of episodes rather than only to the immediately preceding event. A similar pattern may be found in the closely related language Kasua, which likewise favors the use of summary linkage at the beginning of a "new thematic paragraph" (Logan 2008: 24).

Bridging constructions may be found with similar form and function in other languages of Papua New Guinea, and the patterns observed in Eibela may represent a general regional trend. Jendraschek (2009) observes that bridging constructions allow for switch reference marking between discourse units that would not otherwise be possible, and therefore contribute to reference tracking in the Iatmul language. He also observes that languages which feature prominent use of bridging constructions generally do not feature a native class of conjunctions, and that bridging constructions may be serving the same functional role of a conjunction in linking independent clauses. This follows from de Vries (2005: 367) and Longacre (2007: 374–375), who argues that languages of Papua New Guinea tend to avoid noun phrases and argument anaphors as a means of referent tracking, and instead rely on verbal morphology and switch reference marking in dependent (or cosubordinate) clauses. Bridging linkage may therefore be a general coordination strategy for those languages which feature rich verbal morphology, and a tendency to use fewer overt arguments in discourse.

Bridging constructions in Eibela provide varying ways of reiterating previous discourse before presenting new information. This can be viewed as form of topic setting, where a frame of reference is established by a bridging clause which then serves as the basis for subsequent events. The frame of reference defined by the bridging clause will therefore define the relevance of the following main clause. In the case of a medial clause functioning as a bridging clause, the frame of reference can be relevant to an entire clause chain. Bridging clauses formed by a topic clause, on the other hand, typically provide a frame of reference for a single following main clause. Finally, this topic setting role may be viewed as a means of assisting in reference tracking through verbal switch reference morphology, and coordinating independent clauses or clause chains in discourse where there is no native class of coordinating conjunctions.

Appendix

This Appendix provides an extended excerpt from a narrative told by Edijobi Hamaja, an adult female speaker of Eibela who resides in Lake Campbell, while she describes a bush walk. Bridging constructions are labeled throughout using the familiar notation of underlined text for reference clauses and bold text for bridging clauses.

(A1) $[[ja:-n\varepsilon:]_{pred}]_{medial}$
come-MED;IPFV
'(I) came and...'

(A2) $[[ba:k\varepsilon l\varepsilon \quad du:na]_o \quad [d\varepsilon la:]_{pred}]_{final}$
bush.turkey nest;ABS dig;PST
'(I) dug into a bush turkey nest.'

(A3) $[[ba:k\varepsilon l\varepsilon]_o \quad [d\varepsilon la:]_{pred}]_{final} [[h\varepsilon na: di-si]_{pred}]_{medial}$
bush.turkey dig;PST   DUR   PFV-MED;PFV
'(I) continued to digging into the bush turkey (nest) and then...'

(A4) $[[tila:]_{pred} [ha:na:]_o \quad [mu:du:]_{pred}]_{final}$
descend water;ABS wash;PST
'(I) went down and washed.'

(A5) $[[[ha:na:]_o [mu:lu:-w\varepsilon:]_{pred}]_x [h\varepsilon na: di-si]_{pred}]_{medial}$
water;ABS wash-LOC   DUR   PFV-MED;PFV
'(I) finished washing and then...'

(A6)   [[ɸili:-nɛ:=ja:]topic [owa:lo-wa:]o [sola: di]pred]final
ascend-PST=TOP tree.type-ABS peel.bark PFV
'(I) went up and peeled bark strips from an owa:lo tree.'

(A7)   [[owa:lo]o [sola:-li:-si]pred]medial
tree.type   peel.bark-SIM-MED;PFV
'While (I) was peeling bark off a owa:lo tree...'

(A8)   [[bɛda:-lo:lu=wa:]topic [ɛimɛ]x [o:ɸa:]s [a:nɛ:]pred]final
see-ASS.EV=TOP   already sun;ABS go;PST
'I saw that the sun was already setting.'

(A9)   a. [ɛ-bi:=ja:]topic [[owa:lo-wa:]o [sola: hɛnɛ di-si=ja:]pred]topic
do-DS=TOP   tree.type-ABS peel.bark DUR PFV-MED;PFV=TOP
'It was doing that, so (I) finished peeling the owa:lo bark and then...'
       b. [[hɛna:]pred [to:golɛ:]x [ɛ:sa: ka:]o [o:gɛ: di]pred]final
go   road;LOC bilum;ABS FOC carry.bilum PFV
'(I) went to the road and picked up my bilum (string bag).'

(A10) [[[o:kɛ]x [dija: ti-nɛ:=ja:]pred]topic [ja:-nɛ:]pred]medial
okay   hold descend-PST=TOP DIR;VEN-MED;IPFV
'(I) was coming down carrying (the bilum) and...'

(A11) [[o:lona:]o [ta:-nɛ:]pred]final
NAME   cross-PST
'I crossed the O:lona:.'

(A12) [[[o:lona:]o [ta: do:-ta:]pred]x [no:lo: ho:no:]pred]final
NAME   cross-TEL STAT-TEL other.side DEM;LVL
'I was on that other side having crossed the O:lona:.'

(A13) [[hɛna::]pred]medial
go;DUR
'We were going and...'

(A14) *[[jɛ:-si dɛnɛ ba:lɛ]ₓ [kɛ:-ja: ka:]ₒ [ho:dɛ-si]ₚᵣₑ𝒹]ₘₑ𝒹ᵢₐₗ*
come-PL PROG COORD pig-ABS FOC bark-MED;PFV
'While we were coming, (the dogs) were barking at a pig and then...'

(A15) *[[[kɛ:-ja:]ₒ [ho:dɛ-bi=ja:]ₚᵣₑ𝒹]ₜₒₚᵢ𝒸 [kali:ja:]ₛ [ɛ-ta:]ₚᵣₑ𝒹]ғᵢₙₐₗ*
pig-ABS   bark-DS=TOP   wallaby do-TEL
'We thought the dogs barking at a pig was (actually) a wallaby.'

(A16) *[[hɛnɛ-si dɛnɛ ba:lɛ]ₓ [kɛ: ka:]ₒ [ho:dɛ=ja: la:-bi:=ja:]ₚᵣₑ𝒹]ₜₒₚᵢ𝒸 [ka:]ₚᵣₑ𝒹*
go-PL   PROG COORD pig FOC bark=TOP exist-DS=TOP   FOC
'While we were going the dogs were there barking at a pig.'

(A17) *[[[kɛ: ɛna:]ₒ   [sobo:.o:no:-kɛi]ₓ [sɛbɛ:na:-ta:]ₚᵣₑ𝒹]ₓ   [ka: hɛnɛ-sa:]ₚᵣₑ𝒹]ғᵢₙₐₗ*
pig   DEM;ABS ax-INST   hit;N.SG.A;PURP-TEL FOC go-PL;PST
'We went to hit that pig with an ax anyway.'

(A18) *[[sobo:.o:no:-kɛi]ₓ [sɛda:-lo:lu]ₚᵣₑ𝒹]ₘₑ𝒹ᵢₐₗ*
ax-INST   hit;N.SG.A-ASS.EV
'In hitting it with the ax...'

(A19) *[[moga:gɛ-li sɛdɛ-si]ₚᵣₑ𝒹]ₘₑ𝒹ᵢₐₗ*
bad-SIM   hit;N.SG.A-MED;PFV
'We hit it badly and then...'

(A20) *[[ɸo:sɛ ki:-jɛ:]ₚᵣₑ𝒹]ғᵢₙₐₗ*
back;LOC bone-LOC
'(It was) on the backbone (that we hit it).'

(A21) *[[ɛ=bɛda:-nɛ:]ₚᵣₑ𝒹]ₘₑ𝒹ᵢₐₗ*
do=CONS-MED;IPFV
'We did that so...'

(A22) [[*mi-jɛː=jaː*]ₜₒₚᵢ𝒸 [*soːboː-kɛi*]ₓ [*jaː   doː-si*]ₚᵣₑ𝒹]ₘₑ𝒹ᵢₐₗ
come-PST=TOP knife-INST DIR;VEN STAT-MED;PFV
'I came there with the knife, and then...'

(A23) [[*kɛː ɛnaː*]ₒ   [*ka: oːlaː*]ₚᵣₑ𝒹]ᶠᵢₙₐₗ
pig DEM;ABS FOC shoot;PST
'I stabbed the pig.'

(A24) [[**le hɛnaː**]ₚᵣₑ𝒹]ₘₑ𝒹ᵢₐₗ
do DUR
'I did that then...'

(A25) [[*kɛː-jaː*]ₛ [*ka: guːduː-saː-bi*]ₚᵣₑ𝒹]ᶠᵢₙₐₗ
pig-ABS FOC die-3;DR-DS
'that pig died.'

(A26) [[**kɛː-jaː**]ₛ [*guːdu: hɛnaː doː-si*]ₚᵣₑ𝒹]ₘₑ𝒹ᵢₐₗ
pig-ABS   die   go   STAT-MED;PFV
'The pig had died, and then...'

(A27) [[*joːla:*]ₚᵣₑ𝒹]ᶠᵢₙₐₗ
butcher;PST
'(We) butchered (it).'

(A28) [[*hɛnaː-nɛ*]ₚᵣₑ𝒹]ₘₑ𝒹ᵢₐₗ
go-MED;IPFV
'We went and...'

(A29) [[*haːnɛ sɛː=jaː*]ₜₒₚᵢ𝒸 [*ka: soːlo: di*]ₚᵣₑ𝒹]ᶠᵢₙₐₗ
river   beach=TOP FOC darken PFV
'It got dark, at the riverside.'

(A30) *[[[soːlo   di=jaː]ₚᵣₑ𝒹]ₜₒₚᵢ𝒸 [bɛdaː=nɛgɛː]ₚᵣₑ𝒹]ₘₑ𝒹ᵢₐₗ*
become.dark PFV=TOP   CONS=MED;IPFV

'It had gotten dark, so...'

(A31) *[[kaː taː=nɛgɛː]ₚᵣₑ𝒹]fᵢₙₐₗ*
FOC cross=MED;IPFV

'We still crossed.'

(A32) *[[haːnɛ waːwi-jaː]ₒ [kaː taːlɛ-si...]ₚᵣₑ𝒹]ₘₑ𝒹ᵢₐₗ*
river   name-ABS FOC cross-MED;PFV

'We crossed the Waːwi river and then...'

Abbreviations

;	portmanteau	DEM	demonstrative	N	not
-	affix boundary	DIR	directional	NEG	negation
=	clitic boundary	DS	different subject	NMLZ	nominaliser
1	1st person	DR	direct	NON	non
2	2nd person	DUR	durative	P	patient
3	3rd person	ERG	ergative	PFV	perfective
A	transitive subject	FOC	focus	PL	plural
ABS	absolutive	FUT	future	PRED	predicative
ASS.EV	associated event	HYPOTH	hypothetical	PRF	perfect
ASSER	assertion	IDEO	ideophone	PROG	progressive
ASSOC	associative	IMP	imperative	PRS	present
ATEL	atelic	INDF	indefinite	PST	past
COMP	complement clause	INFER	inferred	PURP	purposive
		INS	instrumental	SG	singular
COMPL	completive	INTER	interrogative	SIM	simultaneous
CONS	consequence	IPFV	imperfective	STAT	stative
CONT	continuous/ continuative	IRR	irrealis	TOP	topic
		ITER	iterative	UP	higher elevation
CONTR	contrastive	LOC	locative	VEN	venitive
COORD	coordinator	LVL	same elevation		
DEF	definite	MED	medial		

Acknowledgements

The author wishes to thank the participants of a two-day workshop entitled *Bridging Linkage in Cross-linguistic Perspective* that was organized by Valérie Guérin and Simon Overall at the Cairns Institute (James Cook University, Australia), on 25–26 February 2015. Without the organization of this workshop and the insightful comments of its participants, this chapter would not have been written. Additional comments from two anonymous reviewers and the editor, Valérie Guérin, were greatly appreciated and substantially improved the quality of this publication.

References

Aiton, Grant. 2014. Grammatical relations and information structure in Eibela: A typological perspective. *Language and Linguistics in Melanesia* 32. 1–25.

Aiton, Grant. 2015. Repetition and anaphora as a cohesive device in in Eibela discourse. *Language and Linguistics in Melanesia* 33(2). 35–44.

Aiton, Grant. 2016. *The documentation of Eibela: An archive of Eibela language materials from the Bosavi region (Western Province, Papua New Guinea)*. London: SOAS, Endangered Languages Archive. https://elar.soas.ac.uk/Collection/MPI1013856, accessed 2018-8-19.

de Vries, Lourens. 2005. Towards a typology of tail-head linkage in Papuan languages. *Studies in Language* 29(2). 363–384.

de Vries, Lourens. 2006. Areal pragmatics of New Guinea: Thematization, distribution and recapitulative linkage in Papuan narratives. *Journal of Pragmatics* 38(6). 811–828.

Dixon, R. M. W. 2009. The semantics of clause linking in typological perspective. In R. M. W. Dixon & Alexandra Y. Aikhenvald (eds.), *The semantics of clause linking*, 1–55. Oxford: Oxford University Press.

Evans, N. J. 2012. Insubordination and its uses. In Irina Nikolaeva (ed.), *Finiteness: Theoretical and empirical foundations*, 366–431. Oxford: Oxford University Press.

Guérin, Valérie & Grant Aiton. 2019. Bridging constructions in typological perspective. In Valérie Guérin (ed.), *Bridging constructions*, 1–44. Berlin: Language Science Press. DOI:10.5281/zenodo.2563678

Haiman, John. 1978. Conditionals are topics. *Language* 54(3). 564–589.

Haiman, John. 1983. On some origins of switch-reference marking. In John Haiman & Pamela Munro (eds.), *Switch reference and universal grammar*, 105–128. Amsterdam: John Benjamins.

Jendraschek, Gerd. 2009. Switch-reference constructions in Iatmul: Forms, functions, and development. *Lingua* 119(9). 1316–1339.

Logan, Tommy. 2008. *Kasua sketch grammar.* Ukarumpa, PNG: SIL. http://www-01.sil.org/pacific/png/abstract.asp?id=50999, accessed 2018-8-10.

Longacre, Robert E. 2007. Sentences as combinations of clauses. In Timothy Shopen (ed.), *Language typology and syntactic description: Complex constructions*, vol. 2, 372–420. Cambridge: Cambridge University Press.

Prince, Ellen. 1981. Towards a taxonomy of given-new information. In Peter Cole (ed.), *Radical pragmatics*, 223–256. New York: Academic Press.

Shaw, Daniel. 1986. The Bosavi language family. *Papers in New Guinea linguistics* 24. 45–76.

Thompson, Sandra A., Robert E. Longacre & Shin Ja J. Hwang. 2007. Adverbial clauses. In Timothy Shopen (ed.), *Language typology and syntactic description: Complex constructions*, vol. 2, 237–300. Cambridge: Cambridge University Press.

Van Valin Jr, Robert D. 1984. A typology of syntactic relations in clause linkage. *Proceedings of the tenth annual meeting of the Berkeley Linguistics Society.* 542–558.

Voorhoeve, Clemens L. 1968. The central and South New Guinea Phylum: A report on the language situation in south New Guinea. *Pacific Linguistics A. Occasional Papers* 16. 1–17.

Wurm, Stephen A. 1978. *New Guinea phylum of languages* (Pacific Linguistics D11). Canberra: Australian National University.

Chapter 7

Online and offline bridging constructions in Korowai

Lourens de Vries

Vrije Universiteit Amsterdam

Korowai has two main types of bridging constructions, recapitulative linkage (also known as "tail-head linkage") and summary linkage with generic verbs of doing, each with two subtypes that follow from the grammatical distinction between chained and adverbial or thematic types of clause combining. Recapitulative linkage with chained, switch reference marked clauses is by the far the most frequent type of bridging construction. It has three functions. First, a processual function, to give the speaker and addressee a processing pause in between two often lengthy clause chains. Second, it creates chains of clause chains, so called chaining paragraphs. The third function is to enable the speaker to continue referential tracking in the transition from one clause chain to the next. Recapitulative linkage with thematic subordinate clauses shares the processual function wih the chained type but it signals discourse discontinuity: it disrupts the event and participant lines and the speaker goes off the event line. Summary linkage allows speakers to be less specific in the scope of their anaphoric linkage, not necessarily taking the final clause of the previous sentence as their reference clause.

1 Introduction

Korowai is a Papuan language of the Greater Awyu family spoken by around 4000 persons in the area between the upper Becking and Eilanden Rivers and east of the headwaters of the Becking River in Indonesian West Papua, in the Boven-Digul regency (van Enk & de Vries 1997; de Vries et al. 2012). Korowai is a synthetic language, with agglutinating morphology and some fusion. Verb morphology is suffixing, but Korowai has a negation circumfix. Verbal affixes mark mood, modality, tense, aspect, negation, person and number of the subject

Lourens de Vries. 2019. Online and offline bridging constructions in Korowai. In Valérie Guérin (ed.), *Bridging constructions*, 185–206. Berlin: Language Science Press. DOI:10.5281/zenodo.2563690

(S and A) and switch reference. The opposition Realis and Irrealis is central to the verb system, and tense is dependent on the Realis and Irrealis distinction, as in all Greater Awyu languages (Wester 2009). Korowai nouns have little morphology. Nouns may take possessive prefixes. Only kinship nouns have plural suffixes.

To understand Korowai bridging constructions and some of the grammatical terminology used in Papuan linguistics, it is crucial to introduce three major Korowai clause linkage patterns, conjoining, adverbial clause combining and chaining. The first two types are cross-linguistically common; the last type, clause chaining, occurs in many Papuan language families (especially in the cluster of families called the Trans New Guinea group) but is cross-linguistically less common. Conjoining of clauses (asyndetic or with coordinating conjunctions) is a relatively infrequent type of clause linkage (compared to clause chaining) in Korowai. Conjoining linkage joins two independent clauses of equal syntactic status, as in (1):

(1) *if-e=xa   abül=efè xoŋgél=xayan waf-e=xa   abül=efè*
     this-TR=CONN man=TOP big=very   that-TR=CONN man=TOP
     be-xoŋgé-tebo-da
     NEG-big-be[NON1.SG.RLS]-NEG

     'This man is bigger than that man.' (lit. 'This man is very big, that man is not big.') (van Enk & de Vries 1997: 71)

When coordinating conjunctions are absent, as in (1), it is only the intonational integration of the two member clauses under a joint contour that distinguishes a single conjoined sentence from two juxtaposed sentences.

Adverbial clause combining, with various subtypes, occurs when a clause functions as a peripheral argument of another clause or when a clause functions as an extra-clausal theme that precedes a clause with which it has a pragmatic relation of relevance. Adverbial (or better: thematic) clauses are marked by the general subordinator *=xa* and present information that the speaker wants the addressee to take for granted, as the given theme for the following assertion. The semantic function of the thematic clause may be explicitly marked as in (11b) but is often left implicit. The informational status of the theme clause is optionally but frequently marked by the topic clitic *=efè* (with allomorphs *=fefè* and *=fè*). There is an example of a thematic clause in (2) *bul-mexo=xa=fefè* 'given that he slaughtered'. The term theme is used here in the sense of Heeschen (1998) to denote thematization strategies found in many Papuan languages where thematic noun phrases or thematic clauses are marked in a loose sense as relevant domains or themes for the information that follows (de Vries 2006: 814–816).

(2) *Faül dadü-ai=to=fexo*   *Faül ül-nè*
Faül swim-go.down[NON1.SG.RLS]=DS=CONN Faül kill-ss
bul-mexo=xa=fefè   *Faül ba-nggolol yaüya=pé fe-nè*
slaughter-do[NON1.SG.RLS]=CONN=TOP Faül chest-bone under=LOC get-ss
fu=to=fexo   *méan dadü-ai*   *méan*
put[NON1.SG.RLS]=DS=CONN dog   swim-go.down[NON1.SG.RLS] dog
ül-nè bul-fo=xa=fè
kill-ss slaughter-make[NON1.SG.RLS]=conn=top
méan-manop-yabén=tompexo di-béa-mo=daxu   *i=fexo*
dog-chest-fat=EMPH   get.out-rub-do[NON1.SG.RLS]=ss here=at
wolaxip wolaxif=exa Faül müfe-xolol di
heaven heaven=CONN Faül back-bone cut.ss
lamé-abo-lu
dance-chase-move.up[NON1.SG.RLS]
'Faül came swimming downstream, after having killed and slaughtered
Faül, he put its chest bone part beneath, and its back bone part he placed
towards the sky and having killed and butchered a dog that came
swimming downstream, he cut out the fat of the dog's chest and greased
the back bone part of Faül and he chased it upward in a hurry.' (van Enk
& de Vries 1997: 165)

Clause chaining combines switch reference marked clauses into often long
sentences (called clause chains in Papuan linguistics) that end in a final clause
with an independent verb form. That verb in the final clause of the chain has
tense and mood scope over the preceding sentence. In canonical clause chaining
languages of New Guinea, the verb types used in the final clauses are different
from the verb types used in non-final or medial clauses. On the one hand, medial
verb types cannot express the full range of tense, mood, person and number distinctions that final verbs encode, on the other hand medial verbs have slots for
categories of interclausal relations absent in final verbs, namely switch reference
(Same Subject – ss – or Different Subject – DS – in next clause of the chain) and
temporality (Sequence versus Simultaneity relations between the events of two
adjacent clauses in the chain).

Like other Greater Awyu languages, Korowai is a non-canonical chaining language compared to many other languages of the Trans New Guinea type because
its dedicated medial verb morphology is weakly developed (de Vries 2010). The
only dedicated medial verb type is the Same Subject verb that consists of a verb
stem plus an optional Same Subject suffix. There are also no dedicated Different Subject medial verbs in Korowai as found in more canonical Papuan clause

chaining languages. Instead, Korowai uses clauses with fully inflected independent verbs (the type that must be used in the final clauses of sentences) with
switch reference clitics. This is the set of switch reference conjunctions in Korowai (van Enk & de Vries 1997: 109):

=do(n) 'different subject'

=daxu(l) 'same subject'

=aŋgu 'same subject/intentional'

=(le)lexu 'different subject/irrealis/anteriority'

Chaining is by far the most used type of clause linkage in the Korowai texts available to us and chained clauses are strongly associated with thematic continuity
within a clause chain.

Thematic adverbial clauses are associated with discontinuity, when speakers discontinue the flow of the main event and participant lines, either within
a sentence, or in the transition from one sentence to another, for special reasons: to present background information, to mention circumstances that formed
the cause or reason for an event of the main line, or to start a new paragraph
(Farr 1999: 337, 363; de Vries 2005: 373). A typical Korowai clause chain, as in
(2), contains switch reference marked chained clauses, with medial verbs (for example *ül-nè*) and with switch reference marked independent verb forms (*dadü-
ai=tofexo*). The final clause of the clause chain (2) contains the independent verb
lamé-abo-lu. Within sentence (2), we find two thematic clauses *bul-fo=xa=fè* and
bul-mexo=xa=fefè. They are not switch reference marked but they are marked for
their informational role as themes by the topic marker *=(fe)fè*. The event line of
(2) is twice disrupted by these thematic clauses. The idiomatic translation of the
first thematic clause reads 'after he had slaughtered' but the semantic functions
that thematic clauses have (temporal, locative and so on) are usually left to be
contextually inferred, and this is also the case in (2). A translation closer to the
sense of the first thematic clause in (2) would be 'given that he slaughtered'.

Such generic thematic clauses are very versatile in terms of the wide range
of interpretations that addressees may contextually infer. Thematic clause combining occurs in many Papuan languages with similar functions and may often
be translated idiomatically with adverbial or relative clauses in English (Haiman
1978; Reesink 2000; Heeschen 1998; Foley 1986: 201). Consider example (3):

(3) *Wa gol ülme-tél=exa=fè*   *noxu-gol*
     that pig kill-NON1.PL[RLS]=CONN=TOP our-pig
     'The pig that they killed, is our pig.' ('given that they killed the pig, it is
     our pig').

If the assertion had been 'we are angry' instead of *noxu-gol* 'our pig', the interpretation would have been 'because they killed the pig, we are angry' (de Vries
2006: 826). Korowai has two main types of bridging constructions, recapitulative linkage (§2) and summary linkage (§3). Both types each have two subtypes
that follow from the two types of clause linkage illustrated in (2) and (3), switch
reference marked chaining linkage and *=xa* marked thematic subordinate linkage. The terms bridging constructions, recapitulative linkage, summary linkage,
reference clause and bridging clause are used in this article as defined in the
introductory chapter of this volume.

2 Recapitulative linkage

There are two subtypes of recapitulative linkage (formerly, tail-head linkage) in
Korowai (de Vries 2005: 372–374). In the first type the bridging clause takes the
form of a switch reference marked chained clause. The bridging clause of the second type is a thematic clause marked with the clitic *=xa* and optionally marked
by the topic marker *=(fe)fè*.

2.1 Recapitulative linkage with chained clauses

Recapitulative linkage with switch reference marked bridging clauses is by far
the most common type of linkage of sentences in Korowai texts. Korowai speakers have a general tendency to prefer minimal clauses, preferably just a verb,
and not to allow more than one argument (whether core or peripheral) to be explicitly expressed by noun phrases or pronouns, a tendency also found in many
other oral languages of New Guinea and elsewhere (Foley 2000; Du Bois 1987).
The preference for minimal clauses is not a grammatical constraint. Speakers
can produce clauses with more than one overt argument and with complex noun
phrases but they do so in specific contexts, for example introductory paragraphs
of stories (de Vries 2005: 369).

Final clauses of sentences are also minimal clauses in most cases and this
means that the reference clause usually has the form [(XP) V]. The same tendency towards minimal clauses also constrains recapitulative linkage with switch
reference marked clauses in terms of what is repeated, omitted or added in the

bridging clause. As a general rule, bridging clauses in recapitulative linkage conform to the [(XP) V] minimal clause constraint and therefore they either repeat the lexical verb and its single overt (core or peripheral) argument or they omit the single argument, repeating just the lexical verb of the reference clause. When speakers choose to repeat arguments in the bridging clause, they probably do that to increase the redundancy of bridging clauses in order to enhance the processual function of bridging, as a badly needed pause or break between two lengthy clause chains packed with information. The presence of pause and hesitation markers, silences after the bridging clause and reduction of the number of syllables per second, all confirm this processual function. Adding arguments to the bridging clause that do not occur in the reference clause does not occur so far in the data available to us.

The text of (4), a small section from a story published in van Enk & de Vries (1997), consists of three sentences, each linked to the next one with recapitulative linkage of the chained type, creating a chain of sentences. The bridging clause in (4d) repeats the reference clause in (4c) including its single (peripheral) argument *melil=an* 'in the fire'. But the single core argument of the reference clause (4d), the object *ye=wafil* 'her husband', is omitted in the bridging clause (4e). By repeating the verb of the final clause of (4a), the reference clause, as the switch reference marked verb of the bridging clause, the switch reference tracking of the two given male participants is continued across the chain boundary between (4a) and (4b). This enables the Korowai listener to identify and keep track of the two male subject referents, the husband and the killer: the husband (he$_i$) is doing the sleeping and the DS marking on the sleep verb *élo-bo=do* signals to the listener that the next verb has a different subject referent, inferred to be the killer (he$_j$)

(4) a. *i   lal   xafén-telo-bo   i   wafil*
         this woman awake-be-stay[NON1.SG.RLS] this man
         élo-bo
         sleep-stay[NON1.SG.RLS]

         'the wife stayed awake, the husband was asleep.'

     b. *élo-bo=do   ül-mexo   duol-mo*
         sleep-stay[NON1.SG.RLS]=DS shoot-do[SS] put.into-do[NON1.SG.RLS]
         'He$_i$. (the husband) was asleep and he$_j$. (the killer, lover of his wife) shot him$_i$.'

     c. *ül-mexo   duol-mo=to=fexo*
         shoot-do[SS] put.into-do[NON1.SG.RLS]=DS=CONN

> *gebelipexo=daxu*   *melil=an felé*
> start.from.sleep[NON1.SG.RLS]=SS fire=LOC fall[NON1.SG.RLS]
> 'He$_i$ started from sleep and fell into the fireplace.'

d. ***melil=an felé=to=fexo***   *i*   *la=to*   *ye-wafil*
fire=LOC   fall[NON1.SG.RLS]=DS=CONN this female=FOC her-husband
atilo
hold[NON1.SG.RLS]
'He fell into the fireplace and the woman held her husband down.'

e. ***atilo=dom=pexo***   *lelip*   *ati-ba-té=daxu*
hold[NON1.SG.RLS]=DS=CONN together hold-stay-NON1.PL[RLS]=SS
ül-me-té=daxu   *mintafi*   *laifa-té=daxu*
kill-do-NON1.PL[RLS]=SS valuables get.out-NON1.PL[RLS]=SS
bando-ai=lo=fexo   *fe-nè*
carry-move.down[NON1.SG.RLS]=IDS=CONN take-SS
fe-té=daxu   *lu*   *xaim*   *melil dimexe-té*
put-NON1.PL[RLS]=SS move.up treehouse fire   set-NON1.PL[RLS]
'She held him down, and together they held him down and killed him and carried the wealth items down (the tree house stairs) and put them there (on the ground) and climbed (back) up and set the tree house on fire.' (van Enk & de Vries 1997: 208–209)

The reference clause is in the majority of cases the final clause of the previous sentence but speakers regularly recapitulate the last two clauses of the chain, as in the two chained bridging clauses of (5b).

(5) a. *gexené gufe-tin-da*   *gexené belén-è*
2PL   demand.compensation-NON1.PL.IRR-NEG 2PL   NEG.IMP-EX
dé=xa   *lexé* *é*   *lenggilé-té=daxu*
say[NON1.SG.RLS]=CONN reason pause be.frightened-NON1.PL[RLS]=SS
yaxati-mexe-té
renounce-do-NON1.PL[RLS]
'Because he said "you must not demand compensation payments, don't you do that", they became frightened and revoked (their claims)'

b. ***lenggilé-té=daxu***   *yaxati-mexe-té=do*   *è*
be.frightened-NON1.PL.RLS=SS renounce-do-NON1.PL[RLS]=DS PAUSE
babo=fexo   *ye-pa fe-nè fo=daxu*
sit[NON1.SG.RLS]=CONN he-self take-SS take[NON1.SG.RLS]=SS
'They were frightened and renounced and..uh...he stayed until he himself married (another woman) and...'

The bridging clause is always the first clause of the sentence that it is part of. But the reference clause in recapitulative linkage occasionally is not the final clause of the previous chain but another clause that precedes the final clause, as in (6). The bridging clause of (6b) repeats the penultimate clause of the sentence (6a), *ébo-do*, and the final clause *nu be-ba-lé* is not chosen as the reference clause for the bridging clause in (6b).

(6) a. *xomboxai dé=do*   *éba-té=do*
      all.right   say[NON1.SG.RLS]=DS sleep-NON1.PL[RLS]=DS
      éba-té=do   *ébo=do*   *nu be-ba-lé*
      sleep-NON1.PL[RLS]=DS sleep[NON1.SG.RLS]=DS 1SG sit-be-1SG[RLS]
      'She agreed and they slept, they slept and he slept and I sat down.'

    b. ***ébo=do***   *ülmexo-ülmexo-ma-té*
      sleep.NON1.SG.RLS=DS shoot-shoot-iter-NON1.PL[RLS]
      'He slept and they gave him several injections.'

From a typological perspective Korowai recapitulative linkage with switch reference marked bridging clauses has an interesting feature: it is not restricted to reference clauses with declarative mood (as in other languages with recapitulative linkage). In a clause chain, all clauses are under the mood, modality and tense scope of the verb of the final clause: for example in (7a) the medial verb *bando-xe-nè* receives an imperative reading under the scope of the imperative verb in the final clause. The following text in (7) shows how imperative final clauses are recapitulated in imperative bridging clauses:

(7) a. *wof-e=xa*   *mbolow=è*   *ge-mba-mbam=pexo*   *if-e=xa*
      there-TR=CONN ancestor=VOC your-child-child=CONN this-tr=CONN
      bando-xe-nè *lé-m=é*
      bring-go-SS eat-IMP.2SG=EX
      'Oh forefather over there, with your children, you should take this and eat it!'

    b. ***lé-m=daxu***   *noxup dél=o*   *füon=o*
      eat-IMP.2SG=SS 1PL   bird=COORD marsupial.species=COORD
      gol=o   *fédo-m=do*   *le-fén=è*
      pig-COORD give-IMP.2SG=DS eat-IMP.1PL=EX
      'Eat and give birds and marsupials and pigs for us to eat!'

c. *damol fo   fe-nè fu   woto=fexa   mbolo=fexo*
   back   get[ss] get-ss put[ss] sacred.place=one grandfather=CONN
   ge-mambüm=pexo   ge-yano=fexo   ge-ni-xül=fexo
   your-children=CONN your-people=CONN your-wife-PL=CONN
   if-e=xa   bando-xe-nè le-mén=é
   here-TR=CONN bring-go-ss eat-IMP.2PL=EX

   'And having put down the back part (of the sacrificial pig) (they say),
   "hey, you forefather of that certain sacred place, with your children,
   your people and your wives, you should take this and eat it!"'

d. *le-mén=daxu [noxu lép-telo-xai=xa]*   *noxu*
   eat-2PL:IMP=SS 1PL   ill-be[NON1SG]-IRR=CONN 1PL
   mano-pa-mon=do   xi-telo-fon=è
   good-CAUS-IMP.2PL=DS healthy-be-IMP.1PL=EX

   'You must eat it and if we fall ill, cure us and let us be healthy.'
   (van Enk & de Vries 1997: 159–162)

The exclamative vowel clitic =è (that strengthens the appellative force of directive speech acts) is not repeated in the bridging clause. Imperative and hortative
bridging clauses also occur in other Greater Awyu languages, for example in
Mandobo in (8):

(8) Mandobo (Greater Awyu)

   a. *Mene mbo urumo e-gen   doro, igia kondep men*
      this TOP little be-RLS[NON1SG] CONN, again another give.IMP
      do   makmo to   agöp ke-n   do   timo-p
      CONN add   CONN much be-[IRR]NON1SG CONN receive-[IRR]1SG

      'This is too little, again give me more, add (until) it is much and let me
      receive it.'

   b. *Timo-p   to   kare   e-gen   do,   imban*
      receive-[IRR]1SG CONN, enough be-RLS[NON1SG] CONN, tooth
      keremo-n   o,   u   mene ande-p.
      become-NON1.SG.IRR CONN pig this eat-1SG.IRR

      'Let me receive it, it will be enough, the teeth will be enough to eat
      this pig with.'

Recapitulative linkage with switch reference marked bridging clauses has
three main functions. The first is referential participant cohesion: it continues the
switch reference monitoring of subject referents from one sentence to the next.

Second, it creates discourse units of a type called "chaining paragraphs" by Farr (1999: 337–341): a chain of clause chains held together by recapitulative bridging constructions with chained bridging clauses. Consider example (9) from a text published by van Enk & de Vries (1997: 159–162), with three sentences, linked by recapitulative linkage in its chained form, creating a chaining paragraph, with internal thematic unity.

(9) a. *Wof=è   gol ül-ma-té=daxu   bando-lu*
there=CONN pig kill-do-[RLS]NON1.PL=SS bring-enter[SS]
xaim=an   fe-nè fu   bume-ma-té
treehouse=LOC get-SS put[SS] slaughter-HAB-NON1.PL[RLS]

'After they have killed a pig there, they use to bring it to the tree house and slaughter it.'

b. **Bume-ma-té=daxu**   *ol   di   fe-nè*
slaughter-HAB-[RLS]NON1.PL=SS intestines get.out[SS] take-SS
fu-ma-té=do   ni-xü=to   bando-xe-nè
put-HAB-NON1.PL[RLS]=DS mother-PL=FOC bring-go-SS
ao-ma-té
cleanse-HAB-NON1.PL[RLS]

'They slaughter it and remove the intestines and put it down and the women take (the intestines) and cleanse them.'

c. **Ao-leful-mexo**   *xaim   gilfo-ma-té=do*
cleanse-end-do[SS] treehouse go.away-HAB-NON1.PL[RLS]=DS
gol-e-xal   di-fu-ma-té
pig-TR-meat cut-put-HAB-NON1.PL[RLS]

'When they have finished washing, they go away to the treehouse and (the males) cut the pig meat out and put it down.'

Chaining paragraphs are found in the main body of narrative texts after the main participants, time and place frames and the main topic of the story have been introduced in the first "thematic" paragraph(s) (de Vries 2005: 369). These initial paragraphs tend to lack recapitulative linkage of the chained type and tend to contain relatively many thematic noun phrases and thematic clauses. In contrast, chaining paragraphs are highly "verby", and consist of a number of (often long) clause chains, with each clause chain connected to the next by recapitulative chained bridging clauses. The third function of recapitulative linkage is processual: the verbatim repetition of information creates redundancy and temporarily lowers the amount of information being communicated. Although repetition in general may have all sorts of functions in discourse (emphasis, aesthetic enhancement, mnemonic functions), the repetition in the context of recapitulative bridging constructions has a processual function: it gives a pause and a slowdown of the information flow (iconically reflected in a reduction of speed of speaking in the bridging clause). The final clause of a sentence, the reference clause of the bridging construction, has a falling intonation, with especially the last words receiving a very low pitch. This final low pitch contour is followed by a pause and then the bridging clause starts with a high pitch over the first words. This creates an intonational low-high pitch contrast between reference clause and bridging clause, as in Figure 1. Figure 1 is a simple PRAAT graph of the pitch contours of the reference and bridging clauses used in the recapitulative linkage of (10a) and (10b). Towards the end of the reference clause there is a sharp fall in pitch, followed by a pause. The bridging clause then starts at a much higher pitch, and this pitch contrast before and after a pause is characteristic for bridging constructions.

(10) a. *nu na=xa   nu ne-yanop   nu na=xa*
          1SG 1SG=CONN 1SG 1SG.POSS-person 1SG 1SG=CONN
          lexeli-bando-xa-xe-le   de-lé
          open-carry-go-IRR-1SG say-1SG
          'he is mine, he belongs to me, let me cut his ties and take him with me, I said'

     b. *na=xa   lexeli-bando-xa-xe-lé de-lé=lo=fexo   tidak gu*
          1SG=CONN open-carry-go-IRR-1SG say-1SG=DS=CONN NEG 2SG
          be-lexeli-bando-xa-in-da
          NEG-open-carry-go-IRR-2SG-NEG
          'what is mine I will unbind and take with me, I said but (they said), no, you are not taking him away'

The narrator, Sapuru, tells a real-life first person narrative about how he tried to cut loose a captured person that his opponents wanted to kill and eat. In (10b) he narrates what he told his opponents and in (10b) the final clause (with the quote-marking verb *de* 'to say') is repeated in the bridging clause, but now there is a DS conjunction attached to the quote-marking verb, to indicate that what follows is the reply from the opponents (what they said). The bridging clause also includes the last clause of the quotation clause.

The very fact that the chain-final reference clause is repeated in the initial clause of the next chain implies that the repeated information is now given and in this sense in the background, just as this is the case in recapitulative linkage with thematic clauses (discussed in the next section). But the key difference

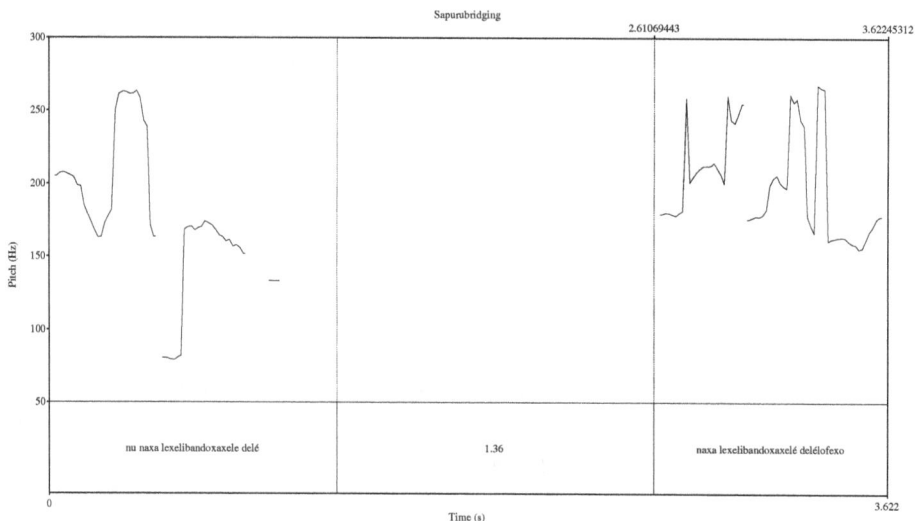

Figure 1: Intonation contour of example (10) extracted with PRAAT.

between the two types of recapitulation is that the chained bridging clause is informationally and syntactically an "online" clause that presents given information, while thematic bridging clauses are "offline" background clauses. The on line nature of chained bridging clauses makes this linkage type one of thematic continuity, both referentially through the continued switch reference monitoring of topical participants and in terms of sequential action continuity (the event line).

2.2 Recapitulative linkage with thematic clauses

This type is a less frequent type of recapitulative linkage in which the bridging clause takes the form of a thematic clause, marked with the subordinator *=xa* (and/or other subordinators), and optionally marked by the topic marker *=(f)efè*. It has two functions. The first function is the processual pause function that it shares with recapitulative linkage with chained bridging clauses.

The second function is to present the repeated information as an *offline* theme, a theme off the continuing event and participants line. The break in thematic continuity with the preceding clause chain is signaled by the discontinuation of switch reference monitoring and the obligatory presence of an independent verb form with TAM specification that is not under the scope of the TAM marking on the verb of the final clause. In contrast, a chained bridging clause presents the repeated clause as *online* information integrated into the continuing event and participant lines. The chained bridging clause cannot be marked by a subordinator or the topic marker =(f)efè. The continuing event and participant lines are carried over the boundary between two consecutive clause chains by obligatory switch reference marking on the repeated verb in the chained bridging clause. In other words, chained bridging clauses form chaining paragraphs, but thematic bridging clauses disrupt and discontinue chaining paragraphs for various purposes, for example because the speaker wants to add important background information or wants to specify a reason why an event on the main event line happened, as in (11b).

Thematic subordinate clauses in Greater Awyu languages behave like noun phrases, and they may take markers that also go with noun phrases to express semantic or pragmatic relations, for example the general subordinator =xa, the reason marker *lexé* that marks the bridging clause of (11b) or the topic marker =(f)efè. It is this noun phrase characteristic that explains the association with disruption or "going offline" when thematic clauses are used as bridging clauses: the events they denote are not part of the main event line expressed by chained clauses.

(11)   a.   *ü   dé=tofexo   a gu ü   du-n-da   gu-pa*
            Ow! say[NON1.SG.RLS]=DS ah you ow! say-INF-NEG you-also

            ü-axa-lé   dé
            kill-IRR-1SG say[NON1.SG.RLS]

            'Ow, he_i said and he_j said, ah you must not say, ow, I will kill you also'

      b.   *dé=xa   lexé lenggilé=daxu*
            say[NON1.SG.RLS]=CONN cause be.frightened[NON1.SG.RLS]=SS

            yaxatimexo
            renounce[NON1.SG.RLS]

            'Because he_j said that, he_i was afraid and renounced'

Compare the recapitulative linkage with thematic subordinate bridging in (11b) and with chained bridging in (12b), both involving the same verb of speaking *de* 'to say'. In (12b) the verb of speaking of the reference clause is repeated in a chained switch reference marked bridging clause, a bridging clause on the continuing event line. But in (11b) the same verb is repeated in a subordinate bridging clause, an offline clause that provides background information with regard to the event line. The switch reference monitoring of participants is carried across the boundary between (12a) and (12b). The chains (12a) and (12b) are chained into a chaining paragraph in which switch reference helps the listener to identify who is doing what from one sentence to the other. But this switch reference monitoring is disrupted by the subordinate bridging clause of (11b) and the listener has to identify the referents of the subjects solely on the basis of the context.

(12) a. *le-bo=to=fexo*   *nggé nabul*   *nu ne-banun*
come-be[NON1.SG.RLS]=DS=CONN friend brother.in.law 1SG my-back

     bimo-m   <u>*dé*</u>
     look-2SG.IMP say.NON1.SG.RLS

     'He came and said, Friend, brother-in-law, you must have a look at my back'

b. **dé=do**   *a ati woxelimexo=do*   *ü yi-pa*
Say[NON1.SG.RLS]=DS ah hold turn[NON1.SG.RLS]=DS ow 3SG-self

     xayo baosa-m-bo   *mé-lai*
     arrow pierce-do-be[NON1.SG.RLS] move-come[NON1.SG.RLS]

     'He said, and as they turned him around, Ow, my!, he had come pierced with arrows!'

3 Summary linkage

There are two types of summary linkage of sentences. Both are used only occasionally. The first is with a demonstrative verb *(w)amo(l)-* 'to do/to be that/thus/in that way' in a chained bridging clause, as in (16b). The second type, rare in our texts, is with the same demonstrative verb but now in a *=xa* marked thematic clause, (18b). The demonstrative verb may also be used in other contexts as in (13) and (14).

(13) *yaxof-exa=lo*   *wof=exa*   *a-mo-mémo?*
who-CONN=FOC that=CONN that-do-IMM[NON1.SG.RLS]
'Who just did that?'

(14) *mülalüp nu-pa amo-ba-lé*
formerly I-self do.thus-PFV-1SG[RLS]
'I myself have done things like that in former times'

    The demonstrative verb *(w)amo(l)-* is used both to link sentences and to link clauses within sentences (as in (15), *wa-mo-nè*), but the latter use is much more frequent than the use as bridging clauses in summary linkage, (16b). For example, the ss medial form of the verb *wamonè* is used to link clauses within the sentence in (15):

(15) *dé=daxu=fexo*   *n-até=lo*   *wa-mo-nè*
say[NON1.SG.RLS]=SS=CONN 1SG.POSS-father=FOC that-do-ss
umo=do   *dai-ba-lé*
tell[NON1.SG.RLS]=DS hear-PFV-1SG[RLS]

'He told it to my father and likewise he (my father) told it and I listened.'

Example (16a) gives just the last two clauses of a chaining paragraph in directive mood, a prayer to the ancestors that accompanies a sacrifice (see examples (8–22) in van Enk & de Vries 1997: 160–162). It looks as if *wamolmo* in (16b) is used as a bridging clause that has the previous paragraph (the prayer as a whole, see 7) as its reference, summarizing and pointing back to it, rather than just the final clause of the prayer episode. The quoted prayer in directive mood with second person verb forms ends in (16a) and the narrator switches to third person subjects and to the habitual aspect in (16b) with summary linkage ('thus they always do') as the bridge between prayer and the continued narration.

(16) a. *le-mén=daxu noxu im-ba-mon=è*
eat-2PL.IMP=SS 1PL see-stay-2PL.IMP=EX

'you must eat and keep taking care of us'

b. **wa-mol-mo** *mamaf bau*
thus-do-do.HAB[SS] a.little sit[NON1.SG.RLS]

'They usually do like that and then after a little while...'

In a summary linkage, the use of the generic demonstrative verb in the bridging clause allows speakers to point back in a vague and general way to what preceded, leaving it to the addressee to infer what the scope of the anaphoric reference is, for example the final clause of the previous chain, or the previous chain as a whole or even a whole episode (a chain of imperative sentences), as in this case where it points back to the whole prayer episode that precedes.

In the next example (17), the generic demonstrative verb seems to refer back to the final clause of the previous clause chain, although it can be taken to have the whole preceding clause chain in its scope:

(17) a. *gexenép anè xa-mén=é*   *dé=do*   *él de-nè xenè*
2PL HORT go-2PL.IMP=EX say[NON1.SG.RLS]=DS yes say-ss next
lapangga=fexo xai-ba-lè=do   *pesau*   *maun=an pesahu*
air.strip=CONN live-be-1PL.RLS=DS aeroplane river=LOC aeroplane

> *lai*
> come[NON1.SG.RLS]
>
> 'She told us to go (home) and we agreed and we waited at the airstrip until the plane landed on the river.'

b. **amo=to=fexo**   *noxu-peninggi*   *bando-ai*   *fe-nè*
   do[NON1.SG.RLS]=DS=CONN 1PL.POSS-evangelist bring-descend take-ss
   fu=to=fexo
   put[NON1.SG.RLS]=DS=CONN

   'It did so and he (=the pilot) brought our evangelist and...'

Example (18b) shows the use of the summary verb in a thematic bridging clause, the second subtype of summary linkage. The narrator of (18) had so far been denied tobacco, although he had tried to get tobacco from them in a friendly, teasing manner and the thematic bridging clause points back to that refusal.

(18) a. *a noxup xeyop é-fu-ba-lè=lo=fexo*   <u>*sü-lexé*</u>
     EX 1PL   house sleep-make-stay-1PL.RLS=DS=CONN tobacco-reason
     <u>*ne*</u> <u>*bu-lelo-ba-lé*</u>
     1SG tease-be-stay-1SG[RLS]

     'In the house we slept and I was teasing (them) for tobacco.'

   b. **amo-xa-tél=exa**   *minya alip=ta*   *alü-xa-léf-é*
     do-IRR-2PL[RLS]-TR=CONN fuel   here=LOC burn-IRR-1SG-EX
     de-ba-lé
     say-stay-1SG[RLS]

     'If you do so, I will raise a fire here by means of petroleum, I said'

4 Other ways to link sentences

Recapitulative linkage with chained bridging clauses is by far the most common device for connecting sentences in Korowai narrative texts but speakers may also use a small set of discourse conjunctions that occur mostly within sentences and mean something like 'next' or 'and'. These conjunctions (or verbs used as conjunctions) can be used also to connect sentences, for example *(me)sé* 'next' and *xenè* 'and'; 'next'. The latter is a medial ss form of the verb of going that can be used both as a lexical verb 'to go' and as a discourse conjunction meaning 'next'. *Xenè* may also precede a recapitulative bridging clause, as in (19b).

(19) a. *Ye loxté=do*   *walüp=ta   walüp=ta*
      3SG go.away[NON1.SG.RLS]=DS half.way=LOC half.way=LOC

      maxaya   au-pexo=do   *wa=fexo   ye xülo   ye*
      maxaya.bat voice-do[NON1.SG.RLS]=DS there=CONN 3SG upstream 3SG

      xe-bo=fexo   *gup=to anè da-mo-m=é*
      go-stay[NON1.SG.RLS]=CONN you=FOC HORT hear-do-2SG.IMP=EX

      dé
      say[NON1.SG.RLS]

      'He went away and halfway a maxaya-bat squeaked and there he
      went upstream and he commanded (the bat), let me know.'

  b. *xe-nè da-mo-m=é*   *dé=do*   *ye*
      go-ss hear-do-2SG.IMP=EX say.NON1.SG.RLS=DS 3SG

      loxté
      go.away[NON1.SG.RLS]

      'And after he commanded, 'you should let me know', he (the bat)
      went away.'

The discourse conjunction *(me)sé* 'next, and' connects (20a) and (20b):

(20) a. *le-mén=daxu   mano-pa-mon=é*
      eat-2PL.IMP =SS good-make-2PL.IMP=EX

      'You should eat it and help (us)!'

  b. *mesé xobül=fcxo woto=fexa*   *fo fe-nè*
      next leg=CONN sacred.place=a.certain get get-ss

      fu-ma-té=daxu
      put-HAB-NON1.P[RLS]=SS

      'And then they usually take another leg and put it down on another
      sacred place, and..'

5 Conclusions

Recapitulative linkage of the chained type is highly frequent in Korowai narrative and procedural texts. It has three functions. First, a processual function, to
give the addressee the time to process the information of the clause chain just
heard and to give the speaker the time to plan his or her following clause chain.
The processual function is also clear from prosodic patterns associated with recapitulative linkage. Second, it creates chains of clause chains, chaining paragraphs

or even chaining episodes. The third function is in the domain of participant cohesion: to carry switch reference monitoring of participants across from one clause chain to the next by chained recapitulative linkage.

In Papuan languages where recapitulative linkage with chained clauses functions in similarly frequent ways in conditions of thematic continuity, the absence of recapitulative linkage is a signal of thematic discontinuity in texts based on sequential event lines (de Vries 2005: 375). For example, Reesink writes how Usan in "paragraphing, then, makes use of a number of criteria, of which absence of tail-head linkage in narrative material is a major one, albeit not a sufficient condition" (Reesink 1987: 332). In Korafe the absence of recapitulative linkage marks various forms of thematic discontinuity such as shifts from speaker orientation to addressee orientation, shifts in time, scene, or character configuration (Farr 1999: 337, 363). This is also true for Korowai.

Recapitulative linkage of sentences with thematic clauses is a deviation from the default option, both formally and functionally, and associated with the disruption of switch reference monitoring of participants and with going off the event line to provide topical background information in relation to one or more events on the event line. It shares the processual function with the chained type of recapitulative linkage. It also shares the givenness of the recapitulated bridging clause with chained bridging but now as part of an explicit, marked presentation of the given clause as offline background, giving the addressee a strong signal that the flow of the narrative is disrupted for special purposes.

Summary linkage allows speakers to be more vague in terms of what the reference is of their anaphoric linkage with demonstrative-derived verbs. Summary linkage may refer back to the final clause of the previous sentence, to the previous sentence as a whole or even to the preceding chain of sentences. This makes it useful in conditions of thematic re-orientation.

Both recapitulative and summary linkage seem to be phenomena restricted in Korowai to event line based genres of texts where the chronology of the reported events is reflected in the order of the narration.

Recapitulative and summary linkage both involve non-main bridging clauses: ss clauses with medial verbs, ss or ds marked clauses with independent verbs and "adverbial" thematic clauses. Switch reference marked clauses with independent verbs are non-main clauses in the sense that, once they are integrated into the sentence by switch reference clitcs, they cannot independently select tense, mood or modality: they depend on the verb of the final clause of the chain for selection of these features.

Mixing of summary and recapitulative linkage has not been found so far in Korowai texts. Recapitulative linkage in the majority of cases implies verbatim repetition of the reference clause(s). However, the only obligatorily repeated element is the verb of the reference clause. Omission of noun phrases, both core and peripheral arguments, occurs with some regularity, as is to be expected given the preference for minimal clauses with only a verb. Addition of nominal material to the bridging clause, elements that do not occur in the reference clause, is very rare.

Appendix

The Korowai text of this appendix was recorded and transcribed by Rev. G.J. van Enk in Yaniruma in the early 1990s. It is part of a folder with unpublished Korowai texts that Rev. G.J. van Enk gave me after his retirement from Papua. I use the text from the van Enk corpus numbered D.1.7 as an illustration of recapitulative linkages in Korowai. It is a short but complete text. I have reglossed the text and deleted the name of the main character because it is a real life story about witchcraft, a very sensitive topic in the Korowai community. The narrator is Fenelun Molonggai who talks about an interrogation of a suspected witch (N.) during a witch trial.

(A1) *noxup N. ati-lame-lè=daxu   gup fala=xo=lolo? xe-nè yanop*
      1PL   N. hold-bind-1PL[RLS]=SS 2SG what=Q=FOC go-SS person
      mé-bol   lé-lé-mba-tèl=exo=lo?   de-lè
      ground-hole.(grave) eat-eat-HAB-NON1.PL=Q=FOC say-1PL[RLS]
      'We had caught and bound N. and we said, what about you, did you use to go to burial places to eat people?'

(A2) **de-lè**=lo=fexo   él yup mündiyop=tanux ye-mayox=fexo
      say-1PL[RLS]=DS=CONN yes 3SG once=only   3SG-companion=CONN
      yanop mé-bol   xe-ba-tè   dé
      person ground-hole go-PFV-NON1.PL[RLS] say[RLS.NON1.SG]
      'We said and, yes he had gone only once with his mates to a grave, he said.'

(A3) *yo anè umo-m   de-lè=lo=fexo   a   gülé alümexon*
      ADH ADH tell-IMP.SG say-1PL.RLS=DS=CONN INJ night full.moon
      alümexon=ta ye-mayox=fexo   yanop mé-bol
      full.moon=in 3SG-companion=CONN person ground-hole

<u>xa-tè</u>   *dé*
go-NON1.PL[RLS] say[RLS.NON1.SG]

'Come on tell us, we said and, uh, on a clear moonlit night with full moon he and his companions had gone to a burial site, he said.'

(A4)   **xa-tè**=*to=fexo*   *yanop laxül ye-lidop=tanux faxte-nè*
go-NON1.PL[RLS]=DS=CONN person corpse 3SG-one=only float-SS
lu-falé-bo   *dé*
come.up-appear-PFV.NON1.SG say[RLS.NON1.SG]

'They had gone and one corpse had floated up and had made an appearance, he said.'

(A5)   *Alo-bo=do=mpexo*   *maun nenilfo-bo=do=mpexo*
stand.up-PFV.NON1.SG=DS=CONN fluid much-sit[NON1.SG]=DS=CONN
sendok=to=mpexo ali-mi-méma-tè=fexo   *yu*
spoon=INS=CONN scoop-drink-IMM-NON1.PL[RLS]=CONN 3SG
ali-féda-té=tofexo   <u>*gololo.*</u>
scoop-give-NON1.PL[RLS]=DS be.afraid[NON1.SG.RLS]

'It (the corpse) stood up and there was much (corpse) fluid and they had just begun to scoop it up with a spoon and drink it and then they scooped it up for him to drink but he was afraid.'

(A6)   **gololo**=*to=fexo*   *ati-ba-té=daxu*
be.afraid[NON1.SG.RLS]=DS=CONN hold-PFV-NON1.PL=SS
ya-xaxolof=an   *ali-mexe-té=do*
3SG.POSS-mouth=LOC scoop-do-NON1.SG[RLS]=DS
me=do=mpexo   *wasü sendok=to=fexo*   *yanop*
drink[RLS.NON1.SG]=DS=CONN there spoon=INS=CONN person
nén-ax   *ali-mi-xami-baxa-ti=fexo*
rotten-water scoop-drink-sit-HOD-NON1.PL[RLS]=CONN
külmexe-té=daxu=fexo   *yexenép xa-un=ngga*
finished-NON1.PL[RLS]=SS=CONN 3PL   go-INF=CONN
lexe-mema-té=to=fexo   *yanop loxül*
aim-IMM-NON1.PL[RLS]=DS=CONN person corpse

xau-meléai=do   *yexenép gilfa-té*
down-descend[NON1.SG.RLS]=DS 3SG   departed-NON1.PL[RLS]
dé
say[RLS.NON1.SG]

'He was afraid and then they held him and scooped the corpse fluid into his mouth and he drank it and they were scooping and drinking corpse fluid there until they were done and then they wanted to go away and when the corpse had sunk, they left, he said.'

Abbreviations

1	first person (speaker)	ITER	iterative
2	second person	IRR	irrealis
ADH	adhortative	LOC	locative
CAUS	causative	NEG	negative
CONN	connective	NON1	second or third person
COORD	coordinator		(non-speaker)
DS	different subject	PFV	perfective
EMPH	emphasis	PST	past
EX	exclamative	PL	plural
FOC	focus	POSS	possessive
HAB	habitual	Q	question marker
HOD	hodiernal past	RLS	realis
HORT	hortative	SG	singular
IMM	immediate	SS	same subject
IMP	imperative	TOP	topic
INF	infinitve	TR	transitional sound
INS	instrument	VOC	vocative

Acknowledgements

I would like to thank Valérie Guérin, Clemens Mayer, and two anonymous reviewers for their helpful critical comments.

References

Boersma, Paul & David Weenink. 2019. *Praat: Doing phonetics by computer. Computer program, version 6.0.46.* http://www.praat.org, accessed 2019-1-3.

de Vries, Lourens. 2005. Towards a typology of tail-head linkage in Papuan languages. *Studies in Language* 29(2). 363–384.

de Vries, Lourens. 2006. Areal pragmatics of New Guinea: Thematization, distribution and recapitulative linkage in Papuan narratives. *Journal of Pragmatics* 38(6). 811–828.

de Vries, Lourens. 2010. From clause conjoining to clause chaining in Dumut languages of New Guinea. *Studies in Language* 34(2). 327–349.

de Vries, Lourens, Ruth Wester & Wilco van den Heuvel. 2012. The Greater Awyu language family of West Papua. *Language and Linguistics in Melanesia* Special Issue, Part I. 269–312.

Du Bois, John. 1987. The discourse basis of ergativity. *Language* 63. 805–855.

Farr, Cynthia J. M. 1999. *The interface between syntax and discourse in Korafe, a Papuan language of Papua New Guinea* (Pacific Linguistics 148). Canberra: Australian National Universtity.

Foley, William A. 1986. *The Papuan languages of Papua New Guinea.* Cambridge: Cambridge University Press.

Foley, William A. 2000. The languages of New Guinea. *Annual Review of Anthropology* 29. 357–404.

Haiman, John. 1978. Conditionals are topics. *Language* 54(3). 564–589.

Heeschen, Volker. 1998. *An ethnographic grammar of the Eipo language (spoken in the central mountains of Irian Jaya (West New Guinea), Indonesia).* Berlin: Reimer.

Reesink, Ger P. 1987. *Structures and their functions in Usan: A Papuan language of Papua New Guinea.* Amsterdam: John Benjamins.

Reesink, Ger P. 2000. Domain-creating constructions in Papuan languages. In Ger P. Reesink (ed.), *Topics in descriptive Papuan linguistics*, 98–121. Leiden: Leiden University.

van Enk, Gerrit J. & Lourens de Vries. 1997. *The Korowai of Irian Jaya. Their language in its cultural context.* Oxford: Oxford University Press.

Wester, Ruth. 2009. *A linguistic history of Awyu-Dumut: Morphological study and reconstruction of a Papuan Language Family.* Amsterdam: Vrije Universiteit PhD Dissertation.

Chapter 8

Recapitulative linkage in Mavea

Valérie Guérin

James Cook University

This chapter concentrates on recapitulative linkage in Mavea, an Oceanic language of Vanuatu. I present the formal characteristics of recapitulative linkage and assess its discourse functions in two texts: a procedural text and a legend. Recapitulative linkage is compared to verbal repetition, another productive discourse strategy in Oceanic languages. I show that recapitulative linkage in Mavea is identified through a constellation of features. Syntactically, it is an instance of main clause coordination; prosodically it is marked with continuation intonation; semantically, it indicates temporal succession; and in discourse, it signals thematic continuity or rhetorical underlining.

1 A brief introduction

Mavea (also spelled Maѵea or Mav'ea) is a moribund Oceanic language spoken by about 30 speakers in Vanuatu.[1] The data for this chapter come from my own field work on Mavea Island (11 months between 2005 and 2007). All files are archived at the Endangered Languages Archive–ELAR (available online, see Guérin 2006). Typologically, Mavea is a head-marking language, mildly agglutinative, mostly prefixing. The language displays an SV/AVO constituent order, with nominative-accusative alignment and the S/A argument obligatorily cross-referenced on the verb as a prefix but optional in canonical imperative sentences (Guérin 2011: 236). This prefix is a portmanteau indicating subject agreement and reality status. However, only two persons (1SG and 3SG) have different realis and irrealis realizations. All other persons have identical forms regardless of the reality status

---

[1]The letters ⟨ѵ̂⟩, ⟨p̂⟩, and ⟨m̂⟩ represent linguo-labials. In this chapter, they are written as ⟨v'⟩, ⟨p'⟩, and ⟨m'⟩ in the figures.

Valérie Guérin. 2019. Recapitulative linkage in Mavea. In Valérie Guérin (ed.), *Bridging constructions*, 207–238. Berlin: Language Science Press. DOI:10.5281/zenodo.2563692

(Guérin 2011: 61). As is widespread in Oceanic languages, Mavea makes extensive use of serial verb constructions (with aspectual and directional meanings) and of clausal coordination (asyndetic or monosyndetic), but less use of subordination to express adverbial clauses.

Of the three types of bridging constructions that were presented in this volume in Chapter 1 (i.e., recapitulative, summary, and mixed linkages), there are in Mavea numerous examples of a construction which I identify as recapitulative linkage, exemplified in (1).

(1)   a. *Tamlo ra-l-to,   mo-v̆a mo-ran tarlavua <u>ra-sopo-one-ra</u>.*
          man   3PL-IPFV-stay 3SG-go 3SG-day morning 3PL-NEG-look-3PL

          'People were waiting until daylight [but] they didn't see them.'

      b. ***Ra-sopo-one-ra** ro   ra-l-aso-ra.*
          3PL-NEG-look-3PL then 3PL-IPFV-search-3PL

          'They didn't see them, then they searched [for] them.'

Summary linkage with light or demonstrative verbs (as described in Chapter 1 of this volume) is not found in Mavea, and at this stage, I venture to say that this type of linkage is not a frequently-employed mechanism to link clauses in the Oceanic languages of Vanuatu. There exists, however, a construction commonly found in Mavea – and in other Oceanic languages such as Ughele (Frostad 2012), Paamese (Crowley 2003: 39), Lolovoli (Hyslop 2001) – involving the verb 'finish' in the bridging clause, following the verb of the reference clause, as shown in (2b).

(2)   a. *Ale ki-lo-to   tuan nira <u>ki-anan</u>.*
          then 1PL:EXCL-IPFV-stay with 3PL 1PL:EXCL-eat

          'Then we stay with them we eat.'

      b. ***Ki-anan**   **mo-ev**   ro ale ki-varvara   nira.*
          1PL:EXCL-eat 3SG-finish and then 1PL:EXCL-speak 3PL

          'Having finished eating, then, we talk with them.'

In such contexts, the verb *ev* 'finish' in (2b) always takes a 3SG agreement marker and it can be said to form an event-argument serial verb construction, in the sense of Aikhenvald (2006: 18) with the preceding verb (here *anan* 'eat') indicating completive aspect (Guérin 2011: 225, 267).[2] Understanding whether constructions involving the verb 'finish' can be treated on a par with bridging constructions, or whether these constructions form another type of clause linkage

---

[2]For an alternative proposal, see Cleary-Kemp (2017: 131, 241)

altogether (e.g., subevent sequencing as serial verbs) can only be addressed once a firm description of the syntax and pragmatics of the more canonical bridging constructions in Mavea is put forth. This chapter is a first step in that direction. In the remaining sections, I concentrate on recapitulative linkage similar to (1). §2 describes the formal characteristics of the bridging clause in detail and §3 discusses the placement of recapitulative linkage in two text genres (procedural and narrative) and the associated discourse functions, in the spirit of de Vries (2005). §4 compares recapitulative linkage to repetition. I conclude that identifying recapitulative linkage in Mavea requires identifying a constellation of features. First, bridging clauses are syntactically main clauses that are often overtly coordinated. Second, they have non-final (or continuation) intonation, indicating that they are in a chain of thoughts. Third, they indicate for the most part sequentiality. And fourth, they have specific discursive functions, the most common being to add emphasis and to track the progression of events in a text.

2 Formal characteristics of recapitulative linkage

In this section, I review the formal properties of recapitulative linkage in Mavea. Questions addressed in §2.1 touch on the composition and content of the bridging clause (what is repeated and how) and on the status of the bridging clause (whether a main or non-main clause, a final or a non-final clause), in §2.2.

2.1 Composition, content, and position

Recapitulative linkage is characterized by the repetition of the reference clause. But what exactly is repeated? Repetition can take different forms as discussed in Guérin & Aiton (2019 [this volume]), and in Brown (2000: 224). In Mavea, I have found so far exact lexical repetition, repetition with addition, with omission, and repetition with substitution. Exact lexical repetition is seen bolded in (3b) where the bridging clause repeats two clauses from the reference clause (underlined), verbatim.

(3) a. *Tamlo vaisesea <u>mo-tapair ro   mo-v</u>   i-valao.*
         man   small   3SG-shake and 3SG-say 3SG:IRR-run
         'The little boy got scared and so he started to run.'

b. ***Mo-tapair ro mo-v i-valao,***   *ro mo-v:* *"Ei! Ko-sopo-valao!"*
3SG-shake and 3SG-say 3SG:IRR-run and 3SG-say hey! 2SG-NEG-run

'He got scared and he started to run, and he (i.e., someone else) said: "Hey! Don't run!"'

Repetition with omission is exemplified in (4): the imperfective aspect marker *lo* is not repeated in the bridging clause. In (5), it is the oblique *na vasao le* which is omitted.

(4)   a. *Mo-v̆a* <u>*mo-lo-sarsar.*</u>
3SG-go 3SG-IPFV-spear.fish

'He went spear-fishing.'

b. ***Mo-sarsar,***   *mo-sop*   *malo...*
3SG-spear.fish 3SG-follow reef

'He spear-fished, he walked along the reef...'

(5)   a. *Ko-v̆a* <u>*ko-oso*</u>   <u>*na vasao*</u>   <u>*le.*</u>
2SG-go 2SG-ashore LOC landing.site DET

'Go ashore to that landing site.'

b. *Ro* ***ko-oso***   *ko-on...*
then 2SG-ashore 2SG-see

'Then, you go ashore, you see...'

Repetition with addition is shown in (6). The bridging clause adds a direct object *re raprapen vatal* 'the banana-log raft' which is not present in the reference clause. Note, however, that 'the raft' is implicit in the reference clause and discussed in the clauses preceding it. Thus, no new information is added in the bridging clause.

(6)   a. <u>*Mo-rave mo-si*</u>   *alao*   *na tasi.*
3SG-pull 3SG-go.down seashore LOC sea

'He pulled (it) down to the seashore.'

b. ***Mo-rave re rap~rape-n***   *vatal mo-si*   *alao*   *na*
3SG-pull PL REDUP~log-3SG:POSS banana 3SG-go.down seashore LOC
tasi, *mo-l-sale-i-a.*
sea   3SG-IPFV-float-TR-3SG

'He pulled the banana-log raft down to the seashore, he put it to float.'

Last, repetition with substitution and addition appear in (7c). The lexical verb of the reference clause *lai* 'take' is replaced in the reference clause by its near synonym *lavi* 'take'. The bridging clause also contain an additional linker, namely *ro* 'and'. Note also that the reference and bridging clause are separated from one another by an intervening clause.

(7) a. <u>*Ko-lai   ko-m̃a   ko-rosi-a.*</u>
      2SG-take 2SG-come 2SG-grate-3SG

      'You bring them, grate them.'

   b. *Ko-mo-osom   i-mo-ngavul   rua te i-ngavul   tol.*
      2SG-COND-husk 3SG:IRR-COND-decade two or 3SG:IRR-decade three

      'You could husk 20 or 30.'

   c. **Ko-lav̆i ko-m̃a   ro ko-rosi-a.**
      2SG-take 2SG-come and 2SG-grate-3SG

      'You bring them and grate them.'

If the content of the bridging clause does not always match the content of the reference clause, one feature that remains constant is the position of the bridging clause: it always occurs after the reference clause (as is the case across languages, see Chapter 1). In the large majority of cases, the reference clause and the bridging clause are contiguous. Most examples adduced so far exemplify this trend. In rarer cases, the bridging clause is not adjacent to the reference clause but separated by one clause as in (7) and also (8).

(8) a. *Kou mo-tur   pos, <u>mo-m̃e-l-sop</u>   <u>sale</u> mo-v̆a na ima*
      fowl 3SG-stand.up turn 3SG-ITER-IPFV-follow road 3SG-go LOC house

      sa-n.
      CLF:LOC-3SG:POSS

      'Fowl turns around, she keeps walking on the road, she goes home.'

   b. **Mo-m̃e-l-sop   sale...**
      3SG-ITER-IPFV-follow road

      'She keeps walking on the road...'

2.2 Grammatical status of the bridging clause

The comparative concept presented in Chapter 1 (this volume) indicates that bridging clauses are non-main clauses. The dependency can be marked grammatically, as in the Oceanic language Erromangan (Vanuatu). In this language, "verbs are obligatorily marked by means of prefixes that express a range of subject categories" (Crowley 1998: 85). In some rare cases, including bridging constructions, the verb occurs without any subject marking. Instead, the verb appears in what Crowley calls the citation form. This is shown in (9) with the verb *tamul-* in bold in the bridging clause.

(9)   Erromangan (Vanuatu)

    a. *Kamu-tetw-i*   *mavel-i ɣi-tamul-i.*

        1DU:EXCL:DIST.PST-BR:wait.for-3SG until-LK 3SG:DIST.PST-BR:send-3SG

        'The two of us waited until he sent it.'

    b. **Tamul-i**   *kamli-vai.*

        CIT:send-3SG 1PL.EXCL:DIST.PST-BR:take

        'Having sent it, we took it.' (Crowley 1998: 118)

In Mavea, on the other hand, bridging clauses do not show any sign of grammatical dependency. They are not restricted in their inflectional possibilities: they show no limitations on the tense, reality status, mood/modality, etc., that they can mark. They can be negated, as shown in (1); they show no restriction on the presence or absence of core arguments. In addition, the bridging clause is often coordinated to the following clause with the coordinator *ro* 'and, and then, then', as shown in (3). This coordinator conjoins verb phrases and clauses, as shown in (10), but not nominals (Guérin 2011: 314ff).[3] Thus, in all morphosyntactic aspects, bridging clauses are just like any other main clause: they do not constitute a separate clause type.

(10)   *Mo-sa*   *mo-sakai ai*   **ro** *mo-otol.*

     3SG-go.up 3SG-sit   LOC:PRO and 3SG-lay.eggs

     'She went up, sat on it, and she laid eggs.' (Guérin 2011: 320)

However, when it comes to prosody, bridging clauses differ significantly from the main clauses that are used as final clauses at the end of a chain of thoughts. They are marked with rising pitch, whereas final clauses have a falling pitch. To illustrate this fact, take Figure 1 as a starting point: a PRAAT graph of the two juxtaposed clauses glossed in (11). There is no semantic linker between these clauses and no semantic link either. Both clauses are main clauses and final clauses. Both have falling intonation (although the second one takes a deeper dip). Throughout the chapter, a number in square brackets such as [0.1s] in the source language indicates a pause, in seconds.

---

[3]Note in passing that the conjunction *ro* generally forms an intonational unit with the first conjunct or with the bridging clause and is followed by a pause (Guérin 2011: 321).

(11) *Arua-ku!*   *Nno ko-l-to.*   *Nao ka-m̃e-l-tapula.*
      friend-1SG:POSS 2SG 2SG-IPFV-stay 1SG 1SG:IRR-ITER-IPFV-return

      'My friend! You stay. I'm going back.'

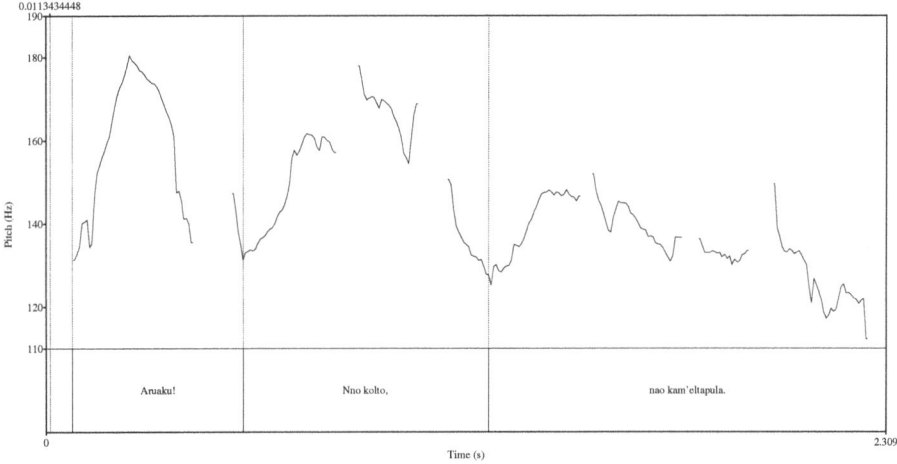

Figure 1: Intonation contour of example (11) extracted with PRAAT.

We can now compare (11) and Figure 1 to (12) and Figure 2 (from the same story and same male speaker). Example (12) contains a recapitulative linkage. (12a) is the reference clause, (12b) is the bridging clause, which is juxtaposed (after a pause) to the following clause in (12c). The graph accompanying this example (Fig. 2) represents the reference and the bridging clauses. It clearly shows that the bridging clause ends on a much higher pitch than the reference clause, which is a final clause.

(12) a. *Mo-vir*   *sun no-n*   *kou mo-si.*   *[1.35s]*
         3SG-throw hat CLF-LK fowl 3SG-go.down

         'He throws down Fowl's hat.'

      b. ***Mo-vir*   *sun no-n kou mo-si***   *[3.4s]*
         3SG-throw hat CLF-LK fowl 3SG-go.down

         'He throws down Fowl's hat,'

      c. *sun mo-si*   *mo-tikel atano.*
         hat 3SG-go.down 3SG-reach ground

         'the hat goes down onto the ground.'

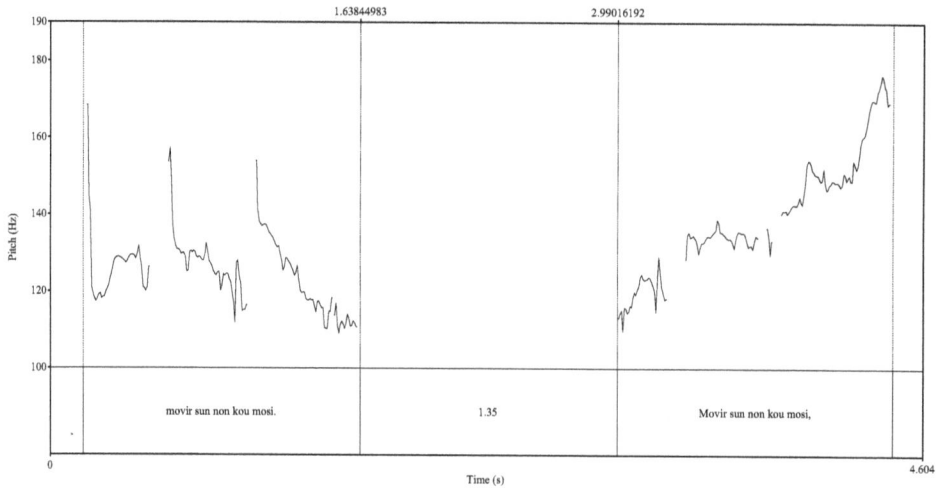

Figure 2: Intonation contour of examples (12a) and (12b) extracted with PRAAT.

Example (13) also contains a recapitulative linkage, but this time, the bridging clause (13b) is overtly coordinated to the following clause. All three clauses are represented in Figure 3.

(13) a. <u>*ko-viris*</u>   <u>*i-si*</u>   <u>*na*</u> <u>*kuku.*</u> *[1s]*
         2SG-squeeze 3SG:IRR-go.down LOC pot

         'You squeeze (out the juice) down into a pot.'

      b. **Ko-viris**   **i-si**   **na** **kuku** ro   *[1.09s]*
         2SG-squeeze 3SG:IRR-go.down LOC pot   then

         'You squeeze (out the juice) down into a pot then,'

      c. *ko-[0.2s]*   *ku-a.*
         2SG-[pause] boil-3SG

         'you...boil it.'

The difference between the bridging clause and the other clauses in (13) is visually striking. The reference clause ends with a falling intonation. The bridging clause ends on a high pitch with rising intonation. The main clause following the bridging clause also has falling intonation.

The intonation contour of a bridging clause is not always so visually striking. For example, the bridging clause in (14b) shown in Figure 4 does not rise as much as the one in (13b), although the female speaker is the same in both instances. This is possibly due to the fact that the linkage in (14) is a bit unusual: the

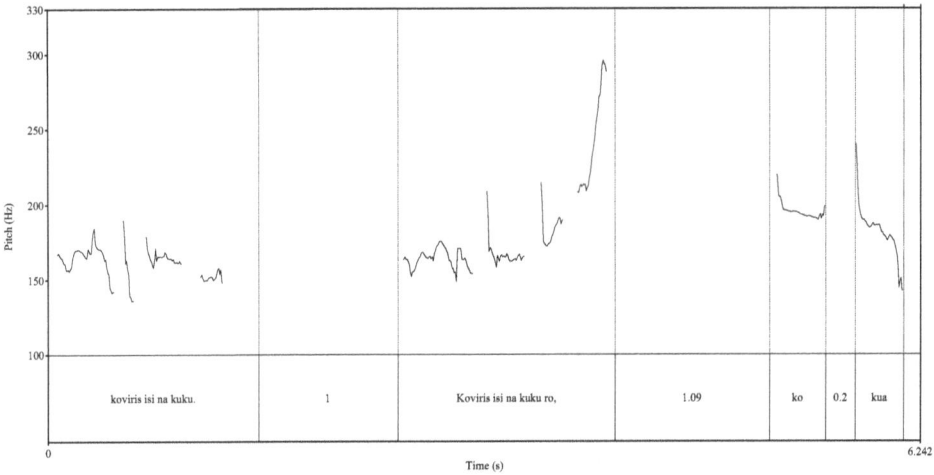

Figure 3: Intonation contour of example (13) extracted with PRAAT.

reference clause is an exclamative clause and not a declarative. There is no pause between the bridging clause and the clause following it. The pitch is much higher throughout. Nevertheless, the bridging clause ends on a pitch higher than the final clause preceding it and the final clause following it. Based on all examples presented so far, I extrapolate the fact that although bridging clauses are morphologically main clauses, they indicate continuation and are non-final clauses. Their non-final status is indicated by their prosody.

(14) a. *Ko-pos ko-si ko-sev!* [1.11s]
        2SG-turn 2SG-go.down 2SG-hang

        'Turn upside down and hang!'

    b. **Ko-pos ko-si ko-sev ro**
        2SG-turn 2SG-go.down 2SG-hang then

        'Turn upside down and hang, then'

    c. *da-r-sev da-r-lala lang.*
        1PL:INCL-DU-hang 1PL:INCL-DU-take.in wind

        'we both hang [and] enjoy the wind.'

Needless to say, a rising tune is not specific to bridging clauses. When used in paragraph-initial position, time adverbials have a similar intonation contour, as shown in Figure 5, since they too indicate continuation.

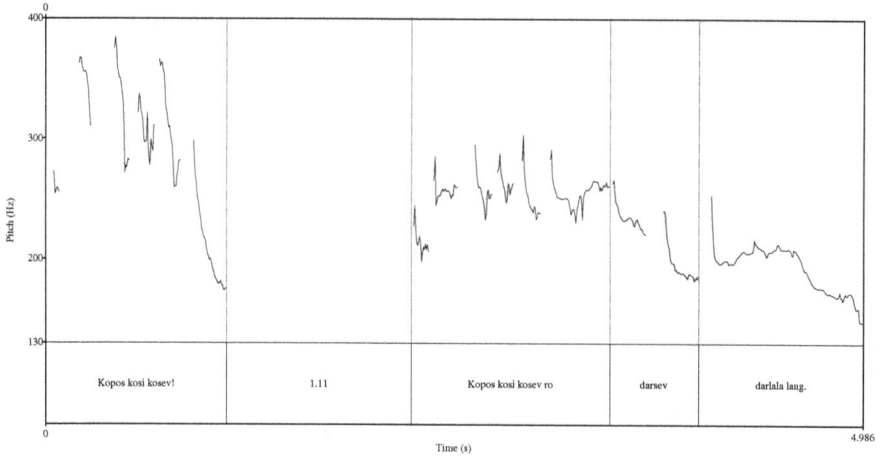

Figure 4: Intonation contour of example (14) extracted with PRAAT.

(15) *Sur   pong aite [2.30s] tina-na   mo-sao.*
      about night one [pause] mother-3SG:POSS 3SG-sick
      'One day, his mother was sick.'

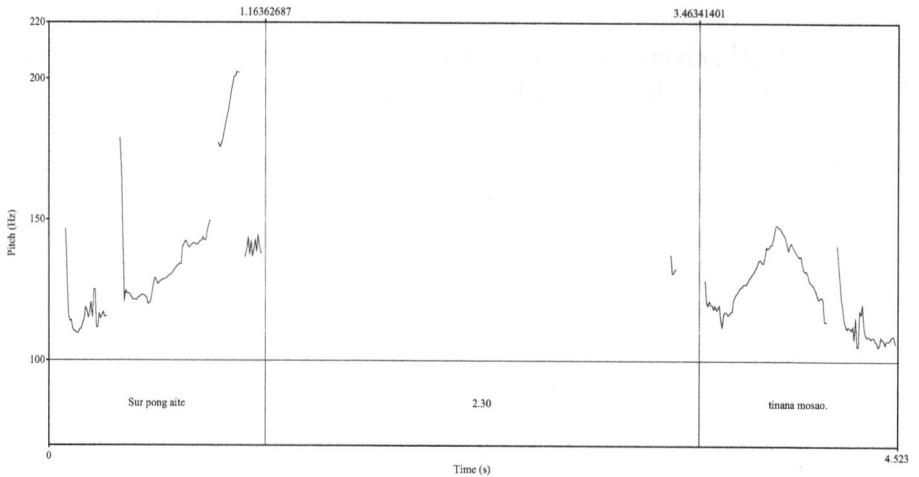

Figure 5: Intonation contour of example (15) extracted with PRAAT.

    In addition, clauses which are considered part of a chain of thought and thus non-final also have a rising intonation contour, regardless of their morphosyntactic features. This is the case, for example, of lines (A25) and (A26) of the Appendix, shown in Figure 6.

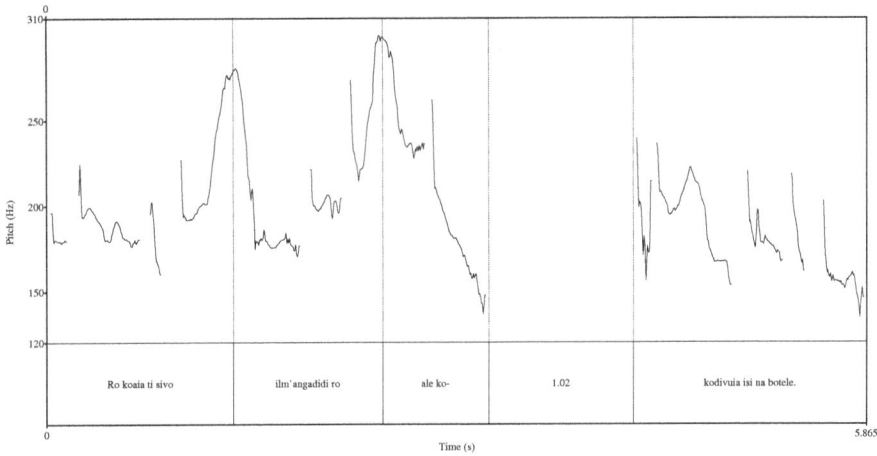

Figure 6: Intonation contour of examples (A25) and (A26) of the Appendix extracted with PRAAT.

I have not found so far cases where a clause with rising intonation ends a paragraph, a text, or a chain of thoughts, indicating that a rising intonation is the preferred contour to expresses continuation in Mavea as is the case elsewhere in the Oceanic subgroup: in Manam (Lichtenberk 1983: 521), in Paluai (Schokkin 2013: 63), and in Abma (Schneider 2010: 38), to name a few. Final clauses on the other hand have falling intonation.

3 Bridging constructions in discourse

Understanding the function of recapitulative linkage in discourse rests on two points. First, the discourse genre in which the linkage occurs requires defining given that the function of a bridging construction can vary depending on the text genre (de Vries 2005). In §3.1, I present a brief description of text genres in Mavea. In line with what is reported in the literature (Longacre 1983: 9, de Vries 2005: 365, Thompson et al. 2007: 274), recapitulative linkage in Mavea is most frequent in narrative and procedural texts.

Second, the placement of the bridging clause in a particular text is important, as different positions can lead to different meanings. In that respect, I assume that a text evolves into the following stages: exposition, development, developing conflict, climax, denouement, conclusion (as discussed in Chapter 1, this volume). I recognize two major textual components: the main event line and the supporting line (Longacre 1983: 14–17) that both help the text progress through the aforementioned stages. To determine the discourse function of recapitulative linkage in Mavea, I evaluate the clauses immediately surrounding the bridging clause: Does the line preceding the bridging clause report on an event on the main line or the supporting line? Is the line following the bridging clause adding new information, i.e., a new event on the main line? Or is it elaborating a previous event, i.e., adding information on the supporting line? In §3.2 and §3.3, I provide a structural study of two texts in Mavea (a procedural text and a narrative) to determine the placement and function of recapitulative linkage in each of these text genres. Needless to say, this analysis and the conclusions reached are provisional. More texts of each genre will need to be analyzed before any definite conclusions can be reached.

3.1 Text genres and token frequency of recapitulative linkage

Texts are classified based on external criteria such as topic, intended audience, purpose, and activity type (Lee 2001: 38). In my Mavea dataset, I arrive at the following division:

Conversations: unplanned dialogues between two speakers

Anecdotal narratives: personal stories, where the speaker narrates episodes of his/her life

Traditional life narratives: depiction (and to some extent explanation) of cultural events and practices such as engagement ceremonies, bride price payment, circumcision, etc.

Fiction narratives: stories about fictional protagonists (humans and anthropomorphic characters), sometimes associated with mythical events, which can reveal human nature and sometimes end with a moral lesson. As part of the traditional folklore, these stories are known by everyone in the community.

Elicited narratives: invented narratives based on picture books. Participants are given a picture book and asked to invent the story depicted.

Procedural texts: elicited texts describing the step-by-step processes to accomplish a task.

To determine the token frequency of recapitulative linkage across text genres, I formed a corpus in each genre of the same approximate length (around 25 minutes long). The texts were randomly chosen with one exception: there are only six procedural texts in my entire dataset (of about 160 recordings). They are all included in the present corpus but they only yield a total of 8 minutes. The results are summarized in Table 1.

Table 1: Token frequency of recapitulative linkage per text genre

Text genres	Speakers' data	Text length, in min.	# of recap. linkages	Recap. linkage/min.
Conversations	2 ♀ age 35–45	22	3	0.14
Anecdotal narratives	2 ♂ age 30–45	27	2	0.07
Traditional life	1 ♂ age 33	23	5	0.22
Fiction	2 ♂,1 ♀ age 33–50	25	20	0.8
Elicited narratives	4 ♂ age 25–45	24	41	1.71
Procedural texts	2 ♀ age 45–65	8	21	2.63

Overall, across text genres, recapitulative linkage is relatively infrequent. A count per minute reveals that it is more frequent in elicited procedural texts (2.63 occurrences per minute) and elicited narratives (1.7 occurrences per minute) than in any non-elicited texts (with a maximum of 0.8 occurrences per minute in fiction narratives). It could be that the high count of recapitulative linkages per minute in elicited texts (procedural or narrative) gives us indirect evidence that the role of bridging construction is for the speaker to buy (processing) time (de Vries 2005: 378; 2006: 817). As Longacre argues (1983: 9–10), in many non-literate communities, people learn by participating in activities, rather than being told how to do things in a procedural way. The speakers could be in need of time to think about the procedure in order to retell it or to think of the story to invent, as it was not something they were accustomed to doing. Another interesting point is the fact that bridging clauses are often coordinated and followed by a pause (as discussed in §2.2). The speaker can use the recapitulative linkage (with continuation prosody) and the pause (which occurs after the coordinator *ro* 'and, then') to maintain the floor while thinking about the next segment. This could be additional indirect evidence that the speaker buys processing time, as suggested by de Vries (2006: 817).

3.2 Analysis of a procedural text

Procedural texts are goal-oriented texts. They provide a sequence of instructions which are to be closely followed in order to perform a task, to reach a goal. These

instructions (which form the main event line) are usually temporally ordered and may be interspersed with explanatory material (the supporting line), such as elaborations, comments, or advice which provide motivation and justification for the instructions (Adam 2001; Fontan & Saint-Dizier 2008; Delpech & Saint-Dizier 2008).

The procedural text that I analyze in this section (schematized in Table 2) is reproduced in its entirety in the Appendix. Line numbers correspond to the example sentences in the Appendix. The text is a recipe giving instructions on how to make coconut oil. I identify 14 independent events or steps on the main line (mostly action verbs) providing instructions and eight events on the supporting line, consisting of repetitions (as in line A20) and of elaborations of various sorts (to offer advice (line A7) or provide a refining comment (line A5) on a main line event).

Based solely on the formal characteristics identified in §2, I isolate five clear tokens of recapitulative linkage in this text. Two instances of recapitulative linkage, the pairs (A9–A10) and (A12–A13), are what I consider "canonical" examples. In both cases, the reference clauses (lines A9 and A12) are final clauses with falling intonation. The bridging clauses (lines A10 and A13) are coordinated to the following clause with *ro* 'and'. The bridging clauses are immediately adjacent to the reference clauses and repeat the lexical content verbatim. Both bridging clauses have rising intonation contours.[4]

The other three recapitulative linkages appear in the pairs (A6–A8), (A15–A18), and (A23–A24). In the first two linkages, (A6–A8) and (A15–A18), the reference and bridging clauses are not immediately adjacent. The recapitulative linkage (A6–A8) shows addition and substitution. The reference clause (line A6) has three consecutive verbs. The first two are separated from the third verb by the coordinator *ro* 'and' in the bridging clause (line A8). The first verb of the reference clause is replaced in the bridging clause by a synonym (i.e., *lai* 'take' > *laVi* 'take'). The pair (A15–A18) shows addition and omission in the bridging clause. The pronoun *nna* 'it' is added in the bridging clause; the location *na apu* 'on the fire', present in the reference clause, is omitted in the bridging clause. Last, the pair (A23–A24) also shows addition. The bridging clause contains a more complex predicate: *mov* is a phasal predicate (Guérin 2011: 342), added to the predicate of the reference clause *rororo*, an ideophone representing the sound of sizzling food.

---

[4] A reviewer asked why line A11, which I call a repetition, was not taken as the bridging clause of line A9. It is indeed possible to envisage a scenario where line A10 is a false start. The speaker starts the bridging clause line A10, changes her mind, and repeats it as line A11 with added material.

Table 2: Schema of the recipe: How to make coconut oil

Main line	Line #	Recap. Link.	Supporting line
title	A1		
purpose	A2		
	A3		repetition of (A1)
Husk	A4		
	A5		repetition/elaboration of (4)
Grate	A6	reference cl.	
	A7		elaboration of (A4) and (A5)
	A8	bridging cl.	elaboration
Knead	A9	reference cl.	
	A10	bridging cl.	
	A11		repetition of (A10)/elaboration
Squeeze	A12	reference cl.	
	A13	bridging cl.	
Boil	A14		
Put on the fire	A15	reference cl.	
	A16		elaboration of (15)
	A17		elaboration of (16)
	A18	bridging cl.	
Stir	A19		
	A20		repetition of (A19)
Become oil	A21		
Stir	A22		
Hear sizzling	A23	reference cl.	
Cooked	A24	bridging cl.	
Remove	A25		
Cool	A26		
Pour	A27		

With respect to placement, the bridging clauses in lines A13 and A24 are surrounded by main line events, i.e., new steps in the recipe. The bridging clauses in lines A8 and A18 are preceded by advisory comments on the supporting line (lines A7, A16, and A17). They are followed by a new main line event, lines A9 and A19. The reference clause line A9 is preceded by the bridging clause from the previous recapitulative linkage. It does not contain a new event per se but an elaboration of the event on the main event line, on line A6. The bridging clause line A10 is followed by a repetition of itself, line A11, with an added aspectual dimension and continuation intonation.

By looking at the placement of the bridging clauses in the text, we can better deduce their function. The two bridging clauses which appear after material on the supporting line (lines A8 and A18) flag a change of orientation, from background to foreground. They bring the topic and the audience back onto the main event line. On the other hand, the bridging clauses surrounded by main line events (lines A13 and A24) signal that the procedure is continuing. They highlight the sequentiality of each step in the recipe and thrust the recipe forward. Recapping one event on the main line (the reference clause) before the next event (in the clause after the bridging clause) "transform[s] the repeated item from new into given information" (Brown 2000: 224).

The findings are summarized in Table 3. It is interesting to note that there are only five clear cases of recapitulative linkages but 14 events on the main event line and nine on the supporting line, indicating that recapitulative linkages are not obligatory: not all sequences of events are overtly signalled by a bridging clause.

If speakers have the choice to use or not use a recapitulative linkage, we may wonder then what triggers the choice. Events that are not recapped by a bridging clause appear on lines A4, A14, A19, and A24 to A27. They are followed by repetitions (lines A5, A20), elaboration on the main event line (line A15), but they can also continue the procedure. There are new steps (lines 25 to 27) taking place after the end goal of the recipe has been achieved (line 24) but no recapitulative linkage to introduce them. Thus, although both the use and non-use of recapitulative linkage can conspire to add thematic continuity, I conclude that bridging clauses in a procedural text either emphasize a temporal semantic relation (e.g., sequentiality) or mark an important narrative change (back to the main event line).

Note also that, in this text, I do not consider the pair A4–A5 to form a recapitulative linkage. Although line A5 involves the repetition of line A4 with lexical substitution, the intonation of this pair is the opposite of the intonation of a canonical recapitulative linkage: line A4 ends with a rising pitch and line A5

Table 3: Properties of recapitulative linkage in the procedural text

Line # of bridging/ reference	Adjacency bridging/ reference	Coordin. or Juxtapos.	Recapitu- lation type	Clauses before/after the construction: on main/supporting line	Discourse function
A6–A8	no	juxtaposed	substitution and addition	supporting/main	to main event
A9–A10	yes	coordinated	verbatim	main/supporting	?
A12–A13	yes	coordinated	verbatim	main/main	sequencing
A15–A18	no	coordinated	omission and addition	supporting/main	to main event
A23–A24	yes	juxtaposed	addition	main/main	sequencing

a falling pitch. It could be that the speaker is correcting herself. Good coconuts (*m̃atiu du*) are old coconuts (*m̃atiu patu*), but *m̃atiu du* is more of a colloquial term, whereas *m̃atiu patu* is the appropriate term for a coconut which has reached maturity.

In addition, it is unclear at this stage whether the pair A21–A22 forms a recapitulative linkage or not. The second clause (*i-oele* 'it is oil') only partially repeats the first clause, which contains a serial verb construction (*i-m̃a i-oele* 'it will become oil'). In comparison, the bridging clauses lines A8, A13, and A18 repeat the entire serial construction in the reference clause. Could it be that line A21 is not a serial verb construction? Could it be that recapitulative linkage plays a role in differentiating serial verb construction from verb juxtaposition? This line of research is left open at this stage.

3.3 Analysis of a narrative

Narratives are texts that tell a story, imagined or real. Like procedural texts, narratives are built on two organizational positions: the main event line which carries the plot forward, and the supporting line which adds emotive or depictive information. The narrative I analyze here (schematized in Table 4) is a fiction narrative with two anthropomorphized characters: Parrot and Flying Fox. It tells the story of how Parrot tricked Flying Fox into hanging upside down, and how to this day, flying foxes hang upside down. The person narrating this text is the same as the narrator of the procedural text.[5]

---

[5]I think that it is important to keep in mind the composer of the narrative (Longacre 1983: 17) as bridging constructions are also used as stylistic devices, their usage thus varying along individual preferences. For example, in Mavea, I used a picture book to elicit a narrative. Two brothers in their early 30s participated. One of the brothers used just one recapitulative linkage in his narrative, the other more than ten.

Table 4: Schema of the fiction narrative: Parrot and Flying fox

Main line	Line #	Recap. Link.	Supporting line
Title	001		
Exposition: information about the protagonists. They are friends, they live, fly, play, eat together.	002–008		
Inciting moment: One day, they eat. They are satiated.	009–011		
They sit, they play.	012	reference cl.	
	013	bridging cl.	
	014–017		**Background**: Before they were both sitting on branches. Flying Fox was not hanging upside down.
Inciting moment: On that day, they eat. They are satiated, they sit.	018		
Complicating action: Parrot tricks Flying Fox. Parrot hangs upside down.	019		
	020	reference cl.	
	021	bridging cl.	
	022		**Repetition/elaboration**: Parrots hangs upside down, he flaps his wings.
Inciting moment: Parrot asks Flying Fox to hang upside down.	023		
	024	reference cl.	
	025	bridging cl.	
	026–027		**Repetition/elaboration**: They both hang upside down, they play.
Complicating action: Parrot goes back to sitting upright.	028	reference cl.	
	029	bridging cl.	
Inciting moment: Parrot asks Flying Fox to sit upright.	029–031		
Climax: Flying Fox tries but cannot sit upright, she hangs upside down.	032		
	033	reference cl.	**Repetition**: She keeps trying in vain.

Main line	Line #	Recap. Link.	Supporting line
Denouement: Flying Fox hangs upside down for good.	034	bridging cl.	
	035		**Summary**: Parrot tricked Flying Fox. To this day, flying foxes hang upside down.

There are 13 events on the main line, and five events on the supporting line. I identify four clear cases of recapitulative linkage, lines 012–013 shown in (17); 020–021 reproduced in (18); 024–025 in (14); and 028–029 in (19). One pair of sentences is ambiguous between a recapitulative linkage and a repetition (lines 014–015) and is left out of the analysis. The bridging clauses are all coordinated to the following clause using *ro* 'and, then'. The bridging clauses repeat the lexical content of the reference clause verbatim in two cases (012–013; 024–025) while in the other two instances (020–021; 028–029), only the subject noun phrase of the reference clause is not repeated in the bridging clause. All four bridging clauses have rising intonation contour and all four reference clauses have falling pitch. Last, all four bridging clauses are immediately adjacent to the reference clauses.

The end of the narrative contains an interesting case which I treat as a recapitulative linkage (lines 033–034), despite its unconventional feature. The reference clause in (16a) does not have the typical falling intonation of other reference clauses (although it is a final clause) because it is an exclamative clause, marked with a very high pitch. The bridging clause in (16b) has rising intonation, as is expected of this type of clause, as shown in Figure 7.

(16) a. *Mo-dere ro,   mo-sev!*   *[0.87s]*
       3SG-no   then 3SG-hang

       'No, she is hanging!'

   b. **Mo-sev**   ro   *mo-sev*   val v̆aite.
       3SG-hang then 3SG-hang go   once

       'She is hanging, then she hangs once and for all.'

In terms of placement and function, the first instance of recapitulative linkage (lines 012–013), reported in (17), occurs after a short list of descriptive events on the main line. What is interesting is that the following lines 014–017 provide background information about the animals, as an aside.

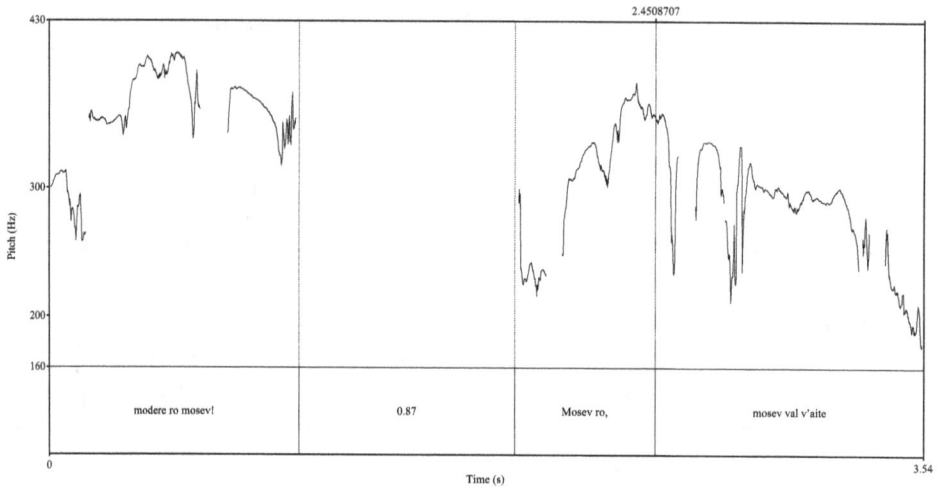

Figure 7: Intonation contour of example (16) extracted with PRAAT.

(17)   a.   *Ra-r-m̊a~m̊av̊an.*   *[0.85s]*
        3PL-DU-REDUP~play
        'They were playing with each other.'

   b.   *Ra-r-m̊a~m̊av̊an*   *ro*   *[1.07s]*
        3PL-DU-REDUP~play then
        'They were playing with each other then,'

   c.   *m̊atan madia ro*   *raruorua*   *ra-r-lo-sakele.*
        because first   then two.together 3PL-DU-IPFV-sit
        'because before, they were both sitting (on branches).'

There is a shift in the narration, from the main line to the supporting line. The question is to know whether this is an instance of thematic discontinuity. Just before the reference clause, the speaker is using hesitation markers and pauses, which I take to indicate that she buys time to think of her next story segment. However, the pauses are not longer than elsewhere in the same text. It is possible that she realizes that a piece of information is missing. She goes on to add the missing information after the bridging clause. I cannot ascertain that she used the bridging clause "deliberately" to mark a change in orientation.

The recapitulative linkage (lines 020–021), reported in (18), occurs at a crucial moment in the story, when Parrot hangs upside down. Many repetitions of the verb *sev* 'hang' appear in this passage. It seems safe to say that it is also a function of the linkage to add emphasis. This example is also interesting as it shows how

a bridging clause in (18b) can be followed by repetitions and elaborations, with
the same intonation pattern, as shown in Figure 8, raising the question of the
boundary between the different types of recapitulation.[6]

(18)   a. *Sivi   mo-si   mo-sev.* *[0.6s]*
              parrot 3SG-go.down 3SG-hang

              'Parrot is hanging upside down.'

   b. **Mo-si**   **mo-sev** *ro*   *mo-sev* *ro*
              3SG-go.down 3SG-hang then 3SG-hang then

              'He is hanging upside down, then he is hanging, then'

   c. *mo-sev   na palo-na   mo-m̃a i rua ro...*
              3SG-hang LOC leg-3SG:POSS 3SG-come LK two then

              'he hangs with both his legs then,...'

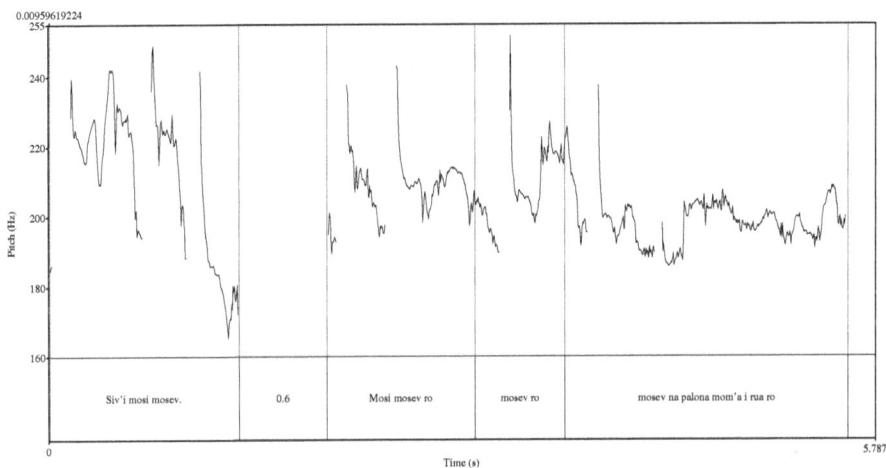

Figure 8: Intonation contour of example (18) extracted with PRAAT.

The recapitulative linkage (lines 024–025) shown in (14) is placed inside the
direct speech report of Parrot. The reference clause functions as a command,
which the bridging clause repeats. This is an important stage in the narrative
which seals the fate of Flying Fox. The recapitulative linkage is interpreted to

---

[6]A reviewer wondered if the repetition and elaboration in (18b) and (18c) could be taken as
bridging clauses. This analysis would entail that a reference clause could be followed by several
bridging clauses.

provide a semantic link between the events (temporal, sequential). It also adds emphasis and force to Parrot's request.

The next recapitulative linkage (028–029) reproduced in (19) also highlights an important stage in the narrative, the fact that Parrot goes back to his normal sitting position (whereas Flying Fox remains upside down). I interpret this recapitulative linkage as functioning like the one before: it adds sequentiality but it also underlines this significant turning point in the story.

(19)   a. *Siṽi   mo-pos   mo-sa   mo-sakele. [1.49s]*
          parrot 3SG-turn 3SG-go.up 3SG-sit

          'Parrot turns back up and sits.'

       b. ***mo-pos mo-sa   mo-sakele** ro   [1.07s]*
          3SG-turn 3SG-go.up 3SG-sit   then

          'He turns back up and sits, then'

       c. *mo-tov karae   mo-v   "ko-pos!"*
          3SG-call flying.fox 3SG-say 2SG-turn

          'he calls Flying Fox and says: "turn!"'

Last, the denouement of the story is reached. The linkage in the denouement (lines 033–034) is reproduced in (16). Again, the bridging clause is followed by an important new stage in the narrative: Flying Fox is trapped for good. Here again, the recapitulative linkage is used to highlight this important event. This is also the final point in the narrative. The following lines simply summarize the story.

My analysis appears in Table 5. In the narrative text, recapitulative linkage may have three functions. (i) It adds temporal sequencing and signals that the event following it is new information on the main event line. (ii) The bridging clause can announce a shift in orientation between foreground and background. (iii) In addition, recapitulative linkage adds emphasis, or what Longacre calls "rhetorical underlining". Around the climactic events, "the narrator does not want you to miss the important point of the story so he employs extra words at that point" (Longacre 1983: 26).

Comparing the two texts and genres, the data suggest that across text genres, a default or unmarked recapitulative linkage in Mavea (i) is one where the bridging clause repeats the lexical content of the reference clause verbatim with continuation intonation; (ii) immediately follows the reference clause; (iii) is overtly coordinated to the following clause; and (iv) functions principally as a highlighter. It draws attention to the temporal sequence of events, to the importance of the events (rhetorical underlining), or to shifts in orientation. This shift can be

Table 5: Properties of recapitulative linkage in the fiction narrative

Line # of bridging/ reference	Adjacency bridging/ reference	Coordin. or Juxtapos.	Recapitu- lation type	Clauses before/after the construction: on main/supporting line	Discourse function
012–013	yes	coordinated	verbatim	main/supporting	to supporting line
020–021	yes	coordinated	omission	main/supporting	rhetorical underline
024–025	yes	coordinated	verbatim	main/main	sequencing/ rhetorical underline
028–029	yes	coordinated	omission	main/main	sequencing/ rhetorical underline
033–034	yes	coordinated	verbatim	main/main	rhetorical underline

from foreground to background and flag thematic discontinuity or the other way around, from background to foreground, and mark thematic continuity, bringing the focus back to the (foregrounded) main sequence of events.

Event sequencing is the most widely acknowledged discourse function of bridging constructions (Halliday & Hasan 1976: 130, 242, 261; de Vries 2005: 370; Thompson et al. 2007: 273). In Oceanic languages, it is found in Nahavaq (Dimock 2009: 259), Lolovoli (Hyslop 2001: 427), Abma (Schneider 2009: 24–26). Whether event sequencing is a function of the recapitulative linkage in Mavea, or of the fact that the bridging clause is usually coordinated to the following discourse (and coordination carries overtones of temporal sequencing), or whether event sequencing is a combination of both strategies requires a more fine-grained analysis (see also Guérin 2011: 325). It seems to me that temporal succession is not just a function of the coordination strategies. The conjunction *(me)ke* in Ughele (Frostad 2012: 242), *ro* in Mavea (Guérin 2011: 322) and *en* in Nahavaq (Dimock 2009: 230–231) indicate that the conjoined clauses occur simultaneously or in sequential order. Similarly, asyndetic coordination can denote simultaneity or sequencing (Frostad 2012: 241, Hyslop 2001: 425–426). A bridging clause, however, does not seem to express simultaneity in Mavea.

4 Recapitulative linkage versus clausal repetition

Both clausal repetition and bridging constructions are common in Mavea discourse, and both repeat a verb phrase or a clause previously mentioned. Both can be coordinated or juxtaposed to the following clause. How can we tease apart these two constructions? First, there seems to be an obvious formal distinction between repetition and recapitulative linkage: the sheer number of repetitions that occur together. Recapitulative linkage involves the repetition of the reference clause just once. In verbal repetitions, on the other hand, the verb or clause can be reiterated three or four times, as in (20), and up to eight times in Tuvaluan (Besnier 2014: 487).

(20) **Mo-tang mo-tang mo-tang** *mo-lo-v̌a.*
     3SG-cry 3SG-cry 3SG-cry 3SG-IPFV-go
     'He cried and cried and kept crying for a while.' (Guérin 2011: 266)

Second, verbal repetition denotes continuous or iterative events. In many Oceanic languages, repetition (and reduplication) has grammaticalized to express aspectual dimensions such as habitual, imperfective, or iterative (Besnier 2014: 487; Guérin 2011: 117; Dimock 2009: 260). Recapitulative linkage, on the other hand, operates on the level of discourse, marking event completion and temporal sequencing, as discussed in §3. Last, repetition and bridging clauses differ in their intonations. Compare the repetition in (21) shown in Figure 9 with the recapitulative linkage in Figure 3, from the same speaker extracted from the same procedural text in the Appendix. It is visually clear that the patterns are very different. The bridging clause in (13b) has a sharp rising pitch, whereas the repetitions in (21b) have a rather flat contour or a falling intonation.

(21)   a. *Ko-l-arvulesi-a.* *[0.88s]*
         2SG-IPFV-stir-3SG
         'You stir it.'
   b. **Ko-arvulesi, ko-arvulesi, ko-arvulesi** *pelmel*
         2SG-stir   2SG-stir   2SG-stir   like.this
         'You stir, stir, stir like this,'
   c. *i-tikel*   *ma...* *[0.82s]*
         3SG:IRR-reach COMP
         'until...'
   d. *i-m̌a*   *i-oele.*
         3SG:IRR-come 3SG:IRR-oil
         'it becomes oil.'

5 Conclusions

This chapter revealed that recapitulative linkage in Mavea are made up of a final reference clause and a bridging clause which is syntactically a main clause, has

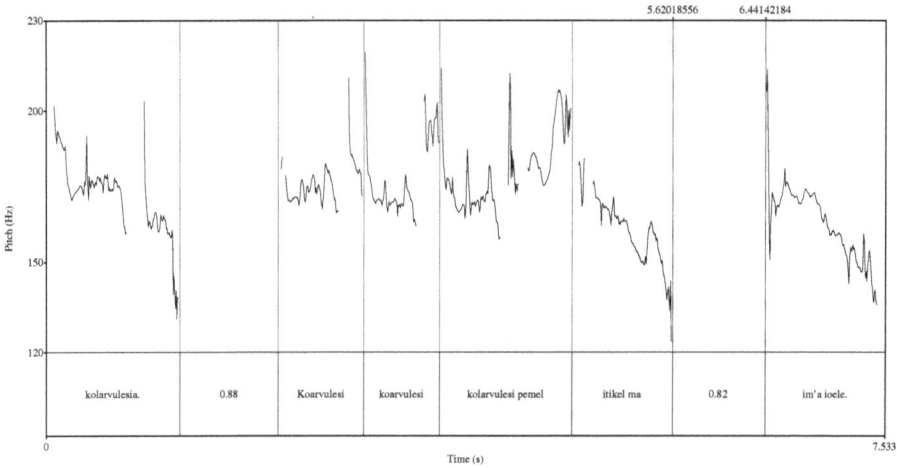

Figure 9: Intonation contour of example (21) extracted with PRAAT.

non-final prosody, and is juxtaposed or overtly coordinated to a following clause. A similar set of features characterizes recapitulative linkage in other languages of Vanuatu (Schneider 2009: 24–26; Thieberger 2006: 327; Hyslop 2001: 426) and elsewhere in the Oceanic language family (Palmer 2009; Frostad 2012; Hamel 1988: 172; Schokkin 2014: 115–116; Lithgow 1995: 94).

A reviewer wonders whether the kind of recapitulation found in Mavea can be considered a "construction", given that there is no special marker in the grammar and no specific condition triggering obligatory use. The point is well taken; recapitulative linkage in Mavea is a stylistic feature which has not grammaticalized. However, the lack of apparent form-meaning pairing is also expected if the syntactic profile of a language influences the formal characteristics of bridging constructions in that language (de Vries 2005; Seifart 2010: 898). First, in many Oceanic languages such as Sobei, Kaulong, Roviana or Manam (reported in Bril 2010; Lichtenberk 1983; Lynch et al. 2002: 53) coordination is preferred over subordination as a clause linking strategy. Therefore, it comes as no surprise that coordination is also the preferred strategy for the recapitulative linkage. Second, bridging clauses have continuation intonation, ending with a rising pitch, which marks them as dependent on the following clause. Even though a rising pitch is by no means a feature peculiar to recapitulative linkages alone, as shown in §2.2, this prosodic pattern separates bridging clauses from verbal repetitions. Last, recapitulative linkage in Mavea is a type of bridging construction given that the pattern has predictable semantic and discourse functions (§3): to flag thematic (dis)continuity, to add rhetorical underlining, and to highlight temporal succession. Thus, identifying recapitulative linkage in Mavea requires identifying a constellation of features: syntactic status, prosodic contour, semantic relation, and discourse function.

Appendix

Reproduced here is the procedural text schematized and analyzed in §3.2. I had asked the speaker, a woman in her 60s, to explain how to make coconut oil. The arrows at the end of a phrase broadly mark the intonation contour. The upper arrow ↑ indicates that the intonation rises, whereas the down arrow ↓ indicates that the intonation falls. No arrow indicates a rather flat intonation contour. Pauses in second appear between square brackets.

(A1) *Oele-n   m̃atiu* ↑ *[0.82s]*
      oil-3SG:POSS coconut [pause]
      'Coconut oil,'

(A2) *ko-rong ko-v   ko-mo-kuk   te   oele* ↓ *[0.6s]*
      2SG-feel 2SG-say 2SG-COND-cook some oil   [pause]
      'suppose you want to make oil,'

(A3) *oele-n   m̃atiu* ↑ *[1.31s]*
      oil-3SG:POSS coconut [pause]
      'coconut oil,'

(A4) *ko-v̆a ko-osom   te   m̃ati   du.* ↑ *[1.25s]*
      2SG-go 2SG-husk some coconut good [pause]
      'you husk some good coconuts.'

(A5) *Ko-v̆a ko-osom   te   m̃ati   patu.* ↓ *[0.7s]*
      2SG-go 2SG-husk some coconut head   [pause]
      'You husk some old coconuts.'

(A6) *Ko-lai   ko-m̃a* ↑ *ko-rosi-a* ↑   *[0.7s]*
      2SG-take 2SG-come 2SG-grate-3SG [pause]
      'You bring them, grate them [i.e., the coconut flesh],'

(A7)   ko-mo-osom   i-mo-ngavul   rua te i-ngavul   tol,
2SG-COND-husk 3SG:IRR-COND-decade two or 3SG:IRR-decade three
[0.9s]
[pause]
'you could husk 20 or 30,'

(A8)   **ko-lav̌i ko-m̌a**   ro   **ko-rosi-a**   i-lo-sisi   na
2SG-take 2SG-come and 2SG-grate-3SG 3SG:IRR-IPFV-go.down LOC
[0.7s]   te   dis ↑ [0.9s]
[pause] some dish [pause]
'you bring them, grate them inside...a dish,'

(A9)   i-v   i-mo-ev   ro ↑ <u>ko-siu-a</u>. ↓   [1.2s]
3SG:IRR-say 3SG:IRR-COND-finish and 2SG-knead-3SG [pause]
'when [grating] is about done, and you knead it [i.e., the coconut flesh].'

(A10)   **Ko-siu-a ↑**   [0.4s]   ro   [0.2s]
2SG-knead-3SG [pause] and [pause]
'You knead it and'

(A11)   **ko-siu-a**   i-lo-v̌a   i-mo-ev   ro ↑
2SG-knead-3SG 3SG:IRR-IPFV-go 3SG.IRR-COND-finish and
'you knead it for a while, and'

(A12)   ale <u>ko-v̌iris</u>   <u>i-si</u>   <u>na</u> <u>kuku</u> ↓ [1s]
then 2SG-squeeze 3SG:IRR-go.down LOC pot   [pause]
'then you squeeze [out the milk] into a cooking pot.'

(A13)   **Ko-v̌iris**   i-si   na **kuku** ro ↑ [1.09s]
2SG-squeeze 3SG:IRR-go.down LOC pot   and [pause]
'You squeeze [out the milk] into a cooking pot and'

(A14)   ko-[0.2s]ku-a. ↓   [1.1s]
2SG-[pause]boil-3SG [pause]
'you...boil it.'

233

Valérie Guérin

(A15) <u>*Ko-ti*   *sa*   *na* *apu*</u> ↓ *[0.6s]*
2SG-put go.up LOC fire   [pause]
'You put it on the fire.'

(A16) *Ko-v   ko-mo-ti   sa   nna ro* ↑
2SG-say 2SG-COND-put go.up 3SG and
'If you put it on [the fire] then'

(A17) *ko-sopo-kuro ti   v̆a.* ↓
2SG-NEG-leave put go
'don't leave it on.'

(A18) **Ko-ti   sa   nna ro** ↑
2SG-put go.up 3SG and
'You put it on [the fire],'

(A19) *ko-l-arvulesi-a* ↓ *[0.88s]*
2SG-IPFV-stir-3SG [pause]
'you stir it.'

(A20) *Ko-arvulesi ko-arvulesi ko-arvulesi pelmel*
2SG-stir   2SG-stir   2SG-stir   like.this
'You stir, stir, stir like this,'

(A21) *i-tikel   ma* ↓ *[0.82s] i-m̆a   i-oele.* ↓   *[0.98s]*
3SG:IRR-reach COMP [pause] 3SG:IRR-come 3SG:IRR-oil [pause]
'until...it becomes oil.'

(A22) *I-oele,   ko-arvulesi i-lo-v̆a*
3SG:IRR-oil 2SG-stir   3SG:IRR-IPFV-go
'It [is becoming] oil, you keep stirring'

(A23) *ko-rong* ↓ <u>*sama-na*</u>   <u>*mo-rororo.*</u>   *[0.6s]*
2SG-hear froth-3SG:POSS 3SG-IDEO.noise [pause]
'[until] you hear its froth sizzling.'

(A24) **Sama-na**   *mo-v* ***i-rororo*** ↑   *mal mo-noa*   *ne* ↓ *[0.88s]*
froth-3SG:POSS 3SG-say 3SG-IDEO.noise DEM 3SG-cooked FOC [pause]
'[When] its froth starts to sizzle, IT is cooked.'

(A25) *Ro ko-aia*   *ti sivo* ↑
and 2SG-remove put go.away
'So you remove [it from the fire]'

(A26) *i-l-m̃angadidi*   *ro* ↑
3SG:IRR-IPFV-cold and
'it cools down and'

(A27) *ale ko-[1.02s]* ↓ *ko-divui-a,   i-si*   *na botele.* ↓
then 2SG-[pause] 2SG-pour-3SG 3SG:IRR-go.down LOC bottle
'then, you pour it down into a bottle.'

Abbreviations

:	portmanteau	DET	determiner	IPFV	imperfective
-	affix boundary	DIST.PST	distant past	IRR	irrealis
1	first person	DU	dual	NEG	negation
2	second person	EXCL	exclusive	PL	plural
3	third person	FOC	focus marker	POSS	possessive
BR	basic root	IDEO	ideophone	PRO	pronoun
CIT	citation root	INCL	inclusive	REDUP	reduplicant
CLF	classifier	ITER	iterative	SG	singular
COMP	complementizer	LK	linker	TR	transitive marker
COND	conditional	LOC	locative		

Acknowledgements

Sincere thanks to both reviewers whose insightful comments helped improve this chapter, and to my consultants, friends, and families on Mavea Island.

References

Adam, Jean-Michel. 2001. Types de textes ou genres de discours ? Comment classer les textes qui disent de et comment faire ? *Langages* 141. 10–27.

Aikhenvald, Alexandra Y. 2006. Serial verb constructions in typological perspective. In Alexandra Y. Aikhenvald & R. M. W. Dixon (eds.), *Serial verb constructions: A cross-linguistic typology*, 1–68. Oxford: Oxford University Press.

Besnier, Niko. 2014. *Tuvaluan: A Polynesian language of the Central Pacific*. London: Routledge.

Boersma, Paul & David Weenink. 2019. *Praat: Doing phonetics by computer. Computer program, version 6.0.46.* http://www.praat.org, accessed 2019-1-3.

Bril, Isabelle. 2010. Informational and referential hierarchy: Clause-linking strategies in Austronesian-Oceanic languages. In Isabelle Bril (ed.), *Clause linking and clause hierarchy: Syntax and pragmatics*, 269–312. Amsterdam: John Benjamins.

Brown, Penelope. 2000. Repetition. *Journal of Linguistic Anthropology* 9(1–2). 223–226.

Cleary-Kemp, Jessica. 2017. *Serial verb constructions revisited: A case study from Koro*. University of California, Berkeley dissertation.

Crowley, Terry. 1998. *An Erromangan (Sye) grammar*. Honolulu: University of Hawai'i Press.

Crowley, Terry. 2003. *Serial verb in Oceanic: A descriptive typology*. Oxford: Oxford University Press.

de Vries, Lourens. 2005. Towards a typology of tail-head linkage in Papuan languages. *Studies in Language* 29(2). 363–384.

de Vries, Lourens. 2006. Areal pragmatics of New Guinea: Thematization, distribution and recapitulative linkage in Papuan narratives. *Journal of Pragmatics* 38(6). 811–828.

Delpech, Estelle & Patrick Saint-Dizier. 2008. Investigating the structure of procedural texts for answering how-to questions. *Proceedings of the International Conference on Language Resources and Evaluation*. 46–51. http://www.lrec-conf.org/proceedings/lrec2008/pdf/20_paper.pdf, accessed 2018-8-8.

Dimock, Laura Gail. 2009. *A grammar of Nahavaq (Malakula, Vanuatu)*. New Zealand: Victoria University of Wellington PhD Dissertation.

Fontan, Lionel & Patrick Saint-Dizier. 2008. Analyzing the explanation structure of procedural texts: Dealing with advice and warnings. *Proceedings of the 2008 Conference on Semantics in Text Processing*. 115–127. https://dl.acm.org/citation.cfm?id=1626491, accessed 2018-8-8.

Frostad, Benedicte Haraldstad. 2012. *A grammar of Ughele: An Oceanic language of Solomon Islands.* Utrecht: LOT.

Guérin, Valérie. 2006. *Documentation of Mavea.* London: SOAS, Endangered Languages Archive. https://elar.soas.ac.uk/Collection/MPI67426, accessed 2018-4-19.

Guérin, Valérie. 2011. *A grammar of Mavea, an Oceanic language of Vanuatu.* Honolulu: University of Hawai'i Press.

Guérin, Valérie & Grant Aiton. 2019. Bridging constructions in typological perspective. In Valérie Guérin (ed.), *Bridging constructions*, 1–44. Berlin: Language Science Press. DOI:10.5281/zenodo.2563678

Halliday, M. A. K. & Ruqaiya Hasan. 1976. *Cohesion in English.* London: Longman.

Hamel, Patricia. 1988. *A grammar and lexicon of Loniu, Papua New Guinea* (Pacific Linguistics C103). Canberra: The Australian National University.

Hyslop, Catriona. 2001. *The Lolovoli dialect of the North-East Ambae language, Vanuatu* (Pacific Linguistics 515). Canberra: The Australian National University.

Lee, David Y. W. 2001. Genres, registers, text types, domains, and styles: Clarifying the concepts and navigating a path through the BNC jungle. *Language Learning and Technology* 5(3). 37–72.

Lichtenberk, Frantisek. 1983. *A grammar of Manam.* Honolulu: University of Hawai'i Press.

Lithgow, David. 1995. Reduplication for past actions in Auhelawa. *Language and Linguistics in Melanesia* 26(1). 89–95.

Longacre, Robert E. 1983. *The grammar of discourse.* New York: Plenum Press.

Lynch, John, Malcolm Ross & Terry Crowley. 2002. *The Oceanic languages.* Richmond: Curzon.

Palmer, Bill. 2009. *Kokota grammar.* Honolulu: University of Hawai'i Press.

Schneider, Cynthia. 2009. Information structure in Abma. *Oceanic Linguistics* 48(1). 1–35.

Schneider, Cynthia. 2010. *A grammar of Abma: A language of Pentecost Island, Vanuatu* (Pacific Linguistics 608). Canberra: The Australian National University.

Schokkin, Dineke. 2014. Discourse practices as an areal feature in the New Guinea region? Explorations in Paluai, an Austronesian language of the Admiralties. *Journal of Pragmatics* 62. 107–120.

Schokkin, Gerda. 2013. *A grammar of Paluai, the language of Baluan Island, Papua New Guinea.* Cairns, Australia: James Cook University PhD Dissertation.

Seifart, Frank. 2010. The Bora connector pronoun and tail-head linkage: A study in language-specific grammaticalization. *Linguistics* 48(2). 893–918.

Thieberger, Nicholas. 2006. *A grammar of South Efate: An Oceanic language of Vanuatu*. Honolulu: University of Hawai'i Press.

Thompson, Sandra A., Robert E. Longacre & Shin Ja J. Hwang. 2007. Adverbial clauses. In Timothy Shopen (ed.), *Language typology and syntactic description: Complex constructions*, vol. 2, 237–300. Cambridge: Cambridge University Press.

Chapter 9

Clause repetition as a tying technique in Greek conversation

Angeliki Alvanoudi

Aristotle University of Thessaloniki and James Cook University

This chapter targets a language in which bridging constructions are not grammaticalized, that is, Greek. It examines instances of same-speaker and cross-speaker clause repetition in informal Greek conversation. The analysis demonstrates that the basic function of clause repetition is to display connectedness between what the current speaker says or does and what the same or previous speaker said or did immediately before. It is argued that clause repetition displays some similarities with recapitulative linkage and it is hypothesized that recapitulative linkage constructions have emerged from repetition practices in conversation.

1 Introduction

Recapitulative linkage is a type of bridging construction in which the bridging clause repeats at least the predicate of the reference clause. Recapitulative linkage is not an integral part of the Greek grammar. Yet clause repetition is one of the cohesive or tying techniques employed in Greek conversation. It consists of a main or non-main clause that repeats a prior main or non-main clause, as in example (1), lines 4–6, and example (2), lines 1 and 3.

(1)   01 Pol: >> Eγó ton ékopsa.

'I stopped drinking coffee.'
02   (1.3)
03 Pol: Vévea éxodas kópsi to tsiγáro o kafés °ítane: (0.5)

'Of course compared to quitting smoking coffee was (0.5)'

Angeliki Alvanoudi. 2019. Clause repetition as a tying technique in Greek conversation. In Valérie Guérin (ed.), *Bridging constructions*, 239–267. Berlin: Language Science Press. DOI:10.5281/zenodo.2563694

04 Ale: >> ↑*De su   kostízi   pá[ra   polí.]*
　　　　　NEG 2SG.GEN cost.3SG.PRS very   much
　　　　　'It doesn't cost you very much.'

05 Pol: >>　　　　　　　　　　　　　　　*[De su   ko]stízi*
　　　　　　　　　　　　　　　　　　　　NEG 2SG.GEN cost.3SG.PRS
　　　　　　　　　　　　　　　　　　　　'It doesn't cost you'

06　　　　>> °*pára polí.=*
　　　　　very   much
　　　　　'very much.'

(2)　01 Mar:>> *Ci áma íse   ce mónos su   ti   na*
　　　　　　　and if   COP.2SG.PRS and by   yourself what SBJV
　　　02　　　*kátsis   na   kánis.=*
　　　　　　　sit.2SG.PFV SBJV do.2SG
　　　　　　　'And if you are alone what are you supposed to do.='
　　03 Our:>> =*Áma íse   mónos su   [ðen éçis   ce]*
　　　　　　　if   COP.2SG.PRS by   yourself NEG have.2SG.PRS and
　　　　　　　'=I think that if you are alone you are not'
　　04 Vag:　　　　　　　　　　　　　　　　　　　[°M: ne.]
　　　　　　　　　　　　　　　　　　　　　　　'Mm yes.'
　　05 Our:　ti ðiáθesi pistévo tin íðja. ektós an íse me á[lus.]
　　　　　　　'in the mood. unless you are together with others.'
　　06 Mar:　　　　　　　　　　　　　　　　　　　　[Ma]: ne.
　　　　　　　　　　　　　　　　　　　　　　　'But of course.'

Clause repetition in Greek conversation shares some of the formal and discursive properties of recapitulative linkage constructions (cf. Guérin & Aiton 2019 [this volume]). First, recapitulative linkage involves repetition of at least the verb of the reference clause; not all elements accompanying the verb of the reference clause are necessarily repeated. Clause repetitions in Greek conversation involve repetition of at least the verb of the first saying and some of the elements accompanying the verb. Second, recapitulative linkage is a discourse strategy that achieves cohesion, by establishing thematic continuity or referential coherence (de Vries 2005), backgrounding the proposition of the reference clause and prefacing discourse-new information that is usually sequentially ordered (Guérin & Aiton 2019 [this volume]). As we will see in this chapter, the basic function of clause repetition in Greek conversation is to display connectedness with the ongoing talk. Yet the two phenomena are not identical. Clause repetition in Greek conversation is a practice widely distributed between speaker and recipient, whereas recapitulative linkage occurs in same speaker's utterance.[1] Unlike bridging clauses that prototypically consist of clauses, which are morphologically, syntactically or intonationally marked as dependent on the reference clauses, repeated clauses in Greek conversation can be grammatically and pragmatically complete utterances. Moreover, recapitulative linkage usually expresses a temporal semantic relation that involves the transition between linked events. Clause repetition in Greek conversation does not express temporal sequentiality or any fixed semantic relationships; it carries different functions in different contexts.

The aim of the present study is to examine instances of clause repetition in two contexts: self-repetition (same-speaker) and repetition of prior turn at talk (cross-speaker) in Greek conversation, and demonstrate that the basic function of clause repetition is to display *connectedness* between what the current speaker says or does and what the same or previous speaker said or did immediately before. It is hypothesized that across languages there is a continuum between repetition as a generic linguistic practice and more or less conventionalized forms of bridging constructions. The outline of the chapter is as follows. In §2, I review previous studies on the forms and functions of repetition in conversation. In §3, I approach the cohesive function of repetition in conversation through the lens of conversation analysis. In §4, I analyse self-repetition (§4.2) and repetition of prior turn (§4.3) in naturally occurring conversations, focusing on the use of clause repetition as a tying technique. §5 contains a discussion of the findings.

2 The role of repetition in conversation

Repetition, in Brown's words (2000: 225), is "a grammatical, stylistic, poetic, and cognitive resource associated with attention." It constitutes part of everyday human conduct and is found in social life, rituals, events, conversation, and grammar (Johnstone 1994; Brown 2000; Wong 2000). In conversation, repetition distinguishes *self-repetition* and *repetition of a prior turn at talk* (Brown 2000). In terms of form, repetition can be exact or modified. Exact repetition involves the exact duplication of words, that is, a "perfect copy" of a first saying, while modified

---

[1]Valérie Guérin pointed out to me that this feature of recapitulative linkage may be an artefact of the data rather than a pattern found in conversation, given that previous studies on bridging constructions did not analyse data from talk-in-interaction.

repetition involves a modified replication of words through addition or omission, that is, a "near copy" of a first saying (Couper-Kuhlen 1996: 368, Brown 2000: 224). Repetition carries multiple functions that depend on the context of use of repeated elements. As Couper-Kuhlen (1996: 368) observes, "replication of form does not necessarily mean replication of function." A similar point is made by Johnstone (1994: 12), who claims that although the referential meaning of repeated elements remains the same, non-referential aspects of their meaning change, given that the context of use of repeated elements changes.

In general, repetition is a mode of focusing the addressee's attention to something. This generic function of repetition can be particularized in different contexts of usage. For instance, speakers use repetition to achieve discourse cohesion (Goodwin & Goodwin 1987; Norrick 1987; Tannen 1987; 1989; Johnstone 1994; Tyler 1994; Sacks 1995; Brown 2000), and implement various social actions in talk-in-interaction, such as:

- Answering a question (Norrick 1987; Raymond 2003; Stivers & Hayashi 2010; Stivers 2011)

- Agreeing or disagreeing with prior speaker (Pomerantz 1984; Goodwin & Goodwin 1987; Norrick 1987; Tannen 1987)

- Claiming more agency with respect to the action they are implementing (Stivers 2005; Heritage & Raymond 2012; Lee 2012)

- Confirming an allusion (Schegloff 1996a)

- Registering receipt of a prior turn (Tannen 1989; Schegloff 1997; Kim 2002)

- Initiating repair (Schegloff et al. 1977; Sorjonen 1996; Kim 2002)

- Sustaining a particular topical focus (Tannen 1989; Kim 2002)

- Resuming a story (Wong 2000)

Repetition is also used for delivering recycled turn beginnings (Schegloff 1987) and dealing with interruption and overlapping talk (Norrick 1987; Johnstone 1994), and it can serve as a stylistic feature used for emphasis or clarification (Norrick 1987; Johnstone 1994). There is often an interrelation between the interactional functions of repetition and "its placement in the turn-taking metric" (Wong 2000: 411). For instance, self-repetitions may deal with overlapping talk, whereas repetitions of prior turn may initiate repair (Wong 2000). The cohesive function of repetition in conversation is the topic of the next section.

3 Repetition as a tying technique in conversation

Discourse cohesion is achieved through a variety of linguistic resources, such as repetition, reference, ellipsis or omission, substitution, conjunction, synonymy and collocation (Martin 2001). Cohesion is usually understood through the lens of systemic functional linguistics (Halliday 1973; Halliday & Hasan 1976), as a relation of dependence between the interpretation of some element and another element in discourse. This study, however, approaches cohesion from a conversation analytic perspective.

Speakers always deal with the problem of cohesion or connectedness with ongoing talk, when they design their turns, given that talk-in-interaction involves contingencies between prior, current and next turns. In talk-in-interaction, speakers take turns, which consist of turn-constructional units (TCUs), i.e., clauses, phrases and lexical items that constitute at least one action (Schegloff 2007: 3–4). Turns form sequences, that is, courses of actions implemented through talk. The unit of sequence organization is the adjacency pair, which is composed of two turns produced by different speakers, adjacently placed and relatively ordered as first pair part and second pair part (Schegloff 2007: 13). First pair parts initiate some exchange, such as a question, a request or an offer. Second pair parts respond to the action of the first pair parts: they deliver an answer to the question, a rejection or an acceptance of the request, or the offer. First pair parts project the relevance of specific second pair parts; they set powerful constraints on what the recipient should do, and on how the action accomplished by the recipient should be understood (Schegloff 2007: 21). Thus, next turns are understood by co-participants to display an understanding of the just prior turn, and to embody an action responsive to the just prior turn so understood (Schegloff 2007: 15). According to Drew (2012: 131), interaction consists of "contingently connected sequences of turns in which we each 'act', and in which the other's – our recipient's – response to our turn relies upon, and embodies, his/her understanding of what we were doing and what we meant to convey in our (prior) turn."

When speakers design their current turn, they need to display how their turn is connected with what came immediately before (Drew 2012: 134), namely how their turn is connected with the prior turn produced by a different speaker, or with the prior TCU within the same speaker's turn. For example, in the beginning of turns speakers may display whether their current turn takes a different stance from the prior turn produced by another speaker (Schegloff 1996b). In the beginning of non-initial TCUs within multi-unit turns, speakers may display whether the current TCU continues the project of the preceding TCU, or whether the current TCU launches or projects another action (Mazeland 2012: 481). Repetition is one of the practices that speakers use to display connectedness with ongoing talk. Couper-Kuhlen & Selting (2017) describe repetition as a generic linguistic practice that "depends on the establishment of a relation of formal similarity between a set of forms in one (current) turn and another set of forms in a prior turn". In conversation, speakers use repetition as a "tying technique" (Sacks 1995) or "format tying" (following the terminology of Goodwin & Goodwin 1987 and Goodwin 1990) to create a relation between a current turn and a prior turn and, thus, achieve cohesion. According to Goodwin (1990: 177), format tying involves participants' strategic use of phonological, syntactic or semantic surface structures of prior turns for tying talk between turns; repetition is an instance of the format tying apparatus. The use of clause repetition as a tying technique in Greek conversation is analyzed in §4.

4 Clause repetition in Greek conversation

4.1 Data

The data analyzed in this study stem from 33 fully transcribed audio-recorded naturally occurring face-to-face conversations among friends and relatives from the Corpus of Spoken Greek of the Institute of Modern Greek Studies.[2] The total duration of the conversations examined is about 22 hours and 23 minutes, and the total number of words is 324,994.

Before moving to the analysis of the data, some basic information on the language profile is required. Modern Greek belongs to the Indo-European group of languages, and is spoken by about 13 million speakers, with approximately 10 million of them living in Greece, and the rest in Cyprus and parts of the Greek diaspora (detailed descriptions of the language can be found in Joseph & Phillipaki-Warburton 1987 and Mackridge 1985). Greek is a fusional, highly inflecting language, in which several grammatical categories are marked morphologically. For instance, nouns inflect for gender, number and case, and verbs inflect for person, number, tense, aspect, voice, and mood. Greek is a pro-drop language with a flexible word order.

Approximately 130 instances of clause repetition were found in the data examined: 73 self-repetitions and 57 repetitions of a prior turn. In terms of form, the large majority of clause repetitions are modified. Most of the modified repetitions involve a change in intonation that contributes to the change in meaning

---

[2]Conversations have been transcribed according to the conventions of conversation analysis. A list of transcription symbols is in the Appendix.

expressed by the repeated clause. Modified repetitions often involve addition or omission whereby speakers go beyond the initial version of the clause or omit something in the repeated clause. In terms of function, most clause repetitions are used as tying techniques. However, variation is found within each category of repetition. Unlike repetitions of prior turn at talk, which are routinely used as tying techniques implementing various actions, self-repetitions do not always have a cohesive function.

Following Wong's 2000 terminology, I refer to the antecedent of the repetition as first saying, and the repetition of the whole clause or part of the clause (at least of the verb) as second saying. I avoid using the terms *reference clause* and *bridging clause* (cf. Guérin & Aiton 2019 [this volume]), since the phenomenon examined here is not a typical bridging construction (cf. §1). First saying and second saying are codified in the excerpts below as FS and SS respectively. Although clause repetition may occur in various turns in each excerpt, special focus is given only to certain usages (marked with bold face). The turns in which these usages occur are followed by glossing.

4.2 Self-repetition

28 out of the 73 self-repetitions found in the data have a cohesive function, as shown in examples (3) to (5). In the lines preceding (3), participants argue about whether Greek taxi drivers drive safely or not. In lines 1–2, Thanos implies that they do not know how to drive through the form of a rhetorical question, and Petros disagrees in lines 3 and 5–8. He uses the negative particle *óçi* 'no' to express his disagreement with the previous speaker, in turn-initial position. In the next TCU, he offers an account for his disagreement: he claims that there are certain standards (*ipárxun meriká stádars* 'there are certain standards'), uttering the noun with emphasis due to increased loudness or higher pitch. The speaker seeks confirmation of understanding by the recipient, and offers another account for his disagreement in the next TCU. He starts the TCU with the discourse particle *ðilaðí* 'that is', and repeats the clause from the previous TCU (>*ipárxun meriká< stádars* 'there are certain standards'). The second saying is modified. The speaker utters part of the clause in a rushed way, with no emphasis on the noun. By repeating the clause, the speaker shows that the current TCU continues the project of the prior one. In this case, clause repetition links different TCUs within the same speaker's turn, and displays connectedness with ongoing talk.

(3) 01 Tha: =e ti: e
    02   [moré. pços kséri na   oðiɣái?]
               '=eh what eh hey. Who knows how to drive?'

```
03 Pet: FS>>   [[Oçi. aplá] θélo          na    po        óti    ipá]rxun
                no    just  want.1SG.PRS SBJV tell.1SG.PFV CONJ  COP.3PL.PRS

                'No. I just want to say that there are'
04 Nef:        [(.............)]
05 Pet: FS>>   meriká              stádars   >vre peðí mu.<
                certain.NEUT.ACC.PL standards PART child my

                'certain standards hey you man.'
06       SS>>  katálaves?         ðilaðí, >ipárxun
                understand.2SG.PST that.is COP.3PL.PRS
07             meriká<
                certain.NEUT.ACC.PL

                'Do you understand? That is, there are certain'
08             stáda[rs, ta opía i taksiʣíðes ðen da sévode.]

                'standards that taxi drivers do not respect.'
09 Tha:             [Eh ↑ ti? pça íne ta- ↑ emís ta        ká]nume

                    'what? What are the- we make'
10             ta stádar.

                'the standards'
```

In (4), participants talk about carnival celebrations in the city of Patra in Greece. In lines 1–2, Vagelis informs his co-participants about volunteers forming groups for the carnival parade (*kánune:::grup*, 'they form groups') and in line 4, Maria interrupts Vagelis before his turn reaches possible completion. In line 8, Vagelis continues the turn that was interrupted. He repeats an almost perfect copy (*kánune grup*, 'they form groups') of his previous clausal TCU (in line 2): the only difference between the first and second saying is the vowel lengthening in the first saying. The turn continues the action of informing that was suspended. The speaker uses clause repetition in turn-initial position. As Schegloff (1987: 72) argues, turn beginnings are "sequence-structurally important places" in conversation, because they project the turn type or shape, and the relation between the current turn and the prior one. The repeated clause prefacing the turn in line 8 conveys that what follows is part of the speaker's prior activity, and connects the same speaker's previous and current turn.

(4)   01 Vag: =Ci éxun ðicéoma na katevúne ó:li, ósi θélune,

                  'And they all have the right to participate, whoever wants
                  to participate,'

```
02    FS >> .hh kánu[ne:]:    [:grup,]
              .hh make.3PL.PRS  group
              '.hh they form groups,'
03 Our:               [(((giggle))]
04 Mar:                           [.h Fad]ázese na min íçes ce ðiçéoma
                                  ((laughing.........................................
                                  'Imagine  if  you  didn't  even  have  the
              right'
05            na katévis séna karnaváli.
              .........................................))
              'to participate in the carnival.'
06 Our:       ((gig[gle............))]
07 Mar:          [(((she laughs][.............))]
08 Vag: SS >>               [kánune]    grup, ci  éçi:
                            make.3PL.PRS group and have.3SG.PRS
                            'they form groups, and it is'
09            e- ci éxun polí pláka:. jatí [parusiázune po]lí protótipa
              'eh- and they are very funny. Because they present very in-
              novative'
10 Mar?:                                  [°A::(h)          ]
11 Vag:       ármata::: me tin [  epi]çerótita,=
              'floats related to current affairs,'
12 Our:                       [°(Ne)]
                              'Yes.'
```

In (5), in line 3, Katia suggests that she and her co-participants cook something. She uses a negative question in the subjunctive (>ðen báme na majirépsume?< 'Shall we go and cook?' or 'Why don't we cook?'), that expects a positive answer. Before recipients respond, and without an expected micro-pause after the delivery of the question, Katia initiates a new sequence by asking Eirini if she wants to eat (line 3), and does a subtopic shift. This sequence is closed down in line 8. In line 11, Katia returns to the initial action that was suspended: she uses the discourse marker *lipón* 'so' to express exhortation, and repeats the clausal TCU that she initially employed, in line 3, to implement the suggestion. The repeated clause is modified (*na páme na majirépsume?* 'shall we go and cook?'): the speaker uses the subjunctive without negation, utters the verb *páme* with emphasis, and does not deliver the clause in a rushed way. The speaker repeats the clausal TCU in the same turn (lines 12, 14) with modifications (*ðen báme stin guzína na majirépsume?* 'shall we go in the kitchen and cook?'). She uses the negative polar question format, and refers to the kitchen, where the activity will take place. In lines 13, 15–16, Eirini and Zoi accept the suggestion. In this excerpt, clause repetition links the same speaker's current and prior turn.

(5) 01 Kat: <u>Pí</u>nasa.
                  'I am hungry.'
      02   (1.1)
      03 Kat:FS>> *>Đen báme   na majirépsume?<*
                  NEG   go.1PL.PRS SBJV cook.1PL.PFV
                  'Shall we go and cook?'
      04   *=Rináci   θa fa::s?=*
                  Eirini.DIM FUT eat.2SG.PFV
                  'Eirini will you eat?'
      05 Eir: =<u>O</u>çi. alá θa voiθí[so ↑sti majirikí sa:s.]=
                  'No. but I will help you with the cooking.'
      06 Kat: [<jatí ðe θa fa:s?>   ]=
                          'Why won't you eat?'
      07 Eir: =[.h ↑jatí <u>é</u>faɣa   sí]mera:. ðe boró álo. éxo <u>ská</u>:si.
                  ((noise starts))
                  '.h because I ate today. I cannot eat any more. I am full.'
      08 Kat: =[avɣá me patá:(tes).]
                  'eggs with potatoes.'
      09 Eir: >ce θa jíno< xo<u>dró</u>. .h o- θa voiθiso ómos sti majirikí sas.
                  ((laughing..))
                  'and I will get fat. .h o- but I will help with your cooking.'
      10   (.)
      11 Kat:SS>> *Lipón. na <u>pá</u>me na majirépsume?*
                  SO   SBJV <u>go</u>.1PL SBJV cook.1PL.PFV
                  'So. Shall we go and cook?'
                    ((noise ends))
      12   SS+>> *θé[lete?   =ðen báme stin guzí]na*
                  want.2PL.PRS NEG go.1PL in   kitchen(F).ACC.SG
                  'Do you want? Shall we go in the kitchen'
      13 Zoi: [Ade. <u>pá</u>me. páme.   ]
                  'Come on. let's go. let's go.'
      14 Kat:SS+>> *na majirépsu[me?]*
                  SBJV cook.1PL.PFV
                  'and cook?'

15 Eir:	[Ne.] =páme stin guzí[na.]
	'Yes. Let's go in the kitchen.'
16 Zoi:	[Pá]me.
	'Let's go.'

In the examples examined above, self-repetition is a tying technique that establishes contiguity between current and prior units or turns. Moreover, in (3) and (4), the repeated clause is followed by discourse-new information. Yet cohesion is not the only function associated with self-repetition. 45 of the self-repetitions found in the data have a non-cohesive function: they deal with overlapping talk, pursue a response, initiate and deliver repair, and add emphasis. These functions are illustrated with examples (6) to (8). In (6), in line 2, Yorgos asks Sotiris a question. His first TCU (*Aftó ðilónete?* 'Is this announced?') overlaps with the talk by Sotiris (line 1), and Yorgos repeats the question (*aftó ðilónete::?* 'is this announced?'), in line 3. The second saying differs from the first saying, as the verb *ðilónete::* is delivered with vowel prolongation and no emphasis. Sotiris answers Yorgos' question in lines 4–5 (*To maθénis °siníθos.* 'Usually you find out about it.'). His first TCU overlaps with Yorgos's prior turn, and Sotiris repeats the answer in the next TCU (*>siníθos< to maθénis.* 'Usually you find out about it.'). The second saying is modified. The order of clause constituents is different, as the adverb precedes the verb phrase, plus the adverb is delivered in a rushed way, and the verb with no emphasis. In this excerpt, clause repetitions compensate for recipient's possible trouble in hearing and understanding, and do not have a cohesive function.

(6)	01 Sot:	[(benun) ðiáfori.]
		'Various people come.'
	02 Yor: FS >>	*[Aftó ðilónete?]*
		this.NEUT.NOM.SG announce.3SG.PASS.PRS
		'Is this announced?'
	03 SS >>	*aftó ðilónete:[:? pos to maθénis?]*
		this announce.3SG.PASS.PRS how it learn.2SG.PRS
		'Is this announced? How do you find out about it?'
	04 Sot: FS >>	*[To maθénis °siní]θos.*
		it learn.2SG.PRS usually
		'Usually you find out about it'
	05 SS >>	*>siníθos< to maθénis.°*
		usually it learn.2SG.PRS
		'Usually you find out about it.'

In example (7), in lines 2–3, Thanasis makes a statement (*˚Esí ti ynórises af-tín.* 'You met her.') that operates as a confirmation-seeking question, and in line 5, Telis initiates repair to resolve trouble in understanding Thanasis's turn due to overlapping talk. In line 6, Thanasis completes the repair by repeating the clause that he used in his prior turn (*˚Ti ynórises.* 'You met her'). Telis answers the question in line 7. Thanasis's second saying is modified: the speaker utters the verb without emphasis, omits the second and third person singular pronouns, while keeping the clitic pronoun *ti* (such omissions are common in Greek conversation). The speaker uses clause repetition to offset the recipient's problem in understanding or hearing.

```
(7)  01 Chr:      [Ne:,] mu ta pe [>°eména.° mu ta pe.<     ]
                  'Yes, he told me. He told me.'
     02 Th: FS >>              [°Esí     ti         [ynó]ri]ses
                               2SG.NOM 3SG.F.ACC meet.2SG.PST
     03                        aftín.
                               3SG.F.ACC
                               'You met her.'
     04 Tel:                                       [°(Ne,)]
                                                    '(Yes,)'
     05 Tel:      Eh?=
     06 Th: SS >> =°Ti      ynó[rises]  .
                  3SG.F.ACC meet.2SG.PST
                  'You met her.'
     07 Tel:                        [.hh   ] >Oçi, alá mu ne san na din gzéro.
                                    '.hh No, but it feels like I know her.'
```

In example (8), clause repetition is a practice for pursuing the recipient's response (Pomerantz 1984). In line 4, Linos asks Mara when she and the others will leave (*Mára, póte févjete (...)* 'Mara, when are you leaving (...)'). His turn overlaps with Mara's answer (line 5) to Roza's question. Mara does not respond, and Linos repeats his question in line 6 (*>Póte θa fíjete.<* 'When are you leaving?'), with modifications. He delivers the turn in a rushed way, with emphasis on the interrogative word, and he uses future tense. His question receives no answer, and Linos delivers the same question again in line 8 (*>Póte θa fíjete esís?<* 'When are you leaving?'), with a few modifications. He repeats what he said in his previous turn, adds the second person plural pronoun, and uses rising intonation. Mara ignores him, and Linos reacts with frustration in line 11. His turn functions as a summons (Schegloff 1968) that aims to secure Mara's attention and availability.

Mara responds to the summons by displaying her attentiveness in line 12. Linos repeats his question in line 13 (*>Póte tha fíjete esís.<* 'When are you leaving.'), with emphasis on the interrogative word and the second person plural pronoun, and falling intonation. Mara answers the question in line 15. In this excerpt, the speaker asks a question that anticipates a response by the recipient but the recipient does not respond. The speaker pursues an articulated response by repeating the clause that he used to implement his question, and thus uses repetition as an attention-getting device.

(8) 01 Mar: <u>Pé</u>mpti íne anixtá. ci i Kalirói éç faɣoθí na páme.

                    'It is open on Thursday. and Kaliroi insists that we go.'

02   stin aɣorá na psonís[i: blú]za.=

                    'to the market, she wants to buy a T-shirt.'

03 Roz: [<u>Sí</u>mera?]

                        'Today?'

04 Lin: FS >> *=**Má**ra, **pó**te [**fé**vjete(.....)]*

          Mara   when leave.2PL.PRS

          'Mara, when are you leaving (...)'

05 Mar: [ðen ↑báo sí]:mera.=

                      'I am not going today.'

06 Lin: SS >> *=>**Pó**[te θa fijete<]*

          when   FUT leave.2PL.PFV

          'When are you leaving?'

07 Mar: [↑Alá: áma]vɣo na psoníso ap ti má:na,=

          'But if I go shopping for mum,'

08 Lin: SS+ >> *=>**Pó**te θa fijete   es[ís?<]*

          when FUT leave.2PL.PFV 2PL.NOM

          'When are you leaving?'

09 Mar: [pu   ] θél

                          'she wants'

10   patá[es,   θél]

          'potatoes, she wants'

11 Lin: [>Re su mi↑lá] o re Dalára.<

          'Hey I am talking to you.'

12 Mar: [Ne.   ]

          'Yes.'

13 Lin: SS+ >> *[>**Pó**te θa] fijete   esís.<*

          when FUT leave.2PL.PFV 2PL.NOM

          'When are you leaving?'

14		(0.8)
15	Mar:	ðe̲n gzéro, Sá̲:vato?

'I don't know, on Saturday?'

(.)

| 16 | Lin: | A̲:: >tha fíjete Sá̲vato.< |

'Ah:: you are leaving on Saturday.'

Finally, self-repetition operates as a stylistic feature used for emphasis. In example (9), participants assess positively a movie they watched. In lines 4–5, Yannis refers to a scene of action that he found exciting, and he uses the interrogative clause *zi i péθane?* 'is he alive or dead?' to express the audience's suspense during the screening. In line 6, he repeats the clause twice with non-falling intonation (*zi i péθane,* 'is he alive or dead') in order to intensify the suspense. This self-repetition is semantically based and iconically motivated (cf. Norrick 1987); it indicates the speaker's emotional involvement, and has a clear emphatic function.

(9) 01 Yan: =[To pos kata]férni [i tenía xorís na] simví [<↑tí̲po]ta,>

'The movie creates such a suspense when nothing is happening,'

02 Ama: =[Polí oréo.]   [Polí̲ oréo.   ]

'Very nice. Very nice.'

03 Nik: [(Foveró.)]

'Fantastic.'

04 Yan: FS >>   esí   na   se   e̲tsi.   zi   i

2SG.NOM SBJV COP.2SG.PRS like.that live.3SG.PRS or

'you are wondering. Is he alive or'

05   péθane?

die.3SG.PST

'dead?'

06   SS/SS+>> zi   i   péθane,   [zi   i   pé]θane,

live.3SG.PRS or die.3SG.PST live.3SG.PRS or die.3SG.PST

'is he alive or dead, is he alive or dead'

07   .hh ce:

hh and

'.hh and'

08 Nik: [(Oréo.)   ]

'(Nice.)'

We now turn to repetitions that build on the prior turn produced by a different speaker.

4.3 Repetition of a prior turn at talk

In next turns, speakers display how their current turn is connected with the prior turn produced by another speaker. Clause repetition is among the resources that speakers employ to display this connectedness. In all 57 instances of repetition of a prior turn at talk found in the data, speakers repeat clauses from prior turns produced by different speakers in order to embody their understanding of what the previous speakers did, and implement actions that respond to the just prior turn. In these cases, clause repetition is a practice that connects speaker's current turn with prior talk.

Answers to polar questions are a common interactional context in which repetitions of prior turn occur, as shown in examples (10) and (11). In this sequential position, repetition connects the speaker's current turn with prior talk and allows the speaker to claim more agency with respect to the action she is implementing (cf. Heritage & Raymond 2012). In (10), in lines 3–4, Roza asks Mara a question (*Ce ðe- ci íne tóso jelío epiçírima?* 'And not- and is it such a ridiculous argument?'). In line 5, Mara replies with the confirmation particle *ne* 'yes', and repeats the clause that Roza used in her prior turn (*íne jelío epiçírima* 'it is a ridiculous argument'), with modifications. She omits the adverb and adds emphasis on the adjective.

(10) 01 Mar: tétça práɣmata.

'such things.'

02   [aftó to len< diá:fori.   ]

'many people say this.'

03 Roz: FS >> [Ce ðe- ci   íne   tó]so jelío

and NEG and COP.3SG.PRS SO   ridiculous

'And not- and is it such a ridiculous'

04   FS >> [epiçírima?   ]

argument(NEUT).NOM.SG

'argument?'

05 Mar: SS >> [Ne íne   jelío   epi]çírima,

yes COP.3SG.PRS ridiculous argument(NEUT).NOM.SG

'Yes it is a ridiculous argument,'

06   [alá (...)]

'but (...)'

07 Roz: [↑Pé:de] çiliáðes Evréi ↓ítan léi:, ecí pu ðúlevan,

'Five thousands Jews are said to have been working there,'

In example (11), Ourania replies (lines 3–4) to Chrysanthi's polar question (lines 1–2). The question is implemented via the interrogative clause *Itan- efiméreve to °Xadzikósta?* 'Was- was the Hatzikosta hospital open?', and the answer is implemented via repetition of the clause with falling intonation (*Efiméreve to Xatzikósta.* 'The Hatzikosta hospital was open.').[3] The clause repetition in this excerpt is modified: the speaker adds emphasis on the verb, and uses falling intonation that turns the clause into a statement.

(11) 01 Chr: FS >> *Itan-*
                         COP.3SG.PST
                         'Was-'

      02   *efi[méreve   to   °Xadzikósta?]*
                   be.on.duty.3SG.PST DEF.NEUT.NOM.SG Hatzikosta
                   'was the Hatzikosta hospital open?'

      03 Our: SS >>   *[.h Efiméreve*   *]*
                   .h be.on.duty.3SG.PST

      04   *to   Xadzikósta.*
                   DEF.NEUT.NOM.SG Hatzikosta
                   'The Hatzikosta hospital was open.'

Clause repetitions are also found in agreement or disagreement with a prior turn. In example (12), lines 1–2, Aleka assesses the neighborhood (*Aplós íne períerji i perioçí.* 'It's just a weird neighborhood.'), and in lines 3–4, Polychronis agrees with the assessment (*Ine períerji i perioçí.* 'It's a weird neighborhood.'). He repeats the copula clause that Aleka used in her previous turn, with emphasis on the adjective, and he omits the adverb. This slightly modified repetition is a practice for implementing an agreement with the prior turn from an "independent agentive position" (Thompson et al. 2015: 285).

(12) 01 Ale: FS >> *=Aplós íne   períerji   i*
                       just   COP.3SG.PRS weird.F.NOM.SG DEF.F.NOM.SG
                       'It's just a weird'

      02   *[perioçí.   ]*
                   area(F).NOM.SG
                   'neighborhood.'

      03 Pol: SS >>   *[Ine   perí]erji*
                   COP.3SG.PRS weird.F.NOM.SG

---

[3]A declarative or subjunctive main clause in Greek can be turned into a polar question through rising intonation toward the end of the utterance.

04   SS >> *i*   *perioçi.*   *jaftó.*

                  DEF.F.NOM.SG area(F).NOM.SG this

                  'It's a weird neighborhood. That's why.'

In example (13), clause repetition is a practice for disagreeing with the previous speaker. In line 3, Aleka makes a claim (*ta: ta riθímzi* ↑*tóra mɲa xará.* 'he keeps things- things in moderation very well.'), and in line 5, Polychronis contradicts the claim (°*ðe ta riθmízi.* 'He doesn't keep things in moderation)'). Polychronis utters the negated proposition expressed in the previous claim, by repeating the clause that Aleka used, omitting the adverbs and adding the negative particle before the clause.

(13)   01 Ale: ↑O̲çi. cítakse. ðilaðí, ta çi riθmísi ta práɣmata se sçési

                         'No. Look. That is, he has kept things in moderation compared to'

       02   me to: pos ítan >(ótan eɣó)< to- to ɣn̲órisa,

                         'how things were (when) I met him,'

       03   FS >>   *ta: ta riθímzi*   ↑*tóra mɲa xará.*

                         them them regulate.3SG.PRS now very well

                         'he keeps things- things in moderation very well.'

       04   (1.2)

       05 Pol: SS >>   °*(ðe ta   riθmízi.)*

                         NEG them regulate.3SG.PRS

                         'He doesn't keep things in moderation.'

Clause repetition is also used in next turns that confirm what the previous speaker said (14), receive information given by the previous speaker (15), or deliver repair within a story telling (16). In (14), participants are engaged in conversational arguing (Muntigl & Turnbull 1998). In the lines preceding the excerpt, Nionios claims that he and his peers never cooked when they were teenagers. Yannis contradicts the previous claim (lines 1–2), and asserts that he and his peers cooked (*emís to k̲áname.* 'we did it.'). In line 4, Nionios initially confirms Yannis's claim by repeating the clause that Yannis used in his previous turn (*To k̲áname:.* 'we did it'). The second saying that implements the confirmation is modified: the first person plural pronoun is omitted. In the next TCU, Nionios delivers a counterclaim that does not directly contradict nor challenge the addressee's claim.

(14) 01 Yan: FS >> *O̱çi. jati̱ ðen do káname   emís. =emís to kániname.*
                    no why NEG it do.1PL.PST 1PL   1PL   it do.1PL.PST

                    'No. Why didn't we do the same? We did it.'
        02   =eɣó ðe ma[ji̱]reva?=

                    'Wasn't I the one cooking?'
        03 Nio: [T-]
        04   SS >> *To kániname:. safós   to kániname*
                       it do.1PL.PST certainly it do.1PL.PST

                       'We did it. We certainly did it'
        05   allá:: ðen do kánan óla ta peðjá::.

                       'but not all kids were doing the same thing.'

In example (15), line 2, Erato asks Yorgos if he switched the kitchen stove off, assuming that the food is ready, and in lines 4–5, Yorgos replies that he didn't because the food is not ready (*majiré°vete (akóma).* 'the food is (still) cooking.'). In line 6, Erato proposes the possible end of the sequence by claiming information receipt. Her turn is composed by three TCUs. The first TCU consists of the free-standing particle *a̱*, uttered with emphasis, which marks a change from not-knowing to now-knowing (similar to the English particle *oh*, Heritage 1984). In the second TCU, the speaker reuses elements from Yorgos's prior turn to express receipt of information. She repeats the adverb *tóra* 'now' and the clause that delivers the informing *majirévete °akómi.* ('it is still cooking.'), with no emphasis on the verb. In the third TCU, the speaker accepts the information via the positive token particle *ne* 'yes'.

(15) 01 Yor: ti [fajitá íçe,   ]

                    'What kind of food they served,'
        02 Era: [Eklises to má]ti?

                       'Did you switch the stove off?'
        03   (.)
        04 Yor: SS >> *O̱çi. ðe   >xriázete   tóra:,*
                       no NEG need.3SG.PASS.PRS now

                       'No. I don't need to switch it off now,'
        05   *majiré°vete   (akóma).<=*
                       cook.3SG.PASS.PRS still

                       'the food is still cooking.'
        06 Era: SS >> *=[A̱. >tóra majiréve][te   akó]mi. ne.<*
                       part now   cook.3SG.PASS.PRS still   yes

                       'Ah. now it's still cooking. yes.'

07 Sot:	=[°(...........................)]	
08 Yor:		[°Ne]
		'Yes'

In example (16), Polychronis tells a story about a funny incident (lines 1–3, 5). He refers to the protagonists in the story via first person plural verbs *ksecinísame* 'we started', *na páme* 'to go', *ðe vríkame* 'we didn't find', *jirnáγame* 'we were wandering around', and the pronoun *mas* 'us'. The collectivity introduced includes the speaker and one of the co-participants. Aleka's participation in the story events establishes her as a story consociate that shares knowledge of the story events (Lerner 1992). Story consociates can participate in the course of story delivery by continuing the story or by repairing aspects of the story and its delivery, such as trouble in the event sequencing of the story, in the delivery of the story, in story elaboration, and in the facts of the story (Lerner 1992). In line 2, Polychronis reports with uncertainty that he, Aleka and the others went to Zythos restaurant (°*ksecinísame na páme sto Zíθo*° 'were we going to Zithos?'). In lines 6–7, Aleka repairs trouble in this fact of the story. She starts her turn with the negative particle *o̱çi* 'no' that expresses her disagreement with what Polychronis said immediately before. She delivers the repair by repeating a clause that Polychronis used to refer to the specific fact of the story (*ksecinísame, h na- na páme* 'we were going'), and she adds the phrase *ja kafé* 'for coffee'.

(16)	01 Pol:	= >Ce mas proécipse cólas< jatí ja̱lú ksecinísame,
		'And it just happened to us because we started heading to another place,'
	02 FS >>	°***ksecinísame na páme** sto Zíθo?*°
		begin.1PL.PST SBJV go.1PL to Zitho(M).ACC.SG
		'were we going to Zithos?'
	03 Pol:	pú ítane. [*ðe*] vríkame trapézi °ecí péra >ce metá,°<
		'where was it? We didn't find a table over there and afterwards,'
	04 Ale:	[Ne]
		'Yes.'
	05 Pol:	(.) ka̱pos jirnáγame, (ékane-) íçe po̱lí krío °ecíni [ti méra,]
		'we were wandering around, it was- it was a very cold day,'
	06 Ale:	[O̱çi.]
		'No.'

07   SS >>   *ksecinísame, h na- na páme ja kafé.*
begin.1PL.PST h SBJV SBJV go.1PL for coffee
'were we going for coffee.'

In the examples examined in this section, repetition of a prior turn at talk is a practice for responding to what the previous speaker did immediately before. Therefore, it displays the relevance between first and second pair part, and the fit between current and prior turn, and it operates as a tying technique.

4.4 Summary

To recapitulate, the analysis of clause repetitions in Greek conversation shows that the basic function of clause repetition is cohesive. Speakers often repeat clauses to display the connectedness between their current unit/turn and prior talk. Being an instance of format tying, clause repetition is deployed in various sequential contexts to carry out different social actions that respond to the just prior turn, such as answer, agreement/disagreement, confirmation, receipt of information, and repair. Moreover, the analysis demonstrates that the sequential position of clause repetition shapes the interactional functions of repetition. Self-repetition achieves cohesion in conversation as well as other interactional tasks, such as dealing with overlapping talk, pursuing a response, initiating and delivering repair and adding emphasis. On the other hand, repetition of a prior turn is routinely associated with a cohesive function. Thus, *who repeats* seems to be important for *what repetition does*. Overall, the findings reported in this study align with the findings reported by previous studies on the functions of repetition in conversation (discussed in §2).

5 From repetition to bridging constructions: Language diversity as a continuum

Although clause repetition and recapitulative linkage differ in substantial ways (cf. §1), they display certain analogies: like recapitulative linkage, clause repetition in Greek conversation involves repetition of at least the verb of the first saying and some of the elements accompanying the verb, and achieves cohesion. Moreover, both recapitulative linkage and repetition practices are discourse practices. I suggest that these analogies point to a *continuum* extending from clause repetition at one extreme to recapitulative linkage at the other extreme. In languages situated at the one extreme of the continuum clause repetition has not been conventionalized, while in languages situated at the other extreme of the continuum clause repetition has grammaticalized into recapitulative linkage.

It is possible that recapitulative linkage constructions have emerged from repetition practices in talk-in-interaction. The hypothesis about the discourse origin of recapitulative linkage aligns with research that examines how discourse or interaction shapes grammar (Givón 1979; Hopper & Thompson 1980; Schegloff et al. 1996; Couper-Kuhlen & Selting 2001). In Bybee's words (2006: 730), "grammar cannot be thought of as pure abstract structure that underlies language use"; grammar emerges in language use and it is "epiphenomenal to the ongoing creation of new combinations of forms in interactive encounters" (Hopper 2011: 26). As a number of studies (Couper-Kuhlen 2011; Gipper 2011; Blythe 2013) demonstrate, discourse contexts motivate the grammaticalization of specific constructions. For instance, Couper-Kuhlen (2011) argues that certain grammatical constructions, such as left dislocation, concession and extraposition, have emerged from the sequential routines of mundane conversational interaction, whereby a succession of (cross-speaker) actions has been "collapsed into" a single speaker's turn. This integrated construction can be said to grammaticalize from the conversational routine. For example, Geluykens (1992), cited in Couper-Kuhlen (2011), suggests that left dislocation, in which a noun phrase is positioned initially and a reinforcing pronoun stands proxy for it in the relevant position in the sentence, has emerged from the recognition search sequence. This sequence consists of three moves in which the speaker introduces a new referent, the hearer acknowledges recognition of the referent, and the speaker elaborates upon the referent. According to Couper-Kuhlen (2011: 429), left dislocation is found in English conversation both in its independent and integrated form (layering, cf. Hopper 1991). In its independent form, the two component parts accomplish two different actions, i.e., they establish referents and elaborate upon them. In its integrated form, the two component parts are coalesced with no intervening turn or pause separating them, and they deliver one single action, that is, they are specialized for listing and contrast.

In line with these views, I suggest that recapitulative linkage emerged from conversational routines: at some point, in certain languages, repetition practices aiming at cohesion were conventionalized and became part of grammar, that is, they grammaticalized into specific resources or patterns with a productive formal representation and a consistent and predictable semantic contribution (cf. Guérin & Aiton 2019 [this volume]). Although it is difficult to provide diachronic evidence for such a hypothesis, given that we lack records of talk-in-interaction in languages with bridging constructions, we have access to some synchronic evidence that point to the discourse origin of recapitulative linkage constructions.

The first type of evidence comes from languages in which repetition is con-ventionalized to some extent. For example, in Tojolabal Mayan conversation, repetition has become the default backchannel response to turns delivered by other speakers (Brody 1986: 260–261). As Brown (2000: 224) claims, "this con-versational practice makes Mayan conversations strike the outside observer as extraordinarily repetitive, drawing attention to the fact that tolerance for rep-etition in speech is *culturally*, as well as contextually, quite variable" (empha-sis added). Clause repetition is a rather common conversational practice among speakers in certain languages. Due to its frequency (Bybee 2003) and cultural salience, clause repetition crystallizes into specific grammatical constructions in these languages.[4]

The second type of evidence comes from languages that employ recapitulative linkage constructions. Guillaume (2011: 112–113) reports that languages vary in terms of the functions of recapitulative linkage. Most languages use recapitula-tive linkage to achieve coherence in context of high thematic continuity, that is, within individual paragraphs. Yet some languages employ additional recapit-ulative linkage constructions specialized for major thematic breaks, that is, be-tween distinct paragraphs. Thus, languages develop formally distinct types of re-capitulative linkage for carrying out different tasks in discourse. This variation further discloses the interactionally motivated and emerging nature of recapit-ulative linkage. More specifically, it shows that the development of recapitula-tive linkage constructions involves the emergence of new forms that coexist and interact with the older forms (layering, Hopper 1991), and the specialization of meanings attached to the forms in particular discourse contexts. Both layering and specialization are distinctive characteristics of grammaticalization (Hopper & Traugott 1993).

The third type of evidence for the discourse origin of recapitulative linkage can be found in universal abstract principles governing linguistic practices in talk-interaction: nextness and progressivity (Schegloff 2006). Nextness is a rela-tion between current and immediately following position. The production of talk is a succession of next elements, such as words, parts of words or sounds. As Sche-gloff (2006: 86) argues, "absent any provision to the contrary, any turn will be heard as addressed to the just prior, that is, the one it is next after". Progressivity refers to the sequential progress of interaction. Recipients orient to each next ele-ment as "a next piece in the developing trajectory of what the speaker is saying or

---

[4]Jarkey (2019 [this volume]) shows that summary linkage in White Hmong (Hmong-Mien, Laos) is limited to first person narratives and reported speech; this finding further points to the conventionalization of linkage constructions.

doing" (Schegloff 2006: 86). These two principles operate in clause repetition and bridging constructions: (a) repeats establish a relation between current and prior turn or TCU (nextness); (b) in reusing prior sayings, repeats disrupt the linguistic progressivity in talk-in-interaction, and, thus, they are examinable for their pragmatic import. That is, universal principles governing talk-in-interaction can function as constraints on "what systems can evolve", and "selectors" generating structures (Evans & Levinson 2009: 446).

By bringing together findings from languages with bridging constructions and a language in which bridging constructions are not grammaticalized, this paper demonstrates the fuzzy boundaries between bridging constructions and verbal repetition and makes a case for the discourse origin of recapitulative linkage.

Abbreviations

1	first person	F	feminine	PFV	perfective
2	second person	FUT	future	PL	plural
3	third person	NEG	negation	PREP	preposition
ACC	accusative	NEUT	neuter	PRS	present
CLIT	clitic	NOM	nominative	SG	singular
CONJ	conjunction	PART	particle	SBJV	subjunctive
COP	copula	PASS	passive		
DIM	diminutive	PST	past		

Appendix: Transcription symbols

The left bracket [is the point of overlap onset between two or more utterances (or segments of them).

The right bracket] is point of overlap end between two or more utterances (or segments of them).

The equal sign = is used either in pairs or on its own. A pair of equals signs is used to indicate the following:
(i) If the lines connected by the equals signs contain utterances (or segments of them) by different speakers, then the signs denote "latching" (that is, the absence of discernible silence between the utterances).

(ii) If the lines connected by the equals signs are by the same speaker, then there was a single, continuous utterance with no break or pause, which

Angeliki Alvanoudi

was broken up in two lines only in order to accommodate the placement of overlapping talk. The single equals sign is used to indicate latching between two parts of the same speaker's talk, where one might otherwise expect a micro-pause, as, for instance, after a turn constructional unit with a falling intonation contour.

Numbers in parentheses (0.8) indicate silence, represented in tenths of a second. Silences may be marked either within the utterance or between utterances.

(.) indicates a micro-pause (less than 0.5 second).

A period indicates falling/final intonation.

A question mark indicates rising intonation.

A comma indicates continuing/non-final intonation.

Colons : are used to indicate the prolongation or stretching of the sound just preceding them. The more colons, the longer the stretching.

Underlining is used to indicate some form of emphasis, either by increased loudness or higher pitch.

The degree sign ° is used to indicate the onset of talk that is markedly quiet or soft. When the end of such talk does not coincide with the end of a line, then the symbol is used again to mark its end.

A hyphen - after a word or part of a word indicates a cut-off or interruption.

Combinations of underlining and colons are used to indicate intonation contours. If the letter(s) preceding a colon is underlined, then there is prolongation of the sound preceding it and, at the same time, a falling intonation contour. If the colon itself is underlined, then there is prolongation of the sound preceding it and, at the same time, a rising intonation contour.

The arrows mark sharp intonation contours. The upper arrow ↑ indicates sharp intonation rises, whereas the down arrow ↓ indicates sharp intonation falls.

The combination of the symbols > and < indicates that the talk between them is compressed or rushed.

The combination of the symbols < and > indicates that the talk between them is markedly slowed or drawn out.

262

Hearable aspiration is shown with the Latin letter h. Its repetition indicates longer duration. The aspiration may represent inhaling, exhaling, laughter, etc.

If the aspiration is an inhalation, then it is indicated with a period before the letter h.

Double parentheses are used to mark meta-linguistic, para-linguistic and non-conversational descriptions of events by the transcriber, e.g. ((laughs)).

Parentheses with dots (...) indicate that something is being said, but no hearing can be achieved.

Words in parentheses represent a likely possibility of what was said.

Acknowledgments

The first version of this paper was presented at the workshop "Bridging linkage in cross-linguistic perspective" at the Language and Culture Research Center, James Cook University, on 25–26 February 2015. I am grateful to the participants of this event for their feedback. I would like to thank the volume editor and two anonymous reviewers for providing insightful comments that helped to improve my arguments.

References

Blythe, Joe. 2013. Preference organization driving structuration: Evidence from Australian Aboriginal interaction for pragmatically motivated grammaticalization. *Language* 89(4). 883–919.

Brody, Jill. 1986. Repetition as a rhetorical and conversational device in Tojolabal (Mayan). *International Journal of American Linguistics* 52(3). 255–274.

Brown, Penelope. 2000. Repetition. *Journal of Linguistic Anthropology* 9(1–2). 223–226.

Bybee, Joan. 2003. Mechanisms of change in grammaticization: The role of frequency. In Brian J. Joseph & Richard D. Janda (eds.), *The handbook of historical linguistics*, 602–623. Oxford: Blackwell.

Bybee, Joan. 2006. From usage to grammar: The mind's response to repetition. *Language* 82(4). 711–733.

Couper-Kuhlen, Elizabeth. 1996. The prosody of repetition: On quoting and mimicry. In Elizabeth Couper-Kuhlen & Margret Selting (eds.), *Prosody in conversation*, 366–405. Cambridge: Cambridge University Press.

Couper-Kuhlen, Elizabeth. 2011. Grammaticalization and conversation. In Heiko Narrog & Bernd Heine (eds.), *The Oxford handbook of grammaticalization*, 366–405. Oxford: Oxford University Press.

Couper-Kuhlen, Elizabeth & Margret Selting. 2001. Introducing interactional linguistics. In Margret Selting & Elizabeth Couper-Kuhlen (eds.), *Studies in interactional linguistics*, 1–22. Amsterdam: John Benjamins.

Couper-Kuhlen, Elizabeth & Margret Selting. 2017. Online Chapter F: Further practices with language. In *Interactional linguistics: Studying language in social interaction*. Cambridge: Cambridge University Press. http://www.cambridge.org/files/2015/1497/6105/Online-Chapter_F.pdf, accessed 2018-8-19.

de Vries, Lourens. 2005. Towards a typology of tail-head linkage in Papuan languages. *Studies in Language* 29(2). 363–384.

Drew, Paul. 2012. Turn design. In Jack Sidnell & Tanya Stivers (eds.), *The handbook of conversation analysis*, 131–149. Boston, MA: Wiley-Blackwell.

Evans, N. J. & Stephen C. Levinson. 2009. The myth of language universals: Language diversity and its importance for cognitive science. *Behavioral and Brain Sciences* 32. 429–492.

Geluykens, Ronald. 1992. *From discourse process to grammatical construction: On left-dislocation in English.* Amsterdam: John Benjamins.

Gipper, Sonja. 2011. *Evidentiality and intersubjectivity in Yurakaré: An interactional account.* Nijmegen: Radboud University PhD Dissertation.

Givón, Talmy. 1979. *On understanding grammar.* New York: Academic Press.

Goodwin, Marjorie H. 1990. *He-said-she-said: Talk as social organization among black children.* Bloomington, IN: Indiana University Press.

Goodwin, Marjorie H. & Charles Goodwin. 1987. Children's arguing. In Susan Philips, Susan Steele & Christine Tanz (eds.), *Language, gender, and sex in comparative perspective*, 200–248. Cambridge: Cambridge University Press.

Guérin, Valérie & Grant Aiton. 2019. Bridging constructions in typological perspective. In Valérie Guérin (ed.), *Bridging constructions*, 1–44. Berlin: Language Science Press. DOI:10.5281/zenodo.2563678

Guillaume, Antoine. 2011. Subordinate clauses, switch-reference, and tail-head linkage in Cavineña narratives. In Rik van Gijn, Katharina Haude & Pieter Muysken (eds.), *Subordination in native South American languages*, 109–140. Amsterdam: John Benjamins.

Halliday, M. A. K. 1973. *Explorations in the functions of language.* London: Edward Arnold.

Halliday, M. A. K. & Ruqaiya Hasan. 1976. *Cohesion in English.* London: Longman.

Heritage, John. 1984. A change-of-state token and aspects of its sequential placement. In J. Maxwell Atkinson & John Heritage (eds.), *Structures of social action,* 299–345. Cambridge: Cambridge University Press.

Heritage, John & Geoffrey Raymond. 2012. Navigating epistemic landscapes: Acquiescence, agency and resistance in responses to polar questions. In Jan P. de Ruiter (ed.), *Questions: Formal, functional and interactional perspectives,* 179–192. Cambridge: Cambridge University Press.

Hopper, Paul J. 1991. On some principles of grammaticalization. In Elizabeth C. Traugott & Bernd Heine (eds.), *Approaches to grammaticalization,* 17–35. Amsterdam: John Benjamins.

Hopper, Paul J. 2011. Emergent grammar and temporality in interactional linguistics. In Peter Auer & Stefan Pfander (eds.), *Constructions: Emerging and emergent,* 22–44. Berlin: Mouton de Gruyter.

Hopper, Paul J. & Sandra A. Thompson. 1980. Transitivity in grammar and discourse. *Language* 56(2). 251–299.

Hopper, Paul J. & Elizabeth C. Traugott. 1993. *Grammaticalization.* Cambridge: Cambridge University Press.

Jarkey, Nerida. 2019. Bridging constructions in narrative texts in White Hmong (Hmong-Mien). In Valérie Guérin (ed.), *Bridging constructions,* 129–156. Berlin: Language Science Press. DOI:10.5281/zenodo.2563686

Johnstone, Barbara. 1994. Repetition in discourse: A dialogue. In Barbara Johnstone (ed.), *Repetition in discourse: Interdisciplinary perspectives,* 1–20. Norwood, NJ: Ablex Publishing Corporation.

Joseph, Brian & Irene Phillipaki-Warburton. 1987. *Modern Greek.* London: Croom Helm.

Kim, Haeyeon. 2002. The form and function of next-turn repetition in English conversation. *Language Research* 38(1). 51–81.

Lee, Seung-Hee. 2012. Response design in conversation. In Jack Sidnell & Tanya Stivers (eds.), *The handbook of conversation analysis,* 415–432. Boston, MA: Wiley-Blackwell.

Lerner, Gene H. 1992. Assisted story telling: Deploying shared knowledge as a practical matter. *Qualitative Sociology* 15(3). 247–271.

Mackridge, Peter. 1985. *The Modern Greek language: A descriptive analysis of Standard Modern Greek.* Oxford: Oxford University Press.

Martin, James R. 2001. Cohesion and texture. In Deborah Schiffrin, Deborah Tannen & Heidi Hamilton (eds.), *The handbook of discourse analysis,* 35–53. Malden, MA: Blackwell.

Mazeland, Harrie. 2012. Grammar in conversation. In Jack Sidnell & Tanya Stivers (eds.), *The handbook of conversation analysis*, 475–491. Boston, MA: Wiley-Blackwell.

Muntigl, Peter & William Turnbull. 1998. Conversational structure and facework in arguing. *Journal of Pragmatics* 29(3). 225–256.

Norrick, Neal R. 1987. Functions of repetition in conversation. *Text* 7(3). 245–264.

Pomerantz, Anita. 1984. Agreeing and disagreeing with assessments: Some features of preferred/dispreferred turn shapes. In J. Maxwell Atkinson & John Heritage (eds.), *Structures of social action: Studies in conversation analysis*, 57–101. Cambridge: Cambridge University Press.

Raymond, Geoffrey. 2003. Grammar and social organization: Yes/No interrogatives and the structure of responding. *American Sociological Review* 68(6). 939–967.

Sacks, Harvey. 1995. *Lectures on conversation*. Oxford: Blackwell.

Schegloff, Emanuel A. 1968. Sequencing in conversational openings. *American Anthropologist* 70(6). 1075–1095.

Schegloff, Emanuel A. 1987. Recycled turn beginnings: A precise repair mechanism in conversation's turn-taking organisation. In Graham Button & John Lee (eds.), *Talk and social organization*, 70–85. Clevedon: Multilingual Matters.

Schegloff, Emanuel A. 1996a. Confirming allusions: Toward an empirical account of action. *American Journal of Sociology* 102(1). 161–216.

Schegloff, Emanuel A. 1996b. Turn organization: One intersection of grammar and interaction. In Elinor Ochs, Emanuel A. Schegloff & Sandra A. Thompson (eds.), *Interaction and grammar*, 52–133. Cambridge: Cambridge University Press.

Schegloff, Emanuel A. 1997. Practices and actions: Boundary cases of other-initiated repair. *Discourse Processes* 23(3). 499–545.

Schegloff, Emanuel A. 2006. Interaction: The infrastructure for social institutions, the natural ecological niche for language, and the arena in which culture is enacted. In N. J. Enfield & Stephen C. Levinson (eds.), *Roots of human sociality: Culture, cognition, and interaction*, 70–96. London: Berg.

Schegloff, Emanuel A. 2007. *Sequence organization in interaction*. Cambridge: Cambridge University Press.

Schegloff, Emanuel A., Gail Jefferson & Harvey Sacks. 1977. The preference for self-correction in the organization of repair in conversation. *Language* 53(2). 361–382.

Schegloff, Emanuel A., Elinor Ochs & Sandra A. Thompson. 1996. Introduction. In Elinor Ochs, Emanuel A. Schegloff & Sandra A. Thompson (eds.), *Interaction and grammar*, 1–51. Cambridge: Cambridge University Press.

Sorjonen, Marja-Leena. 1996. On repeats and responses in Finnish conversations. In Elinor Ochs, Emanuel A. Schegloff & Sandra A. Thompson (eds.), *Interaction and grammar*, 277–327. Cambridge: Cambridge University Press.

Stivers, Tanya. 2005. Modified repeats: One method for asserting primary rights from second position. *Research on Language and Social Interaction* 38(2). 131–158.

Stivers, Tanya. 2011. Morality and question design: 'Of course' as contesting a presupposition of askability. In Tanya Stivers, Lorenza Mondada & Jakob Steensig (eds.), *The morality of knowledge in conversation*, 82–106. Cambridge: Cambridge University Press.

Stivers, Tanya & Makoto Hayashi. 2010. Transformative answers: One way to resist a question's constraints. *Language in Society* 39(1). 1–25.

Tannen, Deborah. 1987. Repetition in conversation: Towards a poetics of talk. *Language* 63(3). 574–605.

Tannen, Deborah. 1989. *Talking voices: Repetition, dialogue, and imagery in conversational discourse.* Cambridge: Cambridge University Press.

Thompson, Sandra A., Barbara A. Fox & Elizabeth Couper-Kuhlen. 2015. *Grammar in everyday talk: Building responsive actions.* Cambridge: Cambridge University Press.

Tyler, Andrea. 1994. The role of repetition in perceptions of discourse coherence. *Journal of Pragmatics* 21(6). 671–688.

Wong, Jean. 2000. Repetition in conversation: A look at "first and second sayings". *Research on Language and Social Interaction* 33(4). 407–424.

Name index

Language index

Subject index